Trade and Employment in Developing Countries

3   Synthesis and Conclusions

Trade and Employment in Developing Countries
1 Individual Studies
2 Factor Supply and Substitution
3 Synthesis and Conclusions

National Bureau of Economic Research

Trade and Employment in Developing Countries

3 Synthesis and Conclusions

Anne O. Krueger

The University of Chicago Press

Chicago and London

ANNE O. KRUEGER is professor of economics at the University of Minnesota (on leave) and vice-president, Economics and Research, of the World Bank, Washington, D.C.

The University of Chicago Press, Chicago 60637
The University of Chicago Press, Ltd., London
© 1983 by The University of Chicago
All rights reserved. Published 1983
Printed in the United States of America
90 89 88 87 86 85 84 83   5 4 3 2 1

Library of Congress Cataloging in Publication Data
Main entry under title:

Trade and employment in developing countries.

"[Results] from the research project sponsored by the National Bureau of Economic Research on alternate trade strategies and employment."
  Includes bibliographies and indexes.
  CONTENTS: v. 1. Individual studies.—v. 2. Factor supply and substitution.
  1. Underdeveloped areas—Foreign trade and employment—Addresses, essays, lectures.   2. Underdeveloped areas—Commerce—Addresses, essays, lectures.   I. Krueger, Anne O.   II. National Bureau of Economic Research.
HD5852.T7   331.12′09172′4   80-15826
ISBN 0-226-45494-0 (v. 3)   AACR1

Relation of the Directors to the
Work and Publications of the
National Bureau of Economic Research

1. The object of the National Bureau of Economic Research is to ascertain and to present to the public important economic facts and their interpretation in a scientific and impartial manner. The Board of Directors is charged with the responsibility of ensuring that the work of the National Bureau is carried on in strict conformity with this object.

2. The President of the National Bureau shall submit to the Board of Directors, or to its Executive Committee, for their formal adoption all specific proposals for research to be instituted.

3. No research report shall be published by the National Bureau until the President has sent each member of the Board a notice that a manuscript is recommended for publication and that in the President's opinion it is suitable for publication in accordance with the principles of the National Bureau. Such notification will include an abstract or summary of the manuscript's content and a response form for use by those Directors who desire a copy of the manuscript for review. Each manuscript shall contain a summary drawing attention to the nature and treatment of the problem studied, the character of the data and their utilization in the report, and the main conclusions reached.

4. For each manuscript so submitted, a special committee of the Directors (including Directors Emeriti) shall be appointed by majority agreement of the President and Vice Presidents (or by the Executive Committee in case of inability to decide on the part of the President and Vice Presidents), consisting of three Directors selected as nearly as may be one from each general division of the Board. The names of the special manuscript committee shall be stated to each Director when notice of the proposed publication is submitted to him. It shall be the duty of each member of the special manuscript committee to read the manuscript. If each member of the manuscript committee signifies his approval within thirty days of the transmittal of the manuscript, the report may be published. If at the end of that period any member of the manuscript committee withholds his approval, the President shall then notify each member of the Board, requesting approval or disapproval of publication, and thirty days additional shall be granted for this purpose. The manuscript shall then not be published unless at least a majority of the entire Board who shall have voted on the proposal within the time fixed for the receipt of votes shall have approved.

5. No manuscript may be published, though approved by each member of the special manuscript committee, until forty-five days have elapsed from the transmittal of the report in manuscript form. The interval is allowed for the receipt of any memorandum of dissent or reservation, together with a brief statement of his reasons, that any member may wish to express; and such memorandum of dissent or reservation shall be published with the manuscript if he so desires. Publication does not, however, imply that each member of the Board has read the manuscript, or that either members of the Board in general or the special committee have passed on its validity in every detail.

6. Publications of the National Bureau issued for informational purposes concerning the work of the Bureau and its staff, or issued to inform the public of activities of Bureau staff, and volumes issued as a result of various conferences involving the National Bureau shall contain a specific disclaimer noting that such publication has not passed through the normal review procedures required in this resolution. The Executive Committee of the Board is charged with review of all such publications from time to time to ensure that they do not take on the character of formal research reports of the National Bureau, requiring formal Board approval.

7. Unless otherwise determined by the Board or exempted by the terms of paragraph 6, a copy of this resolution shall be printed in each National Bureau publication.

(Resolution adopted October 25, 1926, as revised through September 30, 1974)

Contents

Preface

This is the third and final volume emanating from the National Bureau of Economic Research project on alternative trade strategies and employment. It is designed to bring together the theory underlying the trade strategies–employment relationship and the empirical evidence emanating from the project.

The entire project has been devoted to an analysis of the extent to which employment and income distribution are affected by the choice of trade strategies and by the interaction of trade policies with domestic policies and market distortions. The trade strategies in question are, of course, import substitution and export promotion as alternative means of encouraging the growth of domestic industry. While earlier studies, including the NBER project on foreign trade regimes and economic development (see Bhagwati 1978 and Krueger 1978 for details), provided considerable evidence that the economic growth performance of developing countries pursuing export-oriented trade strategies was substantially superior to that of countries under import substitution, little attention was given to the relationship between the choice of trade strategy and conditions in the domestic labor market before this project.

Trade theory, especially the Heckscher-Ohlin-Samuelson (HOS) model, predicts that poor countries will generally have a comparative advantage in the production of relatively labor-intensive commodities. In light of this, failure to have investigated the possible links between different rates of growth of employment and real wages with alternative trade strategies constituted a significant hiatus in our understanding of the trade strategies–growth relationship.

A first stage in the research project on alternative trade strategies and employment consisted of providing an analytical framework within which the links between trade strategies and employment could be identified.

This was done in Krueger (1977) and is partly reproduced here as chap. 4. A next step was to secure a group of researchers willing to undertake investigation of the empirical dimensions of the relationship. Many of the project participants undertook empirical and analytical studies of individual country experiences. Those studies were presented for ten countries in the first volume in this series (Krueger et al. 1981), which also contains a chapter describing the common concepts and methodology employed in all the country studies.

It was clear from the outset that the country studies would provide a great deal of insight into the trade strategies–employment relation, but that there were some interesting questions where comparative analysis, or focus upon a single aspect of the relationship, would yield fruitful results. In addition to the country studies, research was undertaken on these questions as an integral part of the project. The second volume (Krueger 1982) presented the results of those endeavors.

This volume contains an analysis of the trade strategies–employment relationship, especially in the context of factor markets in developing countries. The first four chapters are devoted to underlying theory: of factor, and especially labor, markets; of alternative trade strategies; and of the expected links between trade strategies, growth, and employment. The next two chapters analyze the findings from the project with regard to the observed labor utilization in exportable and import-competing industries. Thereafter, the ways factor market imperfections have affected those coefficients are analyzed in chapters 7 and 8. A final chapter summarizes some main conclusions.

A project of this size and scope is not possible without the contributions of many people. My greatest debt is to Hal B. Lary, whose careful and thoughtful comments on the manuscript, as well as throughout the entire project, were invaluable. All project participants read and commented on treatment of their own countries and topics in earlier drafts of the manuscript. In addition to kindly commenting upon treatment of Argentina, Julio Nogues read the entire manuscript and made many careful suggestions. T. Paul Schultz was especially helpful in commenting on chapter 2. Constantine Michalopoulos and Keith Jay of the United States Agency for International Development provided valuable comments and suggestions throughout the project. Delma Burns not only typed and retyped the manuscript, but also caught numerous inconsistencies and grammatical slips. To all these individuals I express my thanks.

The entire project was financed by the National Bureau for Economic Research, which in turn received funding for the project from the Agency for International Development.

1   Trade and Employment in Less Developed Countries: The Questions

The National Bureau for Economic Research project on alternative trade strategies and employment has had as its objective the understanding of the implications of alternative trade strategies for employment in developing countries. The decision to emphasize import substitution or export promotion has important ramifications for virtually every aspect of economic activity. These effects, which are discussed briefly below and more fully in chapter 3, have been extensively analyzed in a series of studies, including the earlier NBER project on foreign trade regimes and economic development. A significant omission in the earlier research was the employment effects and implications of the alternative trade strategies and the ways they are implemented.

Ironically, just as a considerable body of evidence was emerging demonstrating that there was a significant link between an export-oriented trade strategy and a higher rate of economic growth, disillusionment with the past results of economic growth set in. People began questioning the desirability of higher growth rates, since they noted that in many instances employment opportunities, especially in the industrial sectors of developing countries, failed to grow pari passu with output.

The "employment problem" became a focal point of concern for policymakers and for others interested in improving the well-being of the large majority of poor in developing countries. Interestingly, most studies of the "employment problem," and of ways of increasing the rate of growth of demand for labor, assumed a closed economy and did not recognize the possibility that trade strategy might make a significant difference. Indeed, many development economists believed the goods and services that composed the bulk of expenditure of the residents of developing countries were likely to be more labor intensive than exportable production and thus concluded that a policy implying less trade—

that is, import substitution—would be more favorable to employment than an export-oriented strategy (see Edwards 1974).[1]

To analyze the trade strategies–employment relationship, it was necessary both to provide a fairly careful analysis of the issues and their interrelations and also to undertake empirical investigation of the relevant magnitudes. This volume provides a synthesis of the results of the project, including both the analytical work and the empirical studies. This chapter gives an overview of the project and of the questions that must be addressed and presents a simple framework within which to categorize the links between trade strategies and employment. Chapters 2 and 3 undertake a more detailed analysis first of labor markets in developing countries and then of alternative trade strategies. Chapter 4 then contains a model of trade and development, which provides a rationale for focusing primarily upon trade and employment in industrial projects and also sets forth testable hypotheses that enable a careful examination of the trade strategies–employment relationship.

The second half of the book is devoted to empirical results. Chapter 5 is concerned with the categorization of commodities and industries according to the framework set forth in chapter 4 and presents estimates of direct labor coefficients for these categories found in the countries covered in the empirical analysis. Chapter 6 analyzes some of the main findings with regard to the labor coefficients associated with different industries under alternative trade strategies. Chapters 7 and 8 focus upon domestic factor markets, incentives favoring utilization of capital rather than labor, and other factors that influence these coefficients. The final chapter summarizes the major findings and conclusions.

1.1   The Overall Project

The overall project has had three stages. In the first, preparatory stage, we developed the theory setting forth the relationship between trade strategy and employment and formulated a method for undertaking empirical research. In the second stage, project participants undertook empirical research on individual countries and also on particular topics of special interest for the project as a whole, based upon the papers prepared in the first stage. The third stage, on which this volume is based, is an analysis of the theory and empirical findings for the entire set of individual studies, with a view to ascertaining the extent to which empirical regularities prevail and the lessons learned in the project.

Many of the results from the first stage, in which the underlying theory and method were developed, are incorporated in this volume. Thus the statement of theory in chapter 4 was intended to provide a basis for empirical testing, and it sets forth a model of trade with many countries and many commodities. It is assumed, for purposes of analysis, that there are two distinct sectors of the economy, urban and rural. The rural sector is characterized by its use of labor and land, while the urban sector employs capital and land. Key results, for present purposes, include the theory's prediction that countries will tend to specialize (in the absence of protection) in a range of industrial products that reflects their relative urban capital/labor endowment, and that there should be an association between the labor intensity of production processes and the direction of exports and imports.

The methodology developed in the first stage formed a basis for empirical studies at a later date and was formulated in consultation with all project participants; it first appeared as Project Working Paper no. 1, and much of its contents then became chapter 1 of the first volume of this series, *Trade and Employment in Developing Countries: Individual Studies*, edited by Anne O. Krueger, Hal B. Lary, Terry Monson, and Narongchai Akrasanee. The salient aspects of commodity categorization and other key elements of the methodology are summarized in this volume, especially in chapter 5.

The second stage of the analysis, in which studies were carried out of the empirical aspects of the employment-trade relationship, was undertaken by economists who were already familiar with the functioning of the individual economies. All together, there were fifteen studies of individual countries and four topical analyses.

Turning to the country studies first, there were initially ten sponsored directly by the NBER project. In addition, the Center for Asian Manpower Studies (CAMS) was analyzing certain aspects of the trade strategies–employment relationship, and it was agreed that participants in the CAMS project would join in many of the efforts of the NBER project. Finally, two doctoral dissertations were undertaken at the University of Minnesota within the same framework.

The fifteen countries, the sponsorship of the studies, and the authors, were as follows:

Argentina: Julio Nogues, now of the Central Bank of Argentina, undertook a study of the Argentine economy for his doctoral dissertation at the University of Minnesota (Nogues 1980).

Brazil: José Carvalho and Cláudio Haddad, of the Vargas Foundation, undertook the Brazil study under NBER sponsorship.

Chile: Vittorio Corbo, now of Universidad de Chile, and Patricio Meller, now of the Center for Latin American Development Studies at Boston University, undertook the Chile study under NBER sponsorship.

Colombia: Francisco Thoumi, now with the Interamerican Development Bank, undertook the Colombian study under NBER sponsorship.

Hong Kong: Yun Wing Sung, now of Chinese University of Hong Kong, did an analysis of the Hong Kong economy's experience as his doctoral dissertation at the University of Minnesota (Sung 1979).

India: T. N. Srinivasan, now of Yale University, and V. R. Panchamukhi, now at the Trade Development Authority of India, began a
study of India sponsored by NBER. Unfortunately, Srinivasan left
for a World Bank appointment, and Panchamukhi was appointed to
the Trade Development Authority of India, so the Indian study was
not completed.

Indonesia: Mark Pitt of the University of Minnesota and Soelistyo of
Gadjah Mada University started the Indonesian study under NBER
sponsorship. Soelistyo was pressed by other assignments, and Pitt
carried out the Indonesia study.

Ivory Coast: Terry Monson, of Michigan Technological University,
and Jacques Pegatienan, of the Centre Ivorien de Recherches Econ-
omiques et Sociales, began the project under NBER sponsorship.
Pegatienan's other responsibilities precluded his continuing participation, however, and Monson completed the Ivorian study.

Kenya: Peter Hopcraft and Leopold Murethi, of the Kenyan Center for
Development Studies, began the Kenyan study under NBER sponsorship. It was not completed, owing largely to data difficulties that
increased the time required well beyond the span of the project.

Pakistan: Steve Guisinger, of the University of Texas at Dallas, undertook the Pakistan study under NBER sponsorship.

South Korea: Wontack Hong, of Seoul National University, undertook
the Korean study under CAMS sponsorship.

Taiwan: Kuo-shu Liang, now of the Central Bank of Taiwan, partici-
pated in the first working party under CAMS sponsorship. His
appointment as deputy governor of the Central Bank precluded his
completing the study.

Thailand: Narongchai Akrasanee, now of the United Nations Asian
and Pacific Development Institute, undertook the Thai study under
CAMS sponsorship.

Tunisia: Mustapha K. Nabli, of the University of Tunis, undertook the
Tunisian study under NBER sponsorship.

Uruguay: Alberto Bension and Jorge Caumont, of the Universidad de
la Republica, Montevideo, undertook the Uruguayan study under
NBER sponsorship.

Thus, of the fifteen studies undertaken, twelve were completed. The
results of ten of them are included in Krueger et al. (1981) and the other
two, completed too late to be included, are available as doctoral dissertations. This book relies primarily on the results of those ten, although data
from the other five, especially Hong Kong and Argentina, are included
where they are available and shed additional light on the topic at hand.

The topical studies carried out under the project included an optimizing trade model with variable factor inputs undertaken by James M.
Henderson of the University of Minnesota; an analysis of the links

between rates of effective protection and earnings of workers and employers by T. Paul Schultz of Yale University; an estimate of production functions based on cross-country data by Jere R. Behrman of the University of Pennsylvania; and an analysis of the factor proportions used by multinational corporations done by Robert Lipsey of NBER and by Irving Kravis and Romualdo Roldan, both of the University of Pennsylvania. In addition, two country studies generated results of sufficient general interest beyond their implications for the individual countries to be included in the special studies volume: José Carvalho and Cláudio Haddad provided new estimates of the Brazilian export supply response; and Vittorio Corbo and Patricio Meller estimated Chilean production functions for a sample of forty-four Chilean industries.

This volume, then, attempts to provide an analysis of the trade strategies–employment relationship based upon the preceding analytical and empirical work, including the country studies and the topical studies, as well as other research results where relevant. Although it is not a survey of knowledge in the area (and, in particular, does not attempt to review other empirical results with respect to the trade strategies–employment relationship), it is intended to provide an account of the theoretical and empirical relationships between trade strategies and employment.

1.2 Possible Links between Trade Strategies and Employment

There are several levels at which one can imagine effects of the trade regime upon employment and its rate of growth:

1. One strategy might result in a higher rate of growth of the overall economy owing to superior resource allocation, and faster growth would presumably entail more employment growth.

2. Different trade strategies imply different compositions of output at each point in time. Under an export promotion strategy export industries grow faster, and the opposite is true under import substitution. If employment per unit of output (or value added) is greater in one set of industries than in the other, then employment growth would be faster, on this account, under the strategy that lets the labor-intensive industries grow relatively faster.

3. Alternative trade policies could influence the choice of technique and capital/labor ratio in all industries, as, for example, through implicit subsidization of capital goods imports. If such policies lead to greater capital intensity and fewer jobs per unit of output in all lines of economic activity, then employment opportunities will grow more slowly as there is continued capital deepening.

It is apparent that the three classes of effects need not be in the same direction. It is possible, in particular, that the first effect—a higher rate of growth of employment owing to faster output growth associated with one strategy—might go in one direction, while the second effect could go in the other.

Indeed, the association between higher growth rates and an export-promotion strategy had already been established before the present project began, although additional evidence has since confirmed the results. The earlier NBER project on foreign trade regimes and economic development, in particular, had as its central question the link between trade strategy and growth (see Bhagwati 1978; Krueger 1978).[2] It seemed neither necessary nor desirable to cover that ground again.

Rather, the project on alternative trade strategies and employment was designed to investigate the possibility that faster overall growth under export promotion might be associated with a slower rate of growth of demand for labor owing to the second and third effects. Three alternative, mutually inconsistent hypotheses were all possible given existing knowledge:

1. The amount of employment generated is relatively independent of the trade strategy.

2. Import substitution generates significantly less employment growth than does an export promotion strategy.

3. An export promotion strategy is unlikely to entail significantly more employment growth than an import substitution strategy and may in fact conflict with efforts to expand employment.

The first possibility—that trade strategy does not affect employment very much—might arise for several reasons. First, one might be able to establish the direction of difference in labor intensity of production but find that the difference, if any, was small enough that, within the conceivable range of relative growth rates, the effects on employment would be second-order in size. Second, one might find that a particular policy (such as subsidization of capital goods imports) not really essential to the trade strategy adopted had adverse effects on employment and that a different set of policies could implement the same trade strategy without the adverse employment effects. Finally, it might be that the influences determining the composition of exporting and import substitution industries are independent of factor intensities, and that different relative rates of growth of the two groups of industries would not necessarily affect the rate of growth of employment.

The second possibility—that import substitution industries require considerably less labor per unit of capital and per unit of output—is the forecast that would arise from straightforward interpretation of the two-factor Heckscher-Ohlin model of trade. Developing countries would presumably have their comparative advantage, at least in the early stages of growth, in exporting labor-intensive commodities and importing goods with relatively higher capital (and perhaps skilled labor) requirements.

Finally, there were those who argued that export promotion and employment growth were conflicting objectives. There were several possible reasons given. One view was that developed countries themselves have erected, or would erect if export promotion strategies were seriously adopted, sufficiently high barriers to import of labor-intensive goods that the developing countries can compete only in capital-intensive exports. Another basis for the argument was the casual empiricism suggesting that the exports of some developing countries—notably Colombia and Brazil—were capital intensive. Yet others claimed that most of the exports of manufactured goods originating in developing countries are produced by branches and subsidiaries of multinational corporations that, it was alleged, use the capital-intensive technology of the home country.

If export-promoting growth was capital intensive, there remained a question why it was so: the answer might lie partly in the mix of export incentives granted in the developing country and in domestic policies affecting the relative profitability of different industries. If instead developing countries' potential manufactured export were capital-intensive not because of distortions but because of factors associated with comparative advantage, it was important to ascertain this and to obtain some idea of the empirical magnitude and importance of the phenomenon.

1.3   History of the Debate on Trade Strategies

Chapter 3 is devoted to analysis of alternative trade strategies. Here the purpose is to provide some background on the context of the discussion.

The basic theory of resource allocation under competition and of comparative advantage has long since provided the theoretical rationale for advocacy of relatively free trade with balanced incentives for export promotion and import substitution so that the marginal cost of earning and saving foreign exchange can be equalized (see Bhagwati 1968).

Early advocates of import substitution based their case on some form of pessimism about the prospects for growth of export earnings, a secular tendency for the terms of trade for primary commodities to decline, and the need for "industrialization" (Prebisch 1959). Under the influence of these arguments and foreign-exchange crises induced by excessively ambitious development and other government expenditures and/or the end of the Korean War boom and the consequent drop in export earnings, most developing countries adopted import substitution as a development strategy.

The *practical* shortcomings of such a strategy have become painfully evident to virtually all observers and have been extensively analyzed in research undertaken at Williams College on import substitution and by the National Bureau of Economic Research project on foreign trade regimes and economic development.[3] Briefly, initial emphasis on import substitution led to:

1. Overvaluation of the exchange rate, with consequent disincentives to potential export, failure of foreign exchange earnings to grow, and thus an increasingly stringent exchange-control regime.

2. A series of partial, ad hoc incentives for export, with increasingly complex, often internally inconsistent, bureaucratic regulations, red tape, and complexities that were a consequence of recognition of the scarcity value of foreign exchange. The result was increased demands on the bureaucracy, ever greater incentives for evasion of regulations, and mutual suspicion between the business and government sectors.

3. Increasingly high-cost industries as the "easy" import substitution activities were undertaken first. This led to the loss of any gains that might otherwise have been realized from efficient size of plant, economies of scale, and so on.

4. Lack of competition among newly established firms. Because of the small size of the market, it was seldom feasible to allow many firms in an industry, and licensing of imports of machinery precluded free entry. The result was that import-licensing mechanisms, capital-goods licensing procedures, and other inevitable concomitants of exchange control led to the development of "lazy" entrepreneurs whose inattention to cost consciousness, quality control, and good management was not penalized since profitability stemmed from monopoly positions and the ability to get licenses.

5. Implicit subsidization of capital goods imports. Although one might think that import substitution policies would be across the board in their application, almost all countries with overvalued exchange rates were reluctant to impose surcharges and high duties on machinery and equipment imports for fear of discouraging investment. One of the effects of import substitution policies and consequent currency overvaluation was therefore to provide implicit subsidies for imports of capital goods for such firms as were able to obtain permission to invest.[4]

6. Increased dependence on permitted imports, largely confined to "essentials." Whereas consumption levels were dependent on imports at an earlier stage, import substitution brought about dependence on imports of raw materials and intermediate goods for production, employment, and consumption. "Foreign exchange shortage" led to underutilization of capacity. Economies therefore were sensitive to fluctuations in foreign exchange earnings for production, as well as consumption, levels.

In addition, import substitution policies have often interacted with domestic economic policies in ways that theory might not have forecast. The National Bureau of Economic Research project on foreign trade regimes and economic development has provided documentation on some sorts of interaction: between import licensing and investment licensing; between domestic agricultural policies and the effects of the effective exchange rate in inducing additional exports; in affecting the choice of industry, and so on. A major result of that research effort has been the demonstration of the importance of analyzing the totality of policies affecting a given issue (see Bhagwati 1978).

The advantages of export promotion, by contrast, appear to go somewhat beyond those suggested by the microeconomic theory of optimal resource allocation, although, of course, there can be overemphasis on export promotion as well as on import substitution. Briefly, these additional advantages include the following: (1) competition can be provided by the international marketplace and thus attention to quality control, to new techniques and products, and to good management practices is likely to be encouraged; (2) since export promotion generally entails subsidies in a variety of forms, the costs of excesses are more visible than in import substitution, and there are forces within the government, especially the Ministry of Finance, that therefore place pressures against greatly imbalanced incentives; (3) efficient firms and industries can grow rapidly without being limited to the rate of growth of domestic demand, and whatever economies of scale or indivisibilities there are can be exhausted; and (4) governments cannot achieve their ends by relying upon quantitative restrictions when fostering export growth and must therefore create incentives for exporting.[5]

Thus the argument is strong that an outward-looking export promotion strategy is more conducive to development than an import substitution strategy. In addition, focus upon exports is likely to provide better interaction with domestic policies and variables than import substitution, although, of course, there are better and worse ways of implementing either strategy. Moreover, there has been a significant switch in the emphasis of the developing countries over the past decade, as emphasis on import substitution has gradually lessened and encouragements for the development of exports, particularly of nontraditional products, have begun. The question of how that switch in policy will affect employment is therefore extremely important.

2　Employment and Labor Markets in Less Developed Countries

The purpose of this chapter is to provide the reader with an overview of those aspects of developing countries' labor markets that are important for interpreting data on the trade strategies–employment relationship and to indicate how the countries covered in the project have fared with respect to growth of employment, labor force, and the real wage. To gain insight into the possible order of magnitude of the effect a shift in trade strategy would have on employment, country authors necessarily relied on labor coefficients, average wage rate data, and other observable characteristics of employed workers according to industrial sector. In this chapter, focus is upon the way labor markets function in developing countries and on the ways different institutional characteristics can affect the observed coefficients. Central questions are: (1) what we mean by talking about the determinants of employment; (2) how labor/output ratios may be interpreted; (3) how labor market "distortions" affect the trade strategies–employment relation; and (4) how the role of skills can be analyzed.

The determinants of employment and real wages in LDCs are complex, covering virtually every aspect of the development process. For the rural economy there are questions about the degree to which there may be "disguised unemployment" and about the determinants of average and marginal labor productivity and real incomes. For the urban economy there are extremely difficult questions about the determinants of the structure of real wages, the links between the "formal" and the "informal" sectors, and the factors that influence the level of urban employment and the rate at which it increases. There is another set of issues related to the determinants of migration between rural and urban areas and of the links between the two parts of the economy. Finally, all the factors affecting the rate of population growth are important for analysis of labor markets, largely because it is rapid population growth that underlies concern about the "employment problem" in most developing countries.

Knowledge and understanding of all these factors in developing countries' labor markets has increased rapidly over the past decade, but it is still far from adequate. It would require several sets of country studies at least as complex as the ones undertaken in this project to begin to develop with any degree of confidence estimates of the empirical orders of magnitude involved. Indeed, many of the country authors found it necessary to delve into their countries' labor markets in order to obtain even first approximations to the links between their trade strategies and employment.[1] In this chapter, therefore, focus is on the underlying theory needed to interpret the data. In addition, some estimates of empirical orders of magnitude for population and labor force growth, employment/output elasticities, and related variables for the countries covered by this project are provided. It remains for chapter 7 to examine the country authors' findings with respect to the existence and magnitude of labor market imperfections, and for chapter 8 to analyze the effect of those imperfections on observed coefficients of the trade strategies–employment relation.

The first section of this chapter assesses the nature of the "employment problem" in developing countries. The second then reviews some key aspects of labor market behavior that are relevant for analyzing the effect of alternative trade strategies. The third section focuses upon some pertinent aspects of urban labor markets. The final section summarizes some salient aspects of the experience of the project countries.

2.1 The "Employment Problem" in Less Developed Countries

Everyone agrees that unemployment is a "problem" and that increased employment opportunities are an "objective" in most LDCs. Employment and employment growth are major points of concern in virtually all of them. There is less agreement, however, on the nature and cause of the "problem" and on why employment creation is desirable.

In part this is because the reasons for concern differ from country to country. They include: (1) increasing relatively high-productivity employment opportunities outside the agricultural sector to absorb the low-income agricultural population; (2) increasing employment opportunities in the urban sector to reduce the number of urban unemployed; and (3) providing employment opportunities for the poor to increase their real income and improve the distribution of income.

The first concern, increasing nonagricultural employment opportunities, has been a focal point of development economics ever since W. Arthur Lewis's classic article, "Economic Development with Unlimited Supplies of Labour" (Lewis 1954). Because a very large fraction of the labor force is engaged in agriculture with a very low average productivity of labor in the early stage of development, Lewis characterized the development process as that of creating higher-product nonagricultural employment opportunities at a rate rapid enough first to increase the share of the labor force in nonagricultural activities and then to decrease absolutely the number of persons engaged in agriculture.

Although Lewis's analysis led to the view that there was "disguised unemployment" in agriculture, positing a zero marginal product of labor in agriculture was not really central to his analysis. Rather, the central insight was that additional nonagricultural employment opportunities would raise real income by transferring persons from low-wage/low-product to higher-wage/higher-product employment. Seen in this light, Lewis's concern with the employment problem was that of increasing the productivity associated with the employment activities of the population.

Although subsequent developments have indicated forcefully that there are many opportunities for increasing real output and income within agriculture, to this day one central strand of concern with employment creation in developing countries is that of raising the average and marginal product of the entire labor force. Emphasis is placed upon nonagricultural employment opportunities largely because it is believed that, given pressures of population growth on the land, nonagricultural employment opportunities will (in conjunction with output increases in the agricultural sector) provide the best means for increasing real income and thereby raising the rate of growth of per capita incomes.[2]

The second concern, absorbing the urban unemployed, focuses more specifically upon the social hardships associated with unemployment in the cities in developing countries. It is well known that urban populations have increased very rapidly in most developing countries in the past several decades (see table 2.1). In many countries that growth has been accompanied by an increasing number of urban unemployed, while the rate of increase in employment opportunities, at least in the "formal" sector of the economy, has been sluggish.[3] Individuals concerned with urban unemployment have regarded urban employment creation as a desirable policy goal because they believe this would reduce urban unemployment and its accompanying hardships. It will be seen in section 2.2 that increasing the number of job opportunities in an urban sector does not always reduce unemployment.

The third concern, providing employment opportunities to the poor, has somewhat different origins. Persons concerned with employment creation for this motive have believed that a promising means of alleviating poverty is to provide employment opportunities for the poor. Unlike Lewis's focus, in which employment creation is associated with economic growth and rising per capita real incomes, the objective has been redis-

| Table 2.1 | | | Population, Urban Population, and Labor Force Growth Rates, 1960–70 and 1970–75 (Average Percentage per Annum) | | | | |

	Population		Urban Population		Total Labor Force	
Country	1960–70	1970–75	1960–70	1970–75	1960–70	1970–75
Brazil	2.9	2.9	5.0	4.5	2.8	2.9
Chile	2.1	1.8	3.7	2.7	1.4	2.5
Colombia	2.9	2.8	5.4	4.9	2.7	2.9
Indonesia	2.2	2.4	4.4	4.7	2.2	2.2
Ivory Coast	3.4	4.2	7.3	6.5	1.9	1.9
Pakistan	2.8	3.9	2.9	5.3	1.9	2.6
South Korea	2.6	1.8	6.2	4.9	2.9	2.9
Thailand	3.1	2.9	4.8	5.3	2.1	2.9
Tunisia	2.1[a]	2.3	4.9[a]	4.2	0.7[a]	2.3
Uruguay	0.6	0.4	1.9	1.7	0.8	1.0

Source: International Bank for Reconstruction and Development, *World Development Report*, 1978.
[a]Mustapha Nabli suggests in correspondence that the Tunisian labor force figures, especially for 1960–70, seem too low.

tribution rather than growth. This focus explicitly raises the questions of the extent to which "employment creation" is compatible with economic growth, or whether providing more jobs may not lower the rate of economic growth.

Conflict would arise, of course, only if job creation meant reducing real output, or if creating more jobs with given investible resources implied achieving a lower increment in real output than creating fewer jobs with those same resources. It is beyond the scope of this volume to analyze that issue in detail. Insofar as policies can be identified that would permit a faster rate of increase in employment (especially of the unskilled) with efficient allocation of resources, everyone would agree that those job opportunities would be preferable to ones that reduced real income and output. It is therefore safe to conclude that, if a trade strategy that is optimal from the viewpoint of resource allocation also creates (in the sense to be defined below) as many new job opportunities as a nonoptimal one, or more, the question of "conflict" between real income and employment does not arise.

For the country studies, authors generally focused their research on urban or industrial employment. Table 2.1 gives data on the rates of population growth, urban population, and labor force growth for the periods 1960–70 and the 1970–75. As can be seen, experiences have been markedly different, but all countries have had rapidly growing urban populations. At one extreme, Chile and Uruguay experienced relatively slow overall growth in population and labor force, but urban immigration has resulted in growth rates for the urban population well above population growth rates. However, by 1975, 83 percent of Chile's and 81 percent of Uruguay's population was urban, so future pressures should diminish and the main task is that of creating higher-productivity, predominantly nonagricultural jobs. By contrast, Indonesia has had a more rapid rate of population growth, and her population was only 19 percent urban in 1975. The prospective growth rate of the labor force is substantial for years to come, both because improved health standards should result in increased life expectancies and labor force participation, and because rural out-migration (or at least shifts from agricultural to nonagricultural employment) will continue. Brazil, Pakistan, and Thailand have the highest rates of natural population increase among the countries covered and thus face rapidly growing labor forces; the rate of growth of the labor force was higher from 1970 to 1975 than it was during the decade of the 1960s. The high Ivorian rate of population growth reflects immigration, whereas Tunisia experienced out-migration of workers to Western Europe and Libya, thereby holding down labor force growth up to 1975–76. Future Tunisian labor force growth will probably be more rapid than was the case from 1960 to 1975.

Focus on the link between trade strategies and employment was therefore centered upon the nonagricultural, and often the industrial, sector.[4] This was done partly because we believed that rapid rates of nonagricultural labor force growth made this the pressing policy issue, and partly because most of the key links between choice of trade strategy and employment arise in the industrial sector of developing countries. The rationale for this is spelled out in chapter 4. Suffice it here to point out that this focus is consistent with many views of rural labor markets, including the Lewis viewpoint, and also with the notion that rapidly growing populations must, if per capita incomes are to rise, find productive nonagricultural employment.

The above discussion raises yet another issue. That has to do with what is meant by "job creation" and with what constitute the determinants of (nonagricultural) employment and its growth rate. If labor markets in developing countries functioned well in the neoclassical sense, the "employment problem" would center entirely upon the set of concerns related to productivity and shifting the demand for labor upward. Outward shifts in the demand for labor in excess of the rate of outward shift of supply (owing to population growth and consequent changes in the labor force) would result in rising real wages, since by hypothesis in a well-functioning market all would be employed at a similar wage.[5] Failure to shift the demand curve for labor outward rapidly enough would result not in unemployment, but rather in a decline in the real wage.[6] This provides the motive for concern with shifting the demand for labor outward, which is the interpretation placed on "employment" in this volume.

With a perfectly elastic labor supply from rural areas (either because of the relative constancy of the marginal product of labor within a wide range or because of a divergence between average and marginal product),[7] the motive for concern with employment creation is clearly that additional employment opportunities in the urban sector imply a higher average per capita income (and a more rapid approach to the day when the labor supply from the rural area becomes upward sloping) than would otherwise be the case.[8]

However, there has long been a belief that labor markets do not always function in neoclassical fashion in many developing countries. There are important questions about the determinants of the labor supply to nonrural areas, the degree to which labor markets are fragmented or integrated,[9] and nonmarket influences upon the level and structure of wages. Open unemployment in urban areas has emerged as a major policy problem in some countries, and consideration of the "employment problem" requires a satisfactory analysis of why unemployment exists, who the unemployed are, and what their resources are. Although such an analysis is beyond the scope of this volume, some aspects are crucial to the trade strategies–employment relation.

Table 2.2 gives data on manufacturing employment, the unemployment rate, and the rate of growth of real wages for the project countries and Argentina. As can be seen, recorded urban unemployment was a problem of major magnitude in the mid-1970s for the Ivory Coast, Pakistan, and Tunisia. South Korea experienced very high urban unemployment rates in the early 1960s, and Argentina's and Uruguay's unemployment rates were also rather high at that time. Discussion of employment growth rates and the real wage is deferred until section 2.3.

For purposes of analyzing the trade strategies–employment relation, the presence of open urban unemployment must give the analyst pause. In particular, under some kinds of market imperfections, outward shifts in the demand for labor can generate responses that largely, if not entirely, offset any increase in employment that might otherwise result. This can be seen with two simple examples. If labor markets are sufficiently fragmented, outward shifts in demand for labor in some parts of the market may not result in additional employment but instead may raise wages for those already employed in the sector. Likewise, if unions are sufficiently powerful so that all outward shifts in the demand for labor in unionized sectors are fully offset by increased real wages, policies designed to create jobs in the high-productivity unionized sectors are destined to frustration.

Thus, in interpreting data on labor coefficients and average wage rates the analyst must ascertain whether labor coefficients reflect distortions rather than the inherent "labor intensities" that would be observed in a

Table 2.2   Employment Growth, Unemployment, and Real Wages, 1960–75

Country	Year	Manufacturing Employment	Unemployment Rate	Real Wage (1968 = 100)
Argentina	1963	83.4[a]	8.8	94.4
	1968	100.0	4.9	100.0
	1973	120.3	5.4	106.2
Brazil	1963	93.4[a]	n.a.	90.0
	1968	100.0	n.a.	100.0
	1973	159.5	n.a.	122.1
Chile	1963	96.1[a]	n.a.	65.5
	1968	100.0	n.a.	100.0
	1973	106.7	4.8	82.0
Colombia	1963	98.9[a]	n.a.	95.4
	1968	100.0	n.a.	100.0
	1973	122.7	n.a.	99.0
Indonesia	1961	185.6[b]	5.4	102.5[g]
	1965	205.9	2.3	75.8[g]
	1971	257.3	8.8	109.3[g]
Ivory Coast	1960	36.2[a]	n.a.	99.3
	1968	100.0	n.a.	100.0
	1973	149.8	20.0[c,d]	131.7
Pakistan	1951	93.3[b]	3.2	10.3[h]
	1961	175.8	1.5	100.0
	1972	135.8	13.0	143.0

competitive labor market. Observed trade patterns may be influenced by the existing pattern of wages and may not reflect comparative advantage that would exist under an efficient allocation of resources. Finally, identifying the effect that alternative trade strategies might have upon the demand for labor cannot be equated with identifying its effect on employment when some sorts of distortions are present, as will be seen in the Harris-Todaro model presented in section 2.2.2.

2.2   Labor Markets in Less Developed Countries

2.2.1   Aggregate Employment

In the first two decades after World War II, the analysis of the determinants of the aggregate level of employment in developed countries focused largely on determinants of aggregate demand. Expansionary monetary and fiscal policy was regarded as the appropriate tool to reduce involuntary unemployment. While there is undoubtedly scope for appropriate fiscal and monetary management in developing countries,[10]

Table 2.2 (cont.)

Country	Year	Manufacturing Employment	Unemployment Rate	Real Wage (1968 = 100)
South Korea	1963	52.1[a]	16.4[f]	80.1
	1968	100.0	9.0[f]	100.0
	1973	151.6	6.8[f]	136.2
Thailand	1960	66.0[a]	n.a.	104.7[f]
	1968	100.0	n.a.	100.0[f]
	1973	189.6	6.7	109.3[f]
Tunisia	1961	50.9[a]	n.a.	89.0
	1968	100.0	n.a.	100.0
	1972	122.2	n.a.	102.0
	1975	162.0	14.0[e]	130.3
Uruguay	1963	210.4[b]	10.3	119.1
	1975	205.1	6.7	85.2

Sources: All data are from the country study chapters (Krueger et al. 1981), with the exceptions indicated:

Argentina: data are from national accounts estimates; unemployment pertains to Buenos Aires; real wages are for unskilled labor. Data were provided by Julio Nogues.

Thailand: National Statistical Office. Data were supplied by Narongchai Akrasanee.

Tunisia: real wage is the average industrial real wage. Data were provided by Mustapha Nabli.

[a]1968 = 100.

[b]Thousands of workers.

[c]Urban unemployment rate.

[d]Rate for 1976.

[e]Estimate.

[f]Nonfarm unemployment rate.

[g]1967 = 100.

[h]1954 rate; the real wage is that applicable to large-scale manufacturing.

n.a. = not available.

most analysts of the determinants of aggregate employment have concentrated on other aspects. These have centered upon supply constraints, either technological (as in Eckaus's model) or economic (as in the Chenery-Bruno two-gap model) as limiting output and employment and their growth, at least in the nonagricultural sector. According to the technological hypothesis, there is insufficient scope for substitution between labor and other factors of production to permit full employment at existing levels of factor availability. The empirical validity of this proposition is one of the questions of this project.[11] Under models in the spirit of Chenery-Bruno, a "shortage of foreign exchange" limits the rate of expansion of output and employment; if that model correctly described reality, a trade strategy that generated greater foreign exchange earnings would result in greater aggregate (urban) employment, since more foreign exchange would permit a higher level of investment and production.[12]

In most developing countries, as was seen above, the primary concern is not aggregate demand determination, but rather increasing the demand for labor, especially in the urban sector. It is at this juncture that questions arise about wage determination mechanisms and the link between outward shifts in the demand for labor and employment. In countries where it is generally believed that the labor market is imperfect,[13] there is a sizable wage differential between rural and urban employment (and often also between types of urban employment). There are numerous hypotheses about the causes of the differential,[14] but essentially only two models of the effects on the overall allocation of labor. One is that all those who cannot find employment in the urban sector (given its higher wage) are employed in the rural economy at a lower marginal product and income. The alternative hypothesis is that some persons become unemployed in the urban sector as they seek higher-paying alternatives there. This latter version, known as the Harris-Todaro model, is a convenient basis for outlining the various issues important for analysis of labor market behavior as it affects the trade strategies–employment relation in developing countries.

2.2.2   The Harris-Todaro Model

We start by setting up the model, which can then serve as a framework within which the various aspects of LDC labor markets can be analyzed. Essentially, there are two sectors, rural and urban. In its simplest form, there are six variables in the Harris-Todaro model: the rural labor force, the rural wage, the level of urban employment, the urban wage, urban unemployment, and the number of migrants from the rural to the urban sector. Migration serves as the link (and equilibrating variable) between the two sectors.

The relations in the basic model are as follows:

(1) $$w_a = f(L_a)$$

(2) $$w_e = \bar{w}_e$$

(3) $$L_e = g(w_e)$$

(4) $$pw_e = w_a$$

(5) $$p = L_e/(L_e + L_u)$$

(6) $$L_a + L_e + L_u = \bar{L},$$

where:

L_a is labor employed in agriculture, an endogenous variable
L_e is labor employed in the urban area, also endogenous

L_u is unemployed labor in the urban area, also endogenous
$\bar{L}$ is the total labor force, exogenously given
w_a is the agricultural wage, endogenous
w_e is the urban wage, and $\bar{w}_e$ is the minimum urban wage, exogenous
p is as defined in equation (5), endogenous.

In the form presented, the model describes an equilibrium configuration of variables. It can be used to perform comparative statics exercises, investigating what happens to key variables in response to shifts in the parameters of the model. For any such exercise, the change in the sum of urban unemployed and urban employed is equal to migration.

An equilibrium configuration is given by a circumstance in which, given the predetermined urban wage $\bar{w}_e$ above the rural wage (a decreasing function of the number engaged in agriculture), unemployment is sufficiently high so that additional persons from rural areas do not wish to migrate despite the wage differential. That is, for an equilibrium, out-migrants from rural areas must have flowed to the city in sufficient numbers so that the urban wage times the probability of employment (which is in this representation equal to the fraction of the urban labor force employed) is equal to the rural wage. One can modify the model to allow for any particular variation in the form of the migration relationship.[15]

Figure 2.1 illustrates some of the key properties of the model. The length of the horizontal axis represents the entire labor force, with labor employed in agriculture measured from left to right and labor employed in the urban sector measured from right to left. Wage rates (at assumed fixed terms of trade) are measured on the vertical axis with that in agriculture on the left side and that for the urban sector on the right side. The demand for labor (the marginal product of labor schedules) is drawn downward-sloping. An equilibrium, in the absence of any distortion in the urban wage, is represented by the urban wage w_e^o at which $L_1\bar{L}$ individuals would be employed in industry and OL_1 persons would be employed in agriculture at the same wage.

Assume now that the urban wage is somehow set at w_e'. At that wage, $L_3\bar{L}$ will be employed in the urban sector. If all other workers were engaged in agriculture, the agricultural wage would be w_a'. But, according to the Harris-Todaro model, such a point does not represent an equilibrium, owing to the disparity between the two wage rates. Rural workers will migrate to the city seeking higher-wage employment. Drawing a rectangular hyperbola through the point b (on the urban demand for labor curve at the fixed urban wage) permits finding the point where the average urban wage (taking into account both the employed and the unemployed) is equal to the rural wage. In figure 2.1 that equilibrium is represented by the point c, with OL_2 persons employed in the rural

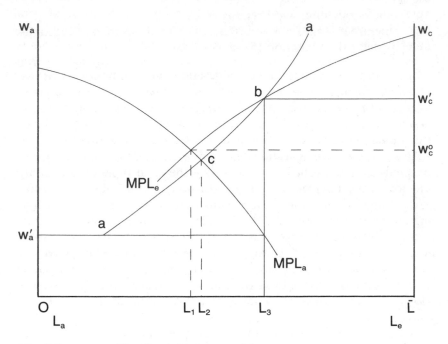

Fig. 2.1   The Harris-Todaro model.

sector, $L_3\bar{L}$ persons employed in the urban sector, and L_2L_3 persons unemployed in the urban sector. It is easy to see that a higher urban wage would result in more urban unemployed. Moreover, depending on the slopes of the two demand for labor curves, it is possible that an upward shift in the urban demand for labor might even result in more urban unemployment as rural workers sought urban jobs.

It should be noted that, in the absence of an exogenously given urban wage, unemployment would not exist and wages would be equated between sectors (allowing for differences in skills and living costs).[16] Indeed, with a sufficiently low urban wage, a zero unemployment level is a feasible outcome of the model. Also, a higher urban wage always leads to greater urban unemployment and hence larger out-migration from the rural sector. In the absence of a mechanism for raising the rural wage to a sufficiently high level, efforts to achieve full employment in the urban sector are doomed to failure: creating additional jobs will induce more immigrants to the urban sector than the number of jobs created. The greater the number of urban employment opportunities, the more unemployed persons there will be to maintain the equality in equation (5) after the upward shift in equation (3).[17]

A number of qualifications and refinements can be made to the model, but its basic structure indicates the factors that must be considered in analyzing developing countries' labor markets: the behavior of rural labor markets and the nature of the out-migration function; the determinants of the urban wage level and structure; and the characteristics of urban unemployment. Even in its simplest form, the model already indicates that the relation between policies to increase employment and policies to reduce unemployment may not be straightforward, and that changing the mechanism by which urban wages are determined may be crucial to domestic employment objectives. It will be seen in chapter 4 that an inappropriate real wage may also significantly distort a country's pattern of trade. All these considerations point to the crucial importance of the wage determination mechanism in analyzing the trade strategies–employment relationship.

2.2.3   Agricultural and Rural Labor Markets

The NBER project on alternative trade strategies and employment was focused primarily on the implications of alternative trade strategies for the commodity composition of trade and production in the industrial sector. In this section, discussion of agricultural and rural labor markets therefore addresses two interrelated issues: why it makes sense to focus on nonagricultural employment opportunities; and the extent to which one can consider the opportunity cost of rural labor to be relatively low.

A key characteristic of almost all LDCs is the high fraction of the population engaged in agriculture.[18] Whether a shift from the rural to the urban areas is necessary in order to shift from agriculture to other economic activities is a difficult question, and no answer is attempted here. What does seem to be the case is that a shift of part of the labor force away from agriculture and into other economic activities, which will be called urban for simplicity, is a necessary concomitant of the process of economic growth. Certainly, in all now-developed economies, the fraction of the labor force engaged in agriculture has rapidly diminished as living standards and productivity have increased.

A key question is the extent to which out-migration is cause or effect. On one view, labor is redundant within the agricultural sector, and any transfer of persons to other lines of economic activity with a positive marginal product constitutes a net gain to society and therefore constitutes part of the growth process. On the other view, agricultural output and productivity must be enhanced in order to release labor for other pursuits: individuals cannot leave the agricultural sector unless there are offsetting sources of productivity and output increases within that sector. Obviously the relationships are simultaneous: higher productivity in agriculture provides a "push," and additional jobs in other sectors of the economy provide a "pull."

The question whether there is "disguised unemployment" in rural areas, in the sense of individuals who can switch from farming to other occupations with no loss in product, has been hotly debated. There is a great deal of evidence suggesting that, at least during peak periods of planting and harvesting, the entire labor force is fully employed, and that more workers would increase the size of the harvest. Individuals may therefore be working fewer hours than they would wish during the nonpeak seasons, and seasonal underemployment may be a factor, but labor is not redundant. On that interpretation, moving an individual from a rural to an urban job does not in fact create "employment," but it may raise output if the urban job has a higher marginal product than the rural one.[19]

Regardless of which interpretation is correct, there is agreement that in countries with large rural sectors agricultural productivity and output must grow if economic development is to be sustained. To the extent that there is success in increasing agricultural output, the rate of increase in nonagricultural employment should substantially exceed the rate of growth of the labor force. This can happen with rising rural employment, since the nonagricultural sector absorbs a greater share of new labor force entrants than its share in the overall labor force. If, for example, a country with 3 percent growth of its labor force initially had three-quarters of its economically active population engaged in agriculture, nonagricultural employment would have to grow at a rate of 12 percent simply to keep the agricultural population constant. Any rate of growth of the nonagricultural labor force in excess of 3 percent but below 12 percent would imply a rising share of the nonagricultural sector in total employment, but an increasing absolute number of persons engaged in agriculture.

To be sure, any sustained rate of growth of the nonagricultural labor force greater than the rate of growth of population will eventually result in declines in the agricultural labor force as the share of the nonagricultural sector rises over time. Nonetheless, the time period during which the agricultural labor force continues increasing, although at a slower rate than population, may be substantial for most developing countries.

For present purposes, the main point is that it can make sense to regard a rapidly growing demand curve for nonagricultural labor as a policy objective provided it is recognized that agricultural production must be increasing simultaneously. Insofar as the demand curve for nonagricultural labor shifts outward reflecting the creation of alternative uses of labor with higher marginal productivity than can be attained in agriculture, the consequent higher incomes will be consistent with development objectives. Whether more nonagricultural employment implies increased total employment may not be important, provided the jobs so created reflect genuinely preferred opportunities for the individuals undertaking them. It was for this reason that the NBER project focused on nonagricultural employment implications of alternative trade strategies.

2.3 Urban Labor Markets

There are several key issues that frequently arise in analysis of urban employment and wage structures. These issues were important in interpreting the results for the individual country studies and therefore merit discussion here. They are the coexistence of "formal" and "informal" sectors within the urban economy; the extent and effectiveness of government-imposed regulations governing employment and wages; and the determinants of the wage structure in relation to characteristics of workers. All are interrelated and hinge in large part on the assumption that institutional or government-imposed constraints prevent the realization of an efficient competitive-market-determined outcome.[20]

2.3.1 Formal and Informal Sectors

Perhaps the most widely accepted modification to the basic Harris-Todaro model has been that suggested by Fields, relating to the characterization of the nonagricultural sector. Fields noted that in the development literature there was widespread recognition that large-scale organized industry usually coexists with small-scale "informal" activity.[21]

There are many characterizations of this split. Some refer to it as "modern" and "traditional," others as large-scale and small-scale, while in yet other instances the characterization is "factory" and "craft." Each of these picks up some of the features, which themselves can vary from country to country, of dichotomization among urban firms into two groups. The "formal" sector usually consists of larger-than-average firms, relying on fairly modern and capital-intensive techniques of production, over which government regulations governing conditions of employment are presumably enforceable. The small-scale sector, by contrast, has a large "craft" component and usually consists of much smaller enterprises, including many one- or two-person operations.

Of the countries covered in the project, Brazil, Chile, Colombia, the Ivory Coast, Tunisia, and Uruguay all had visible and identifiable informal sectors coexisting alongside the large-scale sector.[22] Average wages paid, and the labor intensity of individual activities, differed significantly.[23] For Hong Kong and South Korea the labor market did not seem to have this dichotomy to a noticeable degree.

By its nature, it is difficult to obtain reliable information about the informal sector. In countries for which any data are available, the evidence is that wages paid in the informal sector are considerably below those paid in the formal sector, and important questions arise about the relations between labor markets in the two sectors.

Fields's characterization of the informal sector may be close to the consensus. In his model, wages in the informal sector are flexible, and all who seek employment in that sector find it: the more workers there are, the lower the wage. The traditional-sector worker stands a lower chance of finding modern-sector employment than does an unemployed individual but is nonetheless a job-seeker in the formal sector. The typical migrant in Fields's model might move to a town, live with his cousin, and work in the cousin's shop in return for room and board until he finds modern-sector employment (with a lower probability of finding a job than someone fully unemployed, however). The effective supply of labor to the modern sector therefore includes not only the urban unemployed, but also workers in the urban informal sector and rural workers. However, because the latter two groups have smaller probabilities of locating modern-sector jobs than urban unemployed, they have smaller weights in the pool of job seekers than do the unemployed.

A problem for analysis of the employment implications of alternative trade strategies in the countries covered by the project was that labor coefficients were substantially higher, and wages substantially lower, in the informal sectors of many countries, and no single interpretation of this phenomenon seemed entirely satisfactory. In the Ivory Coast, for example, artisanal workers constitute 88 percent of the labor force and are 62 percent of the labor force even in activities producing HOS goods.[24] Monson provides separate estimates of labor coefficients for the artisanal and the modern sectors and notes that the influence of trade strategies upon employment hinges crucially not only upon which industries expand (although that too is a factor), but even more upon whether the expansion occurs in the modern or in the traditional sector (Monson 1981, table 6.11).

Too little is known about the informal sector in most LDCs for us to be confident that one can identify the size of firm associated with manufacturing for export or for import replacement. In general, country authors chose to use modern-sector coefficients for their estimates. In part this reflects the perhaps defensible belief that production of import-competing goods, or significant expansion of exports, is more likely to occur in large, modern firms than in small ones. Certainly there is considerable impressionistic evidence that import substitution production has expanded mostly in the "modern" sector. It should be recognized, however, that there may be a downward bias in the estimates of employment creation to the extent that small-scale firms might expand output for export markets or for import replacement.[25] If export (traditional) industries have a greater proportion of small-scale firms using labor-intensive techniques than do import substitution industries, the estimates of the differences in employment implications of alternative trade strategies are understated. Without substantial further research on that topic, however, it is difficult to draw any conclusions about the probable magnitude of such biases.

2.3.2   Wage Level Determination

Recall that the basic Harris-Todaro model posits that the urban wage rate is somehow exogenously determined: by hypothesis, endogenous determination of a market clearing wage would result in fewer migrants to the urban sector, more jobs, and a lower rate of unemployment.

Turning back to table 2.2, we see that data on the behavior of real wages in the project countries can be contrasted with data on the growth of manufacturing employment. In some of the project countries, most notably Pakistan, the real wage in large-scale manufacturing grew sharply while employment in manufacturing seems to have declined from 1961 to 1972. In others, such as Chile from 1963 to 1968, very slow employment growth was accompanied by a rapid increase in the real wage.

The country authors' analyses of wage determination mechanisms in their countries are reviewed in chapter 7. At this point the purpose is only to identify the variables crucial to analysis of the phenomenon. Suffice it to indicate that real wage behavior in the urban sector does not appear to have been market determined in all cases.

If the unskilled wage is set exogenously and at a high level—say by minimum wage legislation—two consequences will follow. First, firms attempting to maximize profits are induced to substitute capital for labor (and skilled for unskilled labor) to a greater extent than would be warranted for an efficient use of the country's resources. In addition, for developing countries that are relatively well endowed with unskilled labor, trade theory indicates that an efficient allocation of world resources will be one in which those countries produce and export goods that are relatively intensive in the use of unskilled labor. As will be seen in chapter 4, if too high an unskilled wage rate can be established and maintained, the commodities in which a labor-abundant country should have a comparative advantage will not be competitive on international markets. The source of comparative advantage will be removed as firms in other countries, despite their relatively less labor-abundant situations, become able to compete effectively in international markets. It thus follows that knowledge of the mechanisms by which the wage level for unskilled workers is established is of considerable importance for evaluating the optimality of existing techniques of production and also the pattern of production and trade.[26]

The hypothesis that rising minimum wages and other phenomena might lead to the substitution of capital for labor and to a lower rate of growth of employment than of output is given some preliminary support by inspection of rates of growth of the industrial work force, manufacturing output, and the implied employment/output elasticity for the project countries for the period 1960–70. These are given in table 2.3. As can be seen, most countries' manufacturing output grew fairly rapidly, but in all but two—the Ivory Coast and Pakistan—the rate of growth of employment was considerably lower. Three countries—Chile, Tunisia, and Uruguay, had implied employment elasticities of less than 0.4.[27] These were all countries for which the country authors believed that substantial intervention in wage determination occurred. Pakistan, Indonesia, and South Korea are among the countries in which it is believed that during the 1960s the labor market functioned fairly well:[28] in the first two, employment elasticities were fairly high, while in South Korea, the rate of employment growth—10.8 percent annually, appears to have been so high that real wages rose and capital deepening occurred in response to market forces.

It is for countries with low employment/output elasticities, high real wages, and open unemployment that questions pertaining to the informal labor market, the nature of the "modern" sector, and issues regarding the extent of skills possessed by the "unskilled" workers in the industrial labor force are crucial. For some governments have legislated conditions of work, including wages and salaries, fringe benefits, and working conditions, in a way that has led observers to believe that the resulting labor costs to firms far exceeded an "equilibrium" wage. This was the case in many of the project countries. In other countries it may be that unions have had sufficient market power to permit them to raise wages,[29]

Table 2.3   **Estimates of Industrial Employment Elasticity of Manufacturing Output, 1960–70**

Country	Continuous Average Annual Percentage Rate of Growth		Implied Employment Elasticity
	Industrial Labor Force	Manufacturing Output	
Brazil	4.5	5.6	.833
Chile	1.1	3.2	.343
Colombia	3.8	5.2	.731
Indonesia	3.7	4.2	.881
Ivory Coast	12.2	9.2	1.327
Pakistan	9.0	7.7	1.169
South Korea	10.8	16.6	.651
Thailand	6.0	10.1	.594
Tunisia	1.2	4.5	.267
Uruguay	.6	1.6	.375

Source: Derived from International Bank for Reconstruction and Development, *World Tables 1976*, table 1 of Comparative Economic Data for Manufacturing Output Growth; table 3 of Social Indicators for Industrial Labor Force Growth.

although no country author believed this to be the case for his country. If industrial workers are considerably more skilled than their rural counterparts owing either to more years of formal schooling or to greater experience and on-the-job training, then existing wages may reflect the outcome of market forces rather than government interventions.[30]

Each country author had to form a judgment about the relative importance of government-imposed or union-negotiated floors on wages for unskilled workers. The issue is complicated by a number of considerations. On one hand there are several factors that tend to mitigate the effect of minimum and union-negotiated wages. First, governments (or unions) may not be able to, or may choose not to, enforce minimum wages. Second, the minimum or union-negotiated wage may in fact be set at a level not significantly different from the wage that would prevail in the absence of intervention. In this regard it is noteworthy that the authors for the high-inflation Latin American countries reported that inflation seriously undermined the bite of minimum-wage requirements. On the other hand, there are many legislative measures that affect the costs of hiring or releasing workers and raise the cost of labor as perceived by employers. In several countries the tax on wages for social insurance purposes has risen very sharply; in Brazil it is equal to almost half the wage. In some countries firms are expected to hire more workers than they really need, providing training programs or even accepting redundant labor, in return for "special consideration" in receipt of rationed credit, import licenses, and other administered resources. In other cases housing for workers, health care, and other mandated provisions are costly. Workers fortunate enough to find employment may have high standards of living, but the high labor costs induced thereby may shut off employment opportunities for other potential entrants to the urban sector.

There are those who believe that the key distinction between the formal and the informal sectors in LDCs lies in the enforceability of the minimum wage and other labor legislation over the "formal" sector and their unenforceability in the "informal" sector. It will be seen in chapter 7 that the pattern that emerges from the country studies tends to support this view and to indicate sizable effects on trade and employment.

2.3.3   Labor Force Skills and Wage Structure

Improving the skill composition of the labor force is universally recognized as one of the important factors in the process of raising output and living standards. Developing countries normally are abundantly endowed with unskilled workers but have relatively little "human capital" and physical capital per head.[31] For analysis of the implications of alternative trade strategies, therefore, it was desirable to analyze not only numbers of workers but also skill utilization in different activities.

This led naturally to a desire to estimate the skill coefficients of alternative industrial activities in much the same way as labor coefficients were estimated. In some cases country authors were able to provide estimates of "skill coefficients" with data on such variables as "blue-collar" and "white-collar" or "unskilled" and "skilled" workers per unit of output and value added in different activities. In some instances, including Hong Kong and Tunisia, a more detailed breakdown of skill categories was available.

Even when such data are available, however, using these categories is conceptually equivalent to regarding each worker within a category as a perfect substitute for every other on a one-to-one basis. The "human capital" formulation has shown that there are degrees and degrees of skills and that, in a well-functioning labor market, an "earnings function" for individual workers will reflect years of formal education, on-the-job training, years of experience, and other variables.[32] In such circumstances, data on the average wage paid to workers in a given industry may prove a better indicator of the skill coefficients associated with the industry than a counting of categories of workers.[33]

From the viewpoint of the country authors, this led to a major conceptual difficulty. Insofar as there was reason to believe that urban labor markets in their countries functioned imperfectly, differences in average earnings between activities reflected not only differences in "human capital" but also labor market imperfections. Many of the country authors therefore attempted to use whatever data they had at hand to estimate the degree to which earnings differentials were a function of these two separate influences. In some countries, such as Thailand, so little information was available on worker characteristics that the task proved insurmountable. In other countries, such as Tunisia and Chile, authors chose to take mean earnings by occupational groups and weight the different occupational categories by mean wages to construct industry-specific averages rather than using average wages by industry.

For purposes of analyzing the trade strategies–employment relationship, it was reassuring that physical measures of skills and value measures tended to show much the same pattern and to reinforce each other. The country authors' difficulties in this regard, however, are strong testimony to the need for much further research on the determinants of wage structures in developing countries.

2.4　Summary of Country Characteristics

It is difficult to generalize about experience with employment in each of the project countries, but several patterns seem to appear. First, there are those countries, including Brazil (until 1968), Chile, Colombia (until 1968), Thailand, and Uruguay, where urban employment opportunities grew relatively slowly and where, for one reason or another, real wages paid to urban workers were either very high or rising fairly rapidly. Second, there is a group of countries where real wages have not risen very much, and where the urban labor force has grown at moderate rates. This group includes Argentina, Brazil since 1968, Colombia since 1968, Indonesia, the Ivory Coast, Pakistan, Thailand, and Tunisia. Finally, there are South Korea and Hong Kong, in which there appears to have developed relatively full employment with rising real wages and expanding urban employment opportunities in the 1960s and 1970s. Except for those two, every project country experienced a significant "employment problem" during part of the period under review. Either unemployment was rising along with real wages, or real wages were stagnant and urban employment still grew only moderately. It remains for later chapters to analyze the degree to which the choice of trade strategy interacted with these outcomes.

3 Trade Strategies, Growth, and Employment

As indicated in chapter 1, there are several ways in which the choice of trade strategy (and the policy instruments used to implement it) is linked with the demand for labor. First, the trade strategy may influence the overall growth rate of the economy, thereby influencing employment through a variety of channels. Next, labor/output and labor/value added ratios may differ significantly between industries. Insofar as trade strategy influences the structure of production, differences in factor proportions between exporting and import substitution industries affect the demand for labor. Finally, policy instruments used under alternative trade strategies may affect the choice of technique within all or a subset of industries, inducing more or less demand for labor than would otherwise be the case for the same composition of output.

The focus of the alternative trade strategies and employment project was on the second and third of these links. In part this was because the previous project centered on the relationship between trade regimes and development. More important, however, was the consideration that, difficult as it is to relate changes in the rate of economic growth to choice of trade regimes, it is even more problematic to attempt to delineate the precise relationship between the overall rate of economic growth and employment. The reasons for this difficulty are inherent in the complexity of the characteristics of the labor market and the determinants of wage rates as discussed in chapter 2.

For most of this volume, therefore, attention is on the theoretical and empirical relationships between trade strategies and employment through the effect on composition of output and on factor substitution, without regard to the effect of differences in growth rates arising from alternative trade strategies. Nonetheless, that relationship is too important to be completely overlooked. This chapter, therefore, is devoted to an examination of alternative trade strategies and a review of the results of prior research relating the choice of strategy to the rate of economic growth. In addition, the choice of trade regimes by countries covered in this project and their rates of economic growth are examined. It remains for chapter 4 to spell out the theory underlying the association between alternative trade strategies, the commodity composition of output, and factor proportions.

3.1 Export Promotion and Import Substitution Strategies

3.1.1 The Alternatives

Economic theory indicates that a necessary condition for optimal resource allocation for any country is that the domestic marginal rate of transformation (DMRT) among produced commodities should equal the international marginal rate of transformation (IMRT) among them. For a small country unable to influence its international terms of trade, international prices (f.o.b. for export and c.i.f. for import)[1] can be used to reflect IMRTs. In the absence of distortions in the domestic market, domestic prices can be used to reflect DMRTs.[2]

It is readily shown that any departure from this optimality rule results in a production cost to the economy: when the DMRT between a pair of traded commodities is unequal to the IMRT, switching production toward the item with the relatively lower domestic cost enables a country to receive more of the other commodity through trade than it can obtain through domestic production.

The optimality criterion leads naturally to a definition of bias of alternative trade regimes: bias defines the direction and the degree to which, on average, domestic incentives diverge from those that would prevail under free trade. The notion is most readily formalized in the two-commodity case. Let p's represent international prices, and q's domestic prices, with subscripts m and x denoting the import-competing and export goods respectively. Then, B, the bias of the regime, can be defined simply as:

$$(1) \qquad B = \frac{\dfrac{q_m}{p_m}}{\dfrac{q_x}{p_x}} .$$

If the world and domestic prices of exportables coincide and the domestic price of import-competing goods is above the world price, $B > 1$, and the regime is biased toward import substitution. Conversely, if imports are subsidized, then $B < 1$, and the bias of the regime is toward exports. Naturally, the more B diverges from unity in a particular direction, the more biased is the regime.

When there are many export and many import-competing commodities, a weighting scheme must be employed to estimate the average bias of the regime. In that case both the overall degree and direction of bias and the variance in individual price ratios among commodities are of interest.[3]

One might anticipate that countries would stay fairly close to uniform incentives or that, insofar as they departed from the optimality rule, they might do so partly by encouraging some export industries and partly by protecting some import-competing industries, with an average bias not far from unity. However, while even the countries most oriented toward import substitution encourage some exportable industries (at least more than others) and export promotion countries normally protect some import substitution industries, one rarely encounters a bias of about unity in trade regimes with some high levels of protection for import-competing industries and some large incentives for export promotion. Instead, a number of factors tend to reinforce initial biases in trade regimes and lead to significant overall differences in the direction of bias between the two trade strategies.

Consider first the built-in tendencies under import substitution. Although in principle one could encourage domestic production of an import-competing good with subsidies, in practice encouragement to domestic production is usually given by imposing either tariffs or quantitative restrictions (in the extreme case, import prohibitions) on imports of the commodity. The very act of protecting the domestic industry tends to discourage exports in several ways. First, exporters using the protected commodity as an input to their production process are disadvantaged.[4] Second, it should be noted that the resources employed in the protected industry would otherwise have been employed elsewhere and that, in that sense, protection of import-competing sectors is automatically discrimination against all other sectors, including potential exporting ones. Third, establishment of a new domestic industry usually requires imported capital goods, and in early stages of its development the value of capital goods imported is likely to exceed the international value added of import-substituting production.[5] This tends to put pressure on the foreign exchange markets that could be offset by currency realignment. However, under import substitution regimes, there is resistance to currency depreciation (in order to facilitate the needed capital goods imports, in part), and usually additional quantitative restrictions are employed to reduce the size of the balance of payments deficit, further increasing bias toward import substitution.

None of these tendencies constitutes an inexorable and inevitable outcome of import substitution regimes. In principle, a country could decide to protect, say, the metal products sector while simultaneously encouraging the export of petrochemicals. In practice such an outcome is seldom observed (and, if it is possible at all, it is probably possible only with very moderate levels of encouragement for both sets of activities).[6]

Consider now the sorts of tendencies that are likely to arise under an export promotion strategy. Tariffs cannot induce production for the international market: it requires a production (or an export) subsidy or a realistic exchange rate. Since subsidies are costly to government budgets, and since their heights are clearly visible, excessively high subsidies tend to be politically unpalatable, and there is a tendency to maintain a realistic exchange rate as an alternative (see section 3.1.3.2 for further discussion). That in itself encourages exports (and reduces the "balance of payments" motive for tariff protection), but it limits the degree to which there is a differential incentive for exportable production. Simultaneously, producers in exporting industries must be permitted to purchase their needed intermediate goods and raw materials at world prices (and with world quality) if they are to be competitive. This implies some pressure on the authorities to reduce or remove barriers to imports, which in turn may tend to encourage other producers to enter the export market. Thus a genuine export promotion policy[7] must be accompanied by the maintenance of a fairly open and liberalized trade regime, which tends to be self-reinforcing.

For these reasons it makes sense to talk about export promotion and import substitution trade policies despite the fact that particular aspects of these strategies differ from country to country and that the degree of bias can vary significantly between countries and, within the same country, between industries.

3.1.2   The Trade Strategies of the Countries Included in the Project

Before turning to other properties of import substitution and export promotion trade regimes, it is instructive to examine one or two salient characteristics of the trade regimes used by the countries covered in the project. Table 3.1 gives data that provide a preliminary glimpse of some aspects of the countries' experience. Estimates are given of the mean effective rate of protection (ERP)[8] for all manufacturing activities for sale in the home market for the years indicated.[9] In column 2 the abbreviations give a rough idea of the trade strategy in force at the time the ERP estimates pertain to. As will be seen below (table 3.4), several countries altered trade strategies at one or more times, and their experience permits many inferences about the trade strategies–employment relation. For the periods covered by the ERP estimates, only two countries, the Ivory Coast and South Korea, were following generally export-oriented trade strategies. Several others, including Brazil in 1967 and Colombia in 1969, were in the process of transition to a more outer-oriented set of policies. After 1972, Tunisia also began altering her trade strategy.

Table 3.1   Indicators of Trade Strategy, Various Countries

Country	Period (1)	Trade Strategy (2)	Average ERP for Manufac-turing (3)	Range of ERPs (4)
Brazil	1958	IS	106	17 to 502
	1963	IS	184	60 to 687
	1967	MIS	63	4 to 252
Chile	1967	IS	175[a]	−23 to 1,140
Colombia	1969	MIS	19	−8 to 140
Indonesia	1971	MIS	33[b]	−19 to 5,400
Ivory Coast	1973	EP	41[f]	−25 to 278
Pakistan	1963–64	IS	356[c]	−6 to 595
	1970–71	IS	200[c]	36 to 595
South Korea	1968	EP	−1	−15 to 82[e]
Thailand	1973	MIS	27[d]	−43 to 236
Tunisia	1972	IS	250	1 to 737
Uruguay	1965	IS	384	17 to 1,014

Note: EP = export promotion; IS = import substitution; MIS = moderate import sub-stitution.

[a]Data from Corbo and Meller 1981, table 3.9. Average ERP is an unweighted average for all manufacturing sectors.

[b]Data from Pitt 1981, table 5.A.1. Average ERP is an unweighted average of those rates, excluding manufacturing sectors with negative IVA and canning and preserving of fruits and vegetables (which had an ERP of 5,400).

[c]Calculated from Guisinger 1981, table 7.9. Averages are simple and unweighted, and for 1963–64 they exclude sectors with negative IVA.

[d]Simple average calculated as the mean of realized ERPs from Akrasanee 1981, tables 9.8 and 9.9. ERPs for domestic sale from Akrasanee 1981, table 9.10.

[e]Data from Westphal and Kim 1977, table 2-A.

[f]Data from Monson 1978, appendix table IV B-C (canned coffee and flour are excluded from the mean and the range).

As is evident from column 3, the average effective rate of protection under import substitution was generally fairly high. While some portion of this protection may have served as a partial offset to exchange rate overvaluation, the data in column 4 indicate that high average rates of effective protection were generally accompanied by very wide ranges of individual rates. While the data are not directly comparable between countries (in part because of different degrees of currency overvaluation and in part because data were presented at different levels of disaggregation—and greater disaggregation generally implies more extremes among observations), it is nonetheless highly suggestive that mean protection given manufacturing sector producers exceeded 100 percent in all countries for the year indicated except for Brazil in 1967 (in the process of transition, as already mentioned), Colombia (also in transition), the Ivory Coast, South Korea (both export-oriented countries), and Thailand. Except for Thailand, these countries correspond to the group that eventually eschewed import substitution. Interestingly enough, lower mean rates of effective protection also appear generally to have been accompanied by a relatively narrower range of ERP rates in individual industries and sectors.

The structure of incentives needs to be examined from another angle. A large number of countries provide export incentives as well as tariff protection, so that the same commodity receives a different return when sold abroad than when sold domestically, even if the sale price abroad, translated at the official exchange rate, is the same as the sales price in the domestic market. This reflects the fact that such instruments as tax benefits and direct subsidies per unit of foreign sales are used as export incentives. Carvalho and Haddad estimated for Brazil that it required only 68 percent of the sales price abroad to compensate the firm for the loss of a sale domestically, once tax incentives and other export inducements were taken into account.

Other countries for which there were export incentives that discriminated at least to some extent by place of sale were Argentina, Chile, South Korea, Thailand, and Uruguay. Data on the differences between effective rates of protection for sales in the domestic market and abroad are given in table 3.2. As can be seen, South Korea's export industries received their encouragement as they exported: they received incentives worth about 5 percent of value added when selling abroad and were subject to disincentives when selling domestically equivalent to a negative rate of effective protection of 18 percent.

By contrast with South Korea, Argentina, Chile, and Thailand provided most of their incentives in the form of tariff protection: there were few offsetting export subsidies, as is reflected in the low rates of effective protection for export. For Uruguay as well, discrimination took a number of forms. Data provided by Bension and Caumont (1981) serve primarily to confirm that, despite other incentives, the trade regime continued to be most powerful: in virtually every line of activity, including those where Uruguay presumably has most export potential, the incentives to firms to sell in the domestic market substantially exceeded the incentives to sell on the world market. The only possible exception was leather products, and for that category data were not judged reliable. For Uruguay, as for Argentina and Chile, the bias toward import substitution and sale on the home market was extremely pronounced.

Table 3.2   Effective Rates of Protection, Domestic and Foreign Markets

	Home Market	Export Market
Argentina 1969		
Agriculture	− 13	− 13
Mining	33	− 12
Manufacturing	111	− 40
Chile 1967		
Exportables	37	0
Importables	267	2
Noncompeting imports	155	6
Total	233	4
South Korea 1968		
Agriculture	19	− 16
Mining	3	− 1
Manufacturing		
Export industries	− 18	5
Import-competing	93	− 9
Thailand 1973		
Tapioca flour	− 30	− 30
Veneer and plywood	43	0
Cordage and rope	26	0
Noncotton textile fabrics	64	0
Cotton textile fabrics	8	0
Uruguay 1968		
Food products	150	25
Footwear	892	67
Leather products	20	24
Chemicals	182	43
Metal products	463	37
Electrical machinery	591	45

Sources: Argentina, Nogues 1980, chap. 3, table 2.2; Chile, Corbo and Meller 1981, table 3.10; South Korea, Hong 1981, table 8.9; Thailand, Akrasanee 1981, table 9.10; Uruguay, Bension and Caumont 1981, table 11.7.

Table 3.3 provides yet another way of characterizing the structure of effective protection, this time by end-use category. A hallmark of import substitution regimes seems to be that protection is granted first to industries producing consumer goods. This is reflected in the extremely high level of protection granted to those industries in Brazil in 1958 and in Pakistan in 1970–71. Were comparable data available for Chile and Uruguay, they would no doubt show a similarly high level.[10] South Korea's low overall level of protection, either positive or negative, stands out clearly from the data. Likewise, the Brazilian reforms of the mid-1960s and the fairly moderate nature of Colombia's incentive structure by the late 1960s are reflected in the moderate levels of protection reported

Table 3.3   Effective Protection by End-Use Category

Country	Period	Consumer Goods	Intermediate Goods	Capital Goods
Argentina	1969	96	127	162
Brazil	1958	242	65	53
	1967	66	39	52
Colombia	1969	33	15	80
Pakistan	1970–71	277	158	200
South Korea	1969			
Export		−2	9	−9
Domestic sale		16	0	56
Thailand	1973	19	25	77
Tunisia	1969	74	29	104

Sources: Argentina, Nogues 1980, chap. 3, table 2.2; Brazil, Carvalho and Haddad 1981, table 2.9; Colombia, Thoumi 1981, table 4.4; Pakistan, Guisinger 1981, table 7.9; South Korea, Westphal and Kim 1977, tables 2.A and 2.B; Thailand, Akrasanee 1981, table 9.8; Tunisia, Nabli 1981, table 10.6.

Note: For Argentina, Colombia, South Korea, and Thailand, the numbers are simple averages: of consumer nondurables and consumer durables for consumer goods; of intermediate goods I and II for intermediate goods; of transport equipment and machinery and equipment for capital goods.

for those countries and time periods. Tunisia's levels of protection seem to be subject to a much wider margin of error than most of the others. The ones reproduced here are significantly lower than an alternative set of estimates and nonetheless reflect high levels of protection to both consumer goods and capital goods producers.

Regardless of which indicator of effective protection is used, it seems evident that the differentials in incentives between industries are much larger under import substitution than under export promotion. These incentives are bound to have important influences on the structure of production. While effective rates of production can be high both because of the cost structure of an industry and because of the monopoly power that the trade regime may accord to domestic producers, there can be little doubt that many of the industries protected under import substitution would not, at least with their existing cost structure, be viable under an alternative trade regime. Moreover, given the heavy disincentive to exporting that characterizes some of the more extreme import substitution regimes, import substitution trade strategies must have discouraged the development and expansion of some of the potential export industries. It is left to chapter 5 to report the differences in labor coefficients, and therefore in demand for labor and employment, that are likely to arise from the resulting differences in the commodity composition of output.

3.1.3 Policy Instruments Employed under Alternative Trade Strategies

In principle, the choice of policy instruments for encouraging new industry and rapid economic growth should be largely independent of decisions regarding type of trade policy. Indeed, in the optimal resource-allocation world defined above, one would anticipate that the sorts of incentives offered for establishment and expansion would be indistinguishable between industries whose output competed with imports and industries whose output was destined for export. In practice, however, policy instruments differ markedly. Partly because some trade policy instruments (e.g., tariffs) inherently discriminate between places of sale for the same commodity, and partly for other reasons, the two types of trade strategies generally imply a very different mix of policy instruments.

There are a variety of reasons why understanding these instruments is important. First, knowledge of their magnitude is often a crucial first step in empirical estimates of the incentives offered under a trade and industrialization strategy. Second, the types of instruments employed have a direct influence on the choice of industries that are started and also on factor proportions in individual firms and sectors. Thus there are direct links between the choice of instrument and the implied labor coefficients. Finally, a question of some importance is whether observed differences in labor utilization under alternative trade strategies are inherently the outcome of the strategy choice or whether instead they may not reflect the particular selection of instruments used to achieve that strategy. I shall start by reviewing a "typical" set of instruments employed under an import substitution strategy and then contrast it with the sorts of policies generally adopted to encourage export industries.[11]

3.1.3.1 Policy Instruments under Import Substitutions

For a variety of reasons (including the important fact that the authorities necessarily have greater ability to affect decisions by domestic producers when the economy is relatively less open), measures to promote import substitution tend to consist of a mixture of direct quantitative controls over various aspects of economic activity and of pricing measures.

Quantitative restrictions can be administered in a variety of ways, some more restrictive than others. As Bhagwati (1978) has documented, negative lists of goods that may not be imported tend to be less restrictive than positive lists of items that may be imported; regimes in which there are some items for which licensing approval is automatic and for which bureaucratic delays are avoided tend to be less restrictive than regimes where all licensing applications are individually scrutinized; licensing procedures (and the intervals between granting applications) can also affect the working of the system.

Quantitative restrictions interact with overvalued exchange rates in a variety of ways. That there is excess demand for foreign exchange tends to create incentives for smuggling and evasion of the regime (including over- and underinvoicing), which in turn usually induces the authorities to implement still further regulations aimed at containing illegal and extralegal activities. Those regulations can be exceedingly complex and time-consuming, increasing the restrictiveness of quantitative controls beyond their initially intended levels.

Partly because the exchange rate tends to become increasingly over-valued, and partly for other reasons, there is also a tendency under import substitution to employ a variety of pricing measures to contain excess demand for imports. In addition to tariffs, "handling charges," "port duties," "stamp taxes," and a number of other quasi-tariff measures have been imposed.[12] Although they apparently rely on price, they may sometimes be as prohibitive as any import prohibition. An extreme example, cited by Behrman (1976), is the Chilean practice of imposing requirements in times of foreign exchange difficulties that import license applications be accompanied by a prior deposit equal to 10,000 percent of the value of the license! In Brazil, a law of similars provided that firms importing goods that could be obtained domestically would be ineligible to receive government contracts.

The combined use of quantitative restrictions and quasi-pricing measures can provide almost any industry with sufficient protection to enable it to produce profitably for the domestic market, almost regardless of the degree to which its relative costs exceed those obtaining internationally.[13] Combining use of incentive measures such as prohibitive protection with import licensing can give the government virtually complete control over choice of industries: the fact that many, if not most, capital goods and many intermediate goods are imported means that the authorities can, through import licensing, affect or control the allocation of capital among industries.[14]

Thus the hallmarks of an import substitution regime generally include: high levels of protection to a number of industries, with a very wide range of rates of effective protection; fairly detailed and complex quantitative controls and bureaucratic regulations, both over imports directly and often over a number of areas of domestic economic activity (sometimes through the import regime); and an overvalued exchange rate with associated disincentives for exporting.

3.1.3.2 Policy Instruments under Export Promotion

For policymakers committed to encouraging industrial development and growth through exporting, most of the instruments employed under import substitution are either totally infeasible or demonstrably incompatible with promoting exports. By definition, tariffs cannot be used as an instrument of export promotion, and even tariff rebates do no more than offset the disincentive to export that imposing a tariff would otherwise create.

Likewise, quantitative restrictions upon imports are almost entirely incompatible with export promotion: not only is it administratively extremely difficult to compensate exporters for the excess of domestic over foreign price in the presence of quantitative restrictions, but a genuine export promotion drive must permit exporters ready access to the same quality and variety of inputs that their foreign competitors have.

Furthermore, both because of the visible cost of export subsidies and because of the incompatibility of quantitative controls with export promotion, an overvalued exchange rate is seldom encountered for any substantial period of time among export promotion countries.[15] In South Korea, for example, in the early 1960s export subsidies were introduced between alterations in the exchange rate. But these subsidies decreased in importance over time as the government learned the cost of maintaining them. In 1964 the official exchange rate was 214 won per dollar, while export subsidies were 67 won per dollar, adding about 30 percent to the effective export exchange rate over the official exchange rate. By the early 1970s, export inducements beyond the official rate consisted largely of internal tax exemptions, customs duty exemptions, and interest rate subsidies, none of which had the same direct effect on payments by the government. Even then, the total value per dollar of these inducements had increased only to 105 won per dollar, compared with an official exchange rate of 392 in 1972. Thereafter, the proportionate and absolute value of subsidies declined still further, reaching 81 won per dollar contrasted with an official rate of 485 per dollar in 1975 (see Krueger 1979, tables 22 and 32).

Not only does export promotion have to rely upon pricing incentives rather than quantitative controls, but there are significant and visible constraints on the degree to which incentives can be differentiated among exporting activities,[16] as a substitute for a realistic exchange rate. The major incentives for export promotion found in other countries are similar to those for South Korea: export subsidies (usually expressed as a rate of local currency paid beyond the official exchange rate per unit of foreign currency sales); favorable treatment for exporters with regard to tax liabilities; and availability of credit at below-market rates of interest.[17, 18] In Brazil, for example, domestic tax exemptions were the main instruments used to encourage exports above a realistic (sliding peg) exchange rate policy. Carvalho and Haddad (1981) estimate that selling a product domestically yielded about the same after-tax profit to a firm as selling the item abroad for about two-thirds the price. The important point is that these incentives are provided to anyone who exports. They provide a uniform degree of bias among exporting activities. By contrast, a set of prohibitive tariffs usually entails highly varied protective content for different activites (with a very low, if not negative, degress of effective protection for exports).

The question to which we now turn is what differences there have been in growth performance under the two strategies. Later chapters will consider the effect of each set of policy instruments upon the commodity composition of output and the factor proportions in individual industries.

3.2   Relationship of Trade Strategies to Growth Rates

3.2.1   Growth Rates under Import Substitution and Export Promotion

The determinants of a country's rate of economic growth are numerous, and there is no universally agreed-upon method of quantifying the contribution of any particular factor to the growth rate.[19] This is especially the case when it comes to identifying the role of a variable that may, in part, affect the efficiency of resource allocation. Consider, for example, two economics that both have the same rate of capital formation and initially equal output. In one economy, new capital is employed in less-than-optimal uses, with a consequently high capital/output ratio and a low rate of growth. In the other economy, capital is optimally allocated, with the consequence that the capital/output ratio is considerably lower and the rate of economic growth higher. Without detailed and comparable data for the two countries, it would be difficult, if not impossible, to identify the role of superior resource allocation in affecting the rates of economic growth: capital formation would, in the absence of any other factor contributing to growth, account for 100 percent of the growth in each country. This difficulty illustrates one of the problems of attempting to associate alternative trade strategies with growth rates: the trade strategy itself is but one influence on the effectiveness with which other factors of production are employed.

The matter is further confounded by the consideration that, even in theory, the role of trade, and the optimal fraction of trade in GNP, will differ across countries. South Korea, with her very poor natural resource endowment, for cxample, undoubtedly has a higher optimal share of exports and imports in GNP than does, say, Turkey. It is therefore difficult, if not impossible, to separate export growth, and its contribution to overall economic growth, into that component which is a result of starting from a suboptimal role of trade in GNP and that component which is a consequence of "normal" export growth.

Nonetheless, past research results are highly suggestive of an associaton between trade strategies and growth rates, whether the evidence cited is impressionistic based on the experiences of countries that have altered their trade strategies, or whether the evidence is estimation of the statistical relationship of growth rates with explanatory variables, including the behavior of exports. In this section, some of the evidence is briefly summarized. Thereafter the growth rates and trade strategies of the countries covered in the project are reviewed. Finally, possible reasons for the difference in growth performance are discussed.

3.2.1.1   Results from Prior Research

There are four cross-country estimates of the role of exports in growth. Not surprisingly, in light of the lack of a theoretical underpinning, the estimates differ in techniques used, as well as in countries covered and period of observation. What is perhaps surprising and reassuring is that, despite these differences, the conclusions arising from the four studies are very similar.

The first estimate, by Michalopoulos and Jay (1973), essentially posited an aggregate neoclassical production function with domestic capital, foreign capital, and labor as inputs. They fitted it with data for thirty-nine developing countries for the period covering the 1960s. Having done so, they reestimated including exports as an additional independent variable. Michalopoulos and Jay found that exports were highly significant, and significantly improved the fit of the equation, concluding:

> The growth rate of GNP and the growth rate of exports are highly correlated with each other. Export growth rates explain a significant portion of the variance in income growth rates which remain unexplained by the growth in primary inputs. This empirical relationship is of basic importance to our findings. [Michalopoulos and Jay 1973, p. 22]

The second study was undertaken by Michaely (1977). He estimated the relationship between the change in the proportion of exports to GNP (to eliminate the obvious bias resulting from the fact that an increase of one unit of exports is an increase of one unit in GNP) and the rate of change in GNP for forty-one countries over the period 1950 to 1973. He found a coefficient of Spearman rank correlation between the two of .38, which was significant at the 1 percent level, although there was no correlation between the growth rate and the mean proportion of exports in GNP.[20]

The third estimate was for the countries covered in the NBER project on foreign trade regimes and economic development. Using data for the ten countries over the period roughly covering 1953 to 1972 (depending on data availability for countries' starting and ending points), observations on GNP across countries were fitted on a pooled time-series–cross-section basis. Thus the GNP growth rate for each country was regressed against a time trend in that country's growth and the rate of growth for its exports. A separate coefficient for the time trend was estimated for each country, but the coefficient expressing the contribution of export growth to GNP growth was common for all countries. For the countries covered, an increase in the rate of growth of export earnings of one percentage point annually was associated with an increase in the rate of growth of GNP of about 0.1 percentage point (see Krueger 1978, chap. 11, for details). If this estimate implied causation (which, for econometric reasons as well as because of the analytical difficulties discussed above, it does not), it would imply that the South Korean growth rate in the late 1960s was about four percentage points higher than it would have been had export earnings been stagnant. To be sure, such an inference is far more precise than either the data or the theory warrant. Nonetheless, the results were, once again, strongly indicative of an important link between export growth and the overall growth rate.

Finally, Balassa (1978b) took data for eleven countries (many of them overlapping the countries covered by Krueger 1978) for 1960 to 1973 and reestimated the Michaely relations, incorporating also the Michalopoulos-Jay factors of production. His results generally confirm those of both Michaely and Michalopoulos-Jay, and he noted the similarity of his results to the Krueger results. According to his estimates (based on actual factor accumulation paths),

> the increase in Korea's GNP would have been 37 percent smaller if its export growth rate equalled the average for all countries concerned. The corresponding proportion is 25 percent for Taiwan. At the other extreme, in Chile, India, and Mexico, respectively, the increase in GNP would have been 14, 12 and 8 percent greater if those countries had average export growth rates. [p. 187]

Balassa noted, as did Krueger, that the results obtained, when applied to individual countries, underestimated the effects of export growth on GNP. Despite that, the results are further evidence that the benefits to be derived from an export promotion exceed, perhaps substantially, those from an import substitution trade strategy.

3.2.1.2 Growth Rates in the Project Countries

Table 3.4 gives an indication of each of the ten countries' trade strategies and rates of growth of export earnings and of real GDP. Although the degree of bias of the trade regime has changed from time to time in all countries, some have experienced a much greater degree of

Table 3.4   Trade Strategy, Export Growth,
                   and Real GDP Growth, Project Countries

| | | | Average Annual Rate of Growth | |
| | | Trade Strategy (1) | Export Earnings (2) | Real GDP (3) |
Country	Period			
Brazil	1955–60	IS	−2.3	6.9
	1960–65	IS	4.6	4.2
	1965–70	EP	28.2	7.6
	1970–76	EP	24.3	10.6
Chile	1960–70	IS	9.7	4.2
Colombia	1955–65	IS	−.8	4.6
	1960–65	IS	−1.9	1.9
	1970–76	EP	16.9	6.5
Indonesia	1965–73	MIS	18.9	6.8
Ivory Coast	1960–72	EP	11.2	7.8
Pakistan	1953–60	IS	−1.5	3.5[a]
	1960–70	IS	6.2	6.8
South Korea	1953–60	IS	−6.1	5.2
	1960–70	EP	40.2	8.5
	1970–76	EP	43.9	10.3
Thailand	1960–70	MIS	5.5	8.2
	1970–76	MIS	26.6	6.5
Tunisia	1960–70	IS	6.8	4.6
	1970–76	MIS	23.4	9.4
Uruguay	1955–70	IS	1.6	.7

Sources: Trade strategy: based upon evidence in country studies (Krueger et al. 1981). Export growth rates: computed from data in May 1977 *International Financial Statistics.* GDP growth rates: International Bank for Reconstruction and Development, *World Development Report 1978* and *World Tables 1976*; United Nations *Yearbook of National Accounts Statistics*, vol. 2, for 1971 and 1969.

Notes: EP = export promotion; IS = import substitution; MIS = moderate import substitution.

[a]GNP growth rate is for 1950 to 1960.

stability in their trade orientation than others. Chile, for example, consistently followed import substitution policies until 1974, and fluctuations in the degree of bias toward import substitution were associated primarily with fluctuations in the price of copper (and therefore in export earnings) and with balance of payments crises. Uruguay, too, was consistently strongly biased toward import substitution and has only recently moved toward a more export-oriented policy. For purposes of analysis in the period covered, Uruguay is an import substitution country. The Ivory Coast has also followed a fairly consistent policy over the entire period since independence, but it has had the opposite bias—toward export promotion. Monson notes that in 1974–75 some policies were being adopted that shifted the regime toward somewhat greater encouragement of import substitution industries. Nonetheless, his data are for the earlier export promotion period.

Contrasted with those cases of relatively unaltered trade policy are the countries that radically changed their orientation. As already mentioned, Brazil, South Korea, and Colombia are in that group, since all three switched away from import substitution and toward export promotion. In addition, Indonesia should probably be regarded as a country with an abrupt change, in that the period before 1965 was one of extreme restrictiveness of the system. The inflation rate was more than 100 percent annually, and export earnings were lagging badly. Pitt focuses on the period since 1965, during which Indonesia was moving away from exchange controls toward full currency convertibility. Despite easing exchange controls, Indonesia protected a number of domestic industries. As a consequence, her regime since 1965 is best characterized as "moderate" in its bias toward import substitution.

Tunisia had a fairly strong bias in her trade and payments regime toward import substitution in the 1960s but in the early 1970s began to change incentives toward greater encouragement of exports. However, the period covered by Nabli centers upon the early 1970s. At that time incentives for import substitution remained very strong contrasted with those for exporting. For purposes of analyzing the trade strategies–employment relation, therefore, Tunisia should also be regarded as oriented toward import substitution.

Thailand represents a case very similar to Tunisia, except that the bias toward import substitution was somewhat less than in Tunisia. In the 1960s, the Thai regime appears to have been moderately biased toward import substitution. By the early 1970s, measures were being taken that decreased the magnitude of the bias; Akrasanee's data pertain to the period 1971–73, during which it is probable that the moderate incentive structure of the 1960s was still the dominant influence on the commodity composition of output and pattern of trade. After 1973 government intervention increased and more measures were introduced both to promote manufactured exports and to foster further import substitution.

Finally, Pakistan represents a country moving away from an extreme bias toward import substitution, which was the case in the 1950s, toward a somewhat less unbalanced incentive structure in the 1960s. Guisinger characterizes Pakistan of the 1960s as having a much more liberalized regime, with considerably more balanced incentives, than was true in the 1950s, since the export bonus scheme and related policy moves in the late

1950s removed some of the discrimination against exports that had previously existed in the regime. Nonetheless, as can be seen from table 3.4, bias toward import substitution was still substantial.[21]

Column 2 of table 3.4 gives the rates of growth of export earnings for the periods indicated. It is readily apparent that shifting to export promotion generally resulted in much-improved performance with regard to exports. The shifts in Brazil, Colombia, and South Korea were all highly dramatic, but Pakistan's improved rate of growth of export earnings was also important for that country. The large positive rate of growth of export earnings for Indonesia also represented an abrupt departure from the earlier stagnation experienced under Sukarno. Tunisia's increased rate of growth of export earnings over the period 1970–76 reflects rapid growth of petroleum products, other primary products (especially phosphates), and manufactured exports. Because oil price increases dominate Indonesia's recent export earnings statistics, the Indonesian performance was computed over the period ending in 1973.

The final column of table 3.4 gives the growth rates of real GDP for the same periods as those covered by columns 1 and 2. The overall impression is similar to the results reviewed in section 3.2.1.1. As can be seen, there appears to be a significant association between rates of growth of GDP and of exports, although it is by no means a perfect one. Brazil's export earnings were actually declining between 1955 and 1960, while real GDP grew at an average annual rate of almost 7 percent, and a similar contrast can be seen in the South Korean data for 1953–60. Conversely, Chile's relatively high rate of growth of export earnings in the 1960s was not accompanied by rapid growth of real GDP.[22] Colombia is also a partial exception, in that the rate of growth of exports reversed from a negative 0.8 percent to a positive 17 percent annually, while the increase in real GDP was about two percentage points annually. To be sure, that represented a doubling in the rate of growth of per capita income, but it was far less striking than the change in the Brazilian or South Korean growth rates following their reversals of policy and of trends in export growth.

3.2.2   Reasons for Differences in Performance

An important question is why there are such differences in growth performance. The simple theory of optimal resource allocation is probably not enough, and there is no single, universally agreed-upon diagnosis of the reasons for the difference and the quantitative importance of each factor contributing to differences in growth rates. What instead seems to be possible is an analysis of what has happened under import substitution and under export promotion, which points to some of the factors that must have contributed to the differences in growth rates.

3.2.2.1 Import Substitution

At a descriptive level, the proximate reasons why growth rates tapered off can be traced. There are three important factors. The first concerns the increasing restrictiveness of the trade and payments regime under import substitution; the second is the relatively rapid exhaustion of opportunities for "easy" import substitution; and the third relates to the tendency for import substitution strategies to be administered by detailed and complex quantitative restrictions. Each of these is discussed in turn. Thereafter the descriptive factors are related to the conventional concepts of economic analysis.

Turning to the first factor, in most countries that adopted the import substitution strategy the growth rate of export earnings (and earnings of foreign exchange from other sources) diminished once the strategy had been adopted. In part this diminution in the foreign exchange receipts was the conscious outcome of the import substitution plan: dependence on trade was intended to diminish. However, the growth of export and other foreign exchange earnings was generally slower than anticipated (probably for the reasons discussed in section 3.1.3.1).

Simultaneously with a declining rate of growth of foreign exchange availability, the growth in demand for imports and foreign services should have decelerated, but instead it tended to accelerate. The growing gap between growth in demand and growth in supply of foreign exchange under import substitution caused severe difficulties in many countries.

Meanwhile, virtually every new import substitution industry, and even every expansion of existing import substitution industries, required imports of raw materials, intermediate goods, and machinery and equipment. Policymakers were especially reluctant to deny permission for imports of these goods, since they feared that reducing capital goods imports would reduce the growth rate and that reducing intermediate goods and raw material imports would adversely affect output and employment. "Dependence" upon imports for final consumption goods was replaced with "dependence" upon imports not only for growth via the availability of capital goods but also for employment and output, since the newly established factories could not produce without needed intermediate goods and raw materials.

Structurally, therefore, the level of employment and output and the rate of capital formation within the import substitution sectors became dependent upon the availability of foreign exchange. The import substitution strategy ironically appeared to result in an economy even more dependent upon trade than had been the case under the earlier pattern of primary commodity specialization, while simultaneously discouraging the growth of foreign exchange earnings.

In many import substitution countries, increased dependence upon imports and laggard foreign exchange earnings were reflected in periodic balance of payments crises.[23] These crises, in turn, were associated with intervals during which import licensing became particularly stringent, if not prohibitive. The authorities had run down foreign exchange reserves and borrowed from abroad to the maximum extent in order to maintain the growth rate. Finally, however, resources were exhausted. The period during which import licensing had to be slowed generally was associated with a period of slow growth, if not an outright reduction in output. Proximately at least, foreign exchange was the binding constraint upon the growth rate, and models of "foreign exchange shortage," most notably the two-gap model (see Chenery and Strout 1966), characterized import substitution economies dependent upon imports for their intermediate goods and levels of investment, while simultaneously experiencing slow growth of exports. Very often these periods of severe import restriction ended with a devaluation and stabilization program designed to make exporting more attractive, at least temporarily.[24]

The second factor contributing to the slowing down of growth rates under import substitution was the exhaustion of the "easy" import substitution opportunities. Even in large countries with sizable domestic markets, such as Brazil, the domestic market was not large enough to support the development of industries at economic scales of production after import substitution had taken place in the industries that catered to large numbers of relatively poor consumers. After import substitution in industries such as textiles and shoes, where imports were sizable and outputs fairly standard, it appears that additional industries were generally established at uneconomically small size. Once "easy" import substitution was over, the incremental capital/output ratio in the industrial sector rose sharply, and the "leading growth sector" experienced a diminution in its growth rate.[25]

The third reason for the tapering off of growth rates was the complex nature of the instrument mix under import substitution. Bhagwati (1978) has carefully delineated the reasons why controls tended to multiply: the obviously imperfect across-the-board allocation techniques resulted in ever-finer classifications, as imports were allocated by category of commodity being imported, by type of user of the commodity domestically, by source of foreign exchange, and even by type of use—capital good, intermediate good, or raw material. The proliferation of the control network and its complexity seems to have been a common feature of import substitution regimes and is certainly a characteristic that must have had harmful consequences.

Moving from the descriptive to the analytical level, also, one can link these three tendencies with standard constructs of economic theory. One can fairly well pinpoint some of the things that went wrong, although quantification of their contribution to the outcome is difficult. There are both static and dynamic elements.

In static terms, import substitution proceeds only with a high, and probably increasing, variance among activities in domestic resource costs. As already seen, rates of effective protection of several hundred percent are not infrequent. Instances where the imports for producing domestically exceed the import value of the final product are not unheard of. High-cost, low-quality output is visible to everyone. It may be that this phenomenon is only an economist's characterization of the "exhaustion of easy import substitution," or it may be something more fundamental. Either way, there is a tendency in almost all cases for import substitution to become "indiscriminate," with attendant high costs and low growth rates. Once consumer goods are virtually removed from the eligible import list, each new import substitute implies increasing costs for some domestic consumer goods industry and also for whatever industries might have had export potential. That, in turn, implies higher domestic prices and a lower rate of growth of domestic consumption than would occur if prices did not rise. An almost-universal pattern is the overestimation of the probable size of the domestic market, as entrepreneurs underestimate the extent to which demand is price responsive.

The "indiscriminate," high-cost pattern of import substitution may or may not be inevitable. In large part it arises because policymakers, confronted with "foreign exchange shortage" as described above, understandably want to allocate foreign exchange to capital goods and inputs for existing plants. Incentives are almost always provided to begin domestic production of anything that can be produced; an extremely powerful incentive (and perhaps a necessary one for some high-cost industries that would have little or no hope of becoming profitable even in the face of high tariff walls) is the willingness of the authorities in most import substitution countries to prohibit the importation of goods competing with domestic output. Once a domestic plant is established, the producer is secure in that competing imports are not permitted.

In addition to the high variance in incentives and in domestic resource costs that result from import licensing, quantitative restrictions and their administration impose other costs. In particular, the licensing authorities are caught in a dilemma: if licenses are "fairly" administered, all have to be given equal access to them. Rules are set up for "fair" allocation of valuable licenses. Those rules, in turn, establish new rigidities in the system. Some of these are dynamic and are discussed below. Others, however, affect static resource allocation. For example, in many countries licenses are in one way or another prorated across applicants among existing firms. Most variants of this procedure implicitly grant each producer licenses in proportion to his share of the market; not only are there two few firms for competition, but each producer is really provided with assurance that his share is fixed. This phenomenon is undoubtedly at least partly responsible for the obvious low quality of many of the products produced in import substitution industries, and also for high and rising capital/labor ratios with falling rates of capacity utilization.

The second analytical component has to do with the sorts of market structures created by import substitution policies. The existence of import licensing, together with the fact that firms require imports of intermediate goods, often results in rigid market shares for individual firms under import substitution. Indeed, when the quantity of an imported input stands in fixed proportion to output, even the industry's total sales are rigidly fixed. Profitable firms generally expand little, if at all, more rapidly than others, in part because they are unable to increase their share of import licenses (and thus have little incentive to reduce the price of their output). The small size of the domestic market, which was already seen to tend to lead to firms of smaller than economic size, also implies that the number of firms in any particular industry will be small.

Indeed, policymakers are caught on the horns of a dilemma even if they perceive the difficulties that the absence of competition can create: if there are enough firms to permit a healthy degree of competition, it is highly likely that the size of the individual firms will be so small that industry costs will be high on that account. If, on the other hand, monopoly is permitted in order to avoid uneconomically small firms, a competitive spur to higher productivity will be lacking. Both this consideration and the mechanics of import licensing tend to discourage the establishment of new firms and plants in existing industries: the authorities are naturally reluctant to permit scarce foreign exchange to be used to import capital goods to produce a commodity where domestic production is already believed to be adequate to meet domestic demand (and where indeed excess capacity may exist). The absence of competition or the small size of domestic firms, or both, leads to X-inefficiency and relatively high capital/labor ratios, again tending to reduce growth rates.

Turning from static to dynamic considerations, additional problems arise with an import substitution strategy over time. Stated in its most general way, that quantitative restrictions regulate trade and payments leads to a built-in tendency for relative prices and incentives to diverge from their optimum over time. Currencies tend to become increasingly overvalued, with ever fewer incentives for exporters and greater and greater rewards for those able to obtain import licenses.

Simultaneously, that competititon is fairly well precluded for the reasons indicated above means that producers are not under strong pressures to increase productivity, improve quality, or otherwise become more efficient over time. Indeed, not only are incentives absent for individual firms, but the necessity for "fairness" on the part of the authorities implies that the sorts of mechanisms that operate in market economies to enable the more productive firm to grow more rapidly are inhibited in the import substitution countries. Successful, low-cost producers are generally awarded their share of import licenses on the same basis as are less successful, high-cost producers. Most of the competitive mechanisms for weeding out the less efficient producers (and therefore raising average industry productivity over time) are obviated by the regulations and incentives established in support of the import substitution strategy.

3.2.2.2   Export Promotion

If one turns to the probable reasons why exports have generated generally higher growth rates than import substitutions, one finds they are of two kinds. On one hand, there is the fact that export promotion, by its nature, avoids some of the costs of the import substitution strategy. On the other hand, there are identifiable gains in output for given inputs that are attainable under export promotion. Identification of these elements is not sufficient to permit quantitative estimates of their relative importance. It does, however, increase understanding of the contrasts between the two industrialization strategies.

Perhaps the most important lesson that has been learned from the experience of the successful exporting countries is that identification of industrialization and the development of new industries with the import substitution policy is fundamentally mistaken. For, in all the countries that shifted toward export promotion, a striking feature of their success was the very rapid growth of manufactured exports, and often of exports of newly produced products. While it is obvious that a firm starting to produce a product previously not manufactured in a country is very likely to sell to the domestic market first simply because of transport cost differentials, experience demonstrates that this is not inevitable. In fact, one major way of starting new industries and new product lines in the exporting countries has been for firms in developed countries to subcontract with foreign suppliers to fabricate particular parts and components. In some instances the foreign buyer provides technical specifications, technical assistance, and even capital. The foreign buyer may enter into a joint management or ownership arrangement to produce the subcontracted product, but ownership is not an essential part of the arrangements. In some cases the entire output may be sold abroad initially, with foreign orders filled first and the domestic market satisfied second. Such instances, though recorded, are probably the exception rather than the rule (see Suh 1975). Nonetheless, the exceptions point to the important fact that new industries are developed and expand under an export promotion strategy, and industrialization is by no means synonymous with import substitution.

From an analytical viewpoint, the importance of the recognition that new industries can start under either strategy is severalfold. First, it suggests that the basic criticism of the infant industry argument for tariff protection—that one should subsidize an "infant" product rather than impose a tariff—was empirically very important, although perhaps for different reasons than the "consumption cost" arguments initially put forth. Second, it raises a number of questions about the determinants of productivity growth within individual industries. Third, it raises questions about the determination of comparative advantage within the industrial sector and how it changes in the course of economic growth. The first two questions are addressed here. The third is the subject of chapter 4.

While, as seen above, economic theory indicates that exporting and import substitution industries should both be at sizes where the marginal cost of earning a unit of foreign exchange is equated with the marginal cost of saving a unit of foreign exchange in each line of activity, that precept gives no hint as to the likely proportion of resources going to import substituting and exporting industries at the optimum. One factor of some importance in yielding high-cost import substitution activities has been the very small size of domestic plants. To the extent that there are significant indivisibilities or scale economies in industrial operation, the economic costs of failing to expand plants and industries to sizes adequate to serve more than the domestic market are significantly greater than suggested by consideration of the gains from trade implied by the static comparative advantage model. The lower transport costs between a country and its major trading partners, the greater will be the advantages of longer production runs and of building optimal-sized plants contrasted with the advantages of introducing more, smaller new industries catering to the home market. Conversely, the larger the minimum efficient size of plant, the greater will be the economic costs of catering only to the home market.

The only piece of quantitative evidence available on this point comes from the South Korean experience. There an attempt to estimate the importance of scale economies in manufacturing industries as a factor contributing to the rate of growth of industrial output resulted in an estimate that about 18 percent or one-sixth of the growth in industrial output between 1966 and 1968 was the result of achieving scale economies or overcoming problems associated with small size (Nam 1975). There have also been occasional suggestions that capital-intensive industries tend to have larger minimum efficient sizes and higher costs of operating below those sizes than do labor-intensive industries. If that is the case, and if an import substitution strategy tends to encourage the development of more capital-intensive industries than does an export promotion strategy,[26] that further contributes to the incremental output gains achieved under an export promotion strategy.

That the domestic markets of most developing countries may be too small to support efficient-sized plants makes the traditional criticisms of the infant industry argument for protection—that it imposes costs on consumers and that a production subsidy would be preferable—even more forceful than was earlier thought. Because, to the extent that import substitution is really a way of fostering infant industries, it is inefficient in discriminating between markets based upon place of sale: efficient development of new industries in most cases probably entails an expansion beyond the boundaries of domestic markets. An efficient industrialization strategy is thus seen to be one in which incentives, when granted, induce activity at minimum efficient size, and for that purpose they must be based upon production, not the destination of output.

Before concluding that the gains from export promotion originate largely from the opportunities a larger market provides for minimum-efficient-sized operations, however, we should look at two related considerations. On one hand, export promotion permits the rapid expansion of the most successful new firms and industries, in addition to enabling initial entry at economically efficient size. On the other hand, firms in an exporting environment are generally confronted with international competition and do not face the sheltered domestic markets they face under import substitution.

Little is known about the dynamics of productivity increase: it is not at all clear the extent to which increases in output per head are achieved within existing plants; by new, higher-productivity firms driving out older ones; and by competition among firms with the share of firms with above-average productivity increasing and the shares of firms with below-average productivity decreasing. Even if the contribution of each of these three sources of productivity increase were known, the extent to which productivity gains of any sort were the result of competition among firms would remain an open question. In a monopolistic setting, for example, it might with fairness be asserted that productivity growth could be slow because of the absence of a competitive spur or because the entrepreneurial skill of management was poor, or for other reasons.

3.2.3 Conclusions

The evidence is strong that growth performance seems better under export promotion than under import substitution. Some of the reasons this is so are readily apparent. What is not known is the relative importance of each contributing factor and the interaction among them. It is probable that each of the phenomena discussed above has contributed, perhaps in different degrees in different countries depending upon such factors as size of domestic market, per capita income level, and proximity to the major industrialized countries. What should be borne in mind throughout this volume is that the links between more rapid economic growth and developments in the labor market are not entirely understood. In general there is a fairly strong presumption that factors that tend to increase the rate of economic growth also tend to shift the demand for labor more rapidly to the right. Insofar as the rest of this book focuses upon commodity composition and factor substitution effects of alternative trade regimes, it may be that the single most important effect of choice of trade regimes upon employment is overlooked.

4 The Factor Proportions Explanation of Trade, Distortions, and Employment

At the outset of the project it was readily apparent that existing formulations of the factor proportions explanation of trade, or Heckscher-Ohlin-Samuelson (HOS) model, would not serve as a satisfactory analytical basis for the project. As generally stated, the HOS model was cast in a framework based on two commodities, two countries, and two factors of production.

It is straightforward, however, to extend this framework meaningfully to take into account the realities of agricultural and industrial sectors in developing countries. That framework is set forth in section 4.1. A second task was to analyze the ways domestic factor market interventions might affect observed patterns of trade and associated factor utilization. The theory underlying that relationship is set forth in section 4.2.

4.1 The HOS Model with Many Goods

The basic question explored in this section is how the HOS model can be set forth in a meaningful way to provide testable hypotheses about the relationship between trade strategies and employment in developing countries. Three strands of thought are central to the argument: (1) It has long been recognized that developing economies have large agricultural

Much of this chapter was published in slightly different form in Anne O. Krueger, *Growth, Distortions, and Patterns of Trade among Many Countries*, Princeton Studies in International Finance no. 40 (Princeton: Princeton University, International Finance Section, 1977). Reprinted by permission of the International Finance Section. I am indebted to Stephen P. Magee and to members of the Trade and Development Workshop at the University of Minnesota, especially T. Paul Schultz, for helpful discussions while the research was in progress. William Branson, Carlos Díaz-Alejandro, James Henderson, Ronald Jones, Peter Kenen, Sir Arthur Lewis, Fritz Machlup, and Richard Snape all commented on the original version, and many of their suggestions led to significant improvements.

sectors and that trade in primary commodities cannot be explained by the countries' endowment of labor and capital. (2) Given the observed difference in factor endowments between developing countries and the industrialized world, it seems reasonable to develop a model of complete specialization rather than one of factor price equalization. (3) While numerous theoretical reasons have been advanced in attempts to explain the Leontief (1953) paradox—that American exports were more labor-using than American import competing production—the effects of distortions in goods and factor markets have not been systematically explored in the context of empirical testing of the Heckscher-Ohlin-Samuelson (HOS) factor proportions explanation of trade. While such an omission may be acceptable in dealing with some developed countries, it is surely not so for the developing countries, where market imperfections are thought to be the rule rather than the exception.

First, a simple model of comparative advantage is developed for n commodities, m countries, and two factors of production, under the usual competitive assumptions. Next, that model is amended to incorporate the existence of a primary commodity or agricultural sector. The implications of the analysis for empirical work will then be examined. In section 4.2 distortions in the goods and factor markets are introduced into the model, and consideration is devoted to the way they would alter the observed pattern of trade and factor proportions employed in export and import-competing industries, with particular attention to methods of identifying the effect of those distortions upon the patterns that would otherwise emerge.

Two issues arise in connection with the hypotheses emanating from the HOS model. The first relates to the question whether predictions pertain to the pattern of production or the pattern of trade. For reasons that will become evident below, it proves useful to discuss patterns of production, although there is a close, logical link between production and trade patterns in the n-commodity model.

The second issue relates to alternative interpretations of the predictions arising from the model. On the one hand, they can be interpreted positively, as predictions about the actual pattern of production, in which case they would constitute a set of hypotheses about the observable production patterns. Alternatively, the factor proportions model can be interpreted normatively, as predictions about the properties of an efficient production pattern that will provide society with the largest attainable consumption bundle for any given inputs allocated to traded-goods production. The latter interpretation corresponds, up to a point, to a hypothesis about the nature of an efficient pattern of production. Predictions can then be interpreted as forecasting what would happen under efficient resource allocation.

The two alternative intrepretations coincide, of course, if the structure of production is efficient, but they might not coincide under inefficient allocations. Since one purpose of the project is to consider the effect of market distortions on the observed pattern of trade, it is useful to regard the HOS model and hypotheses as normative. Under this second interpretation, as will be demonstrated, the HOS hypotheses could be correct, while observed production patterns ran counter to them owing to inefficient production patterns. Although the model developed in this chapter assumes a well-functioning competitive market, it can readily be shown that the HOS hypotheses would also be borne out given the assumptions about technology under any economic structure that provided an efficient allocation of resources for production of tradable goods.

4.1.1   The Factor Proportions Model

4.1.1.1   Assumptions and Statement of the Basic Model

There are assumed to be n commodities, m countries, and two factors of production in the basic model considered here. Later the model will be extended to incorporate an agricultural sector, and the n industries under consideration here will then be understood to be those producing n separate commodities within the manufacturing sector. For the moment, however, it is simplest to start by regarding the n commodities, each produced with two factors of production, as constituting the entire economy. Each of the n production functions displays constant returns to scale, with diminishing marginal product to each factor of production.

Consider now the cost-minimizing labor/capital ratio associated in each industry with a particular arbitrarily chosen wage/rental ratio. Order the commodities so that commodity 1 has the highest labor/capital ratio (at that wage/rental ratio), commodity 2 has the next highest, and so on down to commodity n, which has the lowest labor/capital ratio. It will be assumed that, for all wage/rental ratios, repetition of this procedure would result in exactly the same ordering of commodities; that is, there are assumed to be no factor intensity reversals. A sufficient condition for this ordering of commodities to be the same throughout the entire range of wage/rental variation is that all production functions have the same elasticity of substitution. The exclusion of factor intensity reversals implies something fairly important: with undistorted factor markets, one would observe the same ordering of factor intensities across industries in every country, regardless of whether or not goods prices were the same. This proposition will be seen below to be of some importance for testing for the effects of factor market distortions.[1]

We now have a labor intensity ordering of production functions across countries and a specification of technology that is common to all m countries. In addition, it is assumed that within each country perfect competition prevails in every industry in which there are positive production levels, with perfect factor mobility among all producing industries.

The wage rate equals the value of the marginal product of labor, and the rental on capital equals the value of the marginal product of capital for all industries with positive production levels. These assumptions ensure that each country will be producing efficiently on the boundary of its production-possibility set and that the domestic marginal rate of transformation between any pair of produced commodities will equal the price ratio.

These specifications of the nature of the market within each country, and of the production technology, are the same for all countries. What distinguishes each country is its labor/capital endowment. For purposes of simplicity, it is assumed that each country has its own fixed and inelastic supply of labor and of capital. Full employment of both factors prevails in every country. On that basis, one can compute the ratio of the labor to the capital endowment in each country. The countries can then be so numbered that country 1 has the highest endowment of labor to capital, country 2 the next highest, and so on to country m, which has the lowest labor/capital endowment. Thus, commodities are numbered so that a higher number implies a higher capital/labor ratio in production; countries are numbered so that a higher number is associated with a greater abundance of capital relative to labor.

The assumptions made so far are sufficient that, for any given set of prices confronting producers in a particular country, the area along the boundary of the production-possibility set in which competitive equilibrium can occur will be fairly closely circumscribed. For a particular country and set of prices, there are three possibilities. First, it is possible that it will be profitable to produce only one commodity, in which case all labor and capital within the country will be employed in that industry, the wage/rental ratio being determined by the production function for that industry. Second, it may be profitable to produce exactly two commodities, in which case the wage/rental ratio will be determined by the price ratio between the two goods and the precise composition of output will be such that factors are fully employed at the factor proportions implied by the wage/rental ratio. Third, it may be that it is equally profitable to produce three or more commodities, in which case the precise composition of output is indeterminate, although the wage/rental ratio will be determined by the prices of any two of the commodities.[2]

So far, the production side of the model has been specified. To develop a full general-equilibrium model of trade, it would be necessary to add some demand relations to the model and then to establish some properties of the resulting equilibrium price, production, and trade constellation. In exploring the implications of the HOS model, however, it can be assumed that international prices are given. Hypotheses can then be formulated in terms of the structure of production (and later transformed into hypotheses about the factor intensity of trade). As is well known, the only way demand patterns may influence the HOS predictions is through the possibility that they might offset differences in production patterns. It will be seen below that the only role demand patterns can play in this $n \times m \times 2$ model is to determine whether, when more than one commodity is produced by a particular country, produced commodities are exports or import-competing goods.

One way to interpret the assumption that international prices are determined outside the system is to assume that each country under consideration is small relative to the rest of the world and thus does not influence international prices by its production and consumption behavior. It is more satisfactory, however, simply to postulate that there is in the background a price-determining mechanism, via demand and supply relations, that results in the establishment of some constellation of equilibrium prices. The setting, then, is that international prices are given and there are no transport costs or other impediments to trade. Therefore prices are the same in all countries (since there can be no home goods in the absence of transport costs). The zero-transport-cost assumption will be relaxed below, and the implications of the HOS model for factor proportions in the presence of transport costs will be examined.

4.1.2 Implications of the Basic Model

For any particular country, given international prices, either only one commodity is produced or the domestic wage/rental ratio is determined by the commodity/price ratio when two or more commodities are produced. For a pair of countries, the implications of this proposition are straightforward. If both countries produce two or more goods in common (or, at the limit, if producers in both countries are indifferent between their existing production pattern and an output bundle that would entail producing two or more goods in common), there will be a common wage/rental ratio between those two countries. All that can be said about production patterns is that factor proportions in each country will be the same in each industry (with the same wage/rental ratio) and the more labor-abundant country will have a production bundle more heavily weighted toward the labor-intensive commodities. It is possible that the more labor-abundant country might produce a commodity more capital intensive than some commodity produced by the capital-abundant country: as Bhagwati (1972) has shown, only the overall weighting of factor intensities can be predicted when factor rental equalization occurs.

For present purposes, let us assume that there is no factor rental equalization. This does no violence to the basic model: if two countries have overlapping production patterns and factor rental equalization, they can be regarded as one country in an economic sense. Such may be the case, for example, for some of the European Common Market countries.

In effect, the assumption of no equalization of factor rentals implies that no pair of countries produces two commodities (or more) in common; specialization must result.[3] What, then, can be said about the production patterns for two countries between which factor rentals are not equalized? It follows immediately that the more labor-abundant country will specialize in producing more labor-intensive (lower-numbered) commodities than the more capital-abundant country. The more labor-abundant of any pair of countries cannot produce any commodity more capital intensive than the least capital-using commodity produced in the other. The two countries might produce a commodity in common (if they are adjacent to each other in factor endowments), but the wage/rental ratio would be lower in the more labor-abundant country, and it would produce the common commodity using a more labor-intensive technique.

That the wage/rental ratio must be lower in the labor-abundant country follows immediately from the fact that, if the ratio were higher, it would be profitable to produce more capital-intensive goods with more capital-intensive techniques in the labor-abundant country, an impossibility under the assumption of full employment in both countries.

It is evident that the foregoing statements hold independently of the number of commodities under consideration. In a world of one hundred commodities and two countries, it would be quite possible for the more labor-abundant country to specialize in the first forty-nine commodities, while the other country produced 51 or 52.[4]

Figure 4.1 illustrates the possible sorts of production patterns that might emerge under the assumptions set forth above. In figure 4.1, $m = 11$ and $n = 9$, although other numbers are equally plausible. Commodities are listed in the columns and countries in the rows. An X in the ith row and jth column indicates that the production of commodity j is positive in the ith country, and a blank means there is no production of the commodity in question. For expository convenience it is assumed that there are no cases with zero production levels where producers are indifferent to whether or not they produce.

Inspection of the combinations of production patterns between pairs of adjacent countries illustrates the properties of the model. Country 1 produces commodities 1 and 2 and produces commodity 2 in common with country 2. There is, however, no presumption of factor rental equalization between countries 1 and 2, since country 1 may have a considerably lower wage/rental ratio than country 2. Country 2 also produces commodities 3 and 4 (and must be endowed with a higher capital/labor ratio than country 1), producing commodity 4 in common with countries 3, 4, 5, and 6. It is apparent, however, that the capital intensity of production of commodity 4 is greater in each higher-numbered country. Note that country 2 produces one commodity in common with country 1 and one commodity in common with country 3: there is no factor rental equalization because there are not two commod-

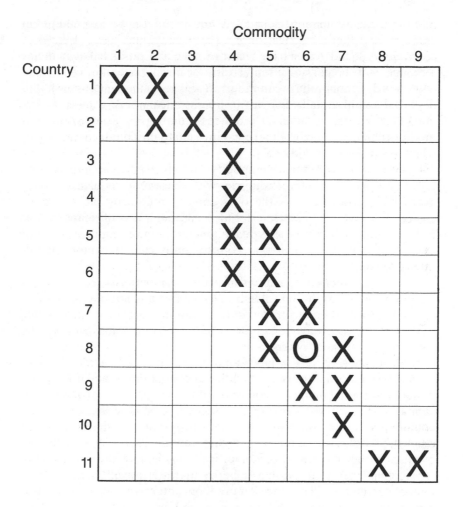

Fig. 4.1   Possible production patterns for eleven countries and nine commodities.

ities produced in common. Countries 5 and 6 produce two commodities in common and therefore must have equal wage/rental ratios. Likewise, countries 7, 8, and 9 must have factor rental equalization between them, although at a higher wage/rental ratio than countries 5 and 6. That country 8 does not produce commodity 6 illustrates the remote possibility of factor rental equalization in a circumstance where a more labor-abundant country (number 7) produces a more capital-intensive commodity (number 6) than a more capital-abundant country (number 8, which produces commodity 5.)[5]

Country 10 also produces commodity 7 but uses more capital-intensive techniques than do the three countries with factor rental equalization. As drawn here, country 11 is the only country producing the two most capital-intensive commodities, 8 and 9, although it could happen that factor rental equalization took place among the most capital-abundant countries, with more than one country producing the most capital-intensive commodity.

Obviously, other constellations of production patterns are also possible, but figure 4.1 sufficiently illustrates the basic possibilities. Generalizing, when there is no factor rental equalization (or when all geographic units with the same wage/rental ratio are treated as a single country), the following conclusions emerge:

1. Production in the most labor-abundant country will be concentrated on the most labor-intensive commodity or commodities, and production in the most capital-abundant country will include production of the most capital-intensive good. Country 1, in other words, is certain to produce commodity 1, and country m is certain to produce commodity n. For countries 2 to $m-1$, those with higher capital/labor endowments will produce higher-numbered commodities than those with lower capital/labor endowments. It will never be so that a relatively more capital-abundant country will produce a more labor-intensive good than any less capital-abundant country (since it is assumed that factor rental equalization cannot occur).

2. If a country produces more than one commodity, the produced commodities will lie adjacent to each other in the factor intensity ordering. Whether the additional commodities produced are import substitutes or exports will depend on the country's factor endowment (in the absence of transport costs) and on demand conditions. It is clear that at least one produced commodity will be exported and that all nonproduced commodities will be imported. It is quite possible that all commodities domestically produced will be made in sufficient quantities to satisfy domestic demand and to export. It is also possible that imports of one or more commodities will result. Except for the most and the least capital-abundant countries, therefore, import-competing industries can lie on either or both sides of the factor intensity of export industries.[6] There will be no essential commodity characteristic that distinguishes import substi-

tutes from exports. The key distinction is between produced and nonproduced commodities.

3. If any two countries produce a common commodity without factor rental equalization between them, the more capital-abundant country will be found employing a more capital-intensive technique of production than the labor-abundant country, and the wage/rental ratio will be higher than in the labor-abundant country.

4. In general, the factor proportions explanation of trade will show up in the pattern of specialization of production rather than in the factor intensity of exports and import-competing goods. Countries in the middle of the factor endowment ranking will tend to specialize in producing commodities in the middle of the factor intensity ranking. They will import labor-intensive commodities from more labor-abundant countries and capital-intensive commodities from countries with relatively higher capital/labor endowments.

4.1.3   Growth in One Country

As a first step in extending the model, it is instructive to examine how the pattern of production and factor prices would change if one relatively labor-abundant country started accumulating capital more rapidly than the rate of growth of its labor force, while international prices and other countries' factor endowments were constant.[7]

Straightforward application of the factor rental equalization and Rybczynski theorems yields the results. Recall that there are three possible initial conditions: (1) the country is specialized in the production of one commodity; (2) the country produces two or more commodities but no more than one in common with any single country; and (3) there is factor rental equalization with another country and two or more commodities are produced in common. Consider first case 1—complete specialization in one commodity. As capital accumulates relative to labor, the production process becomes more capital intensive, with an increase in the wage/rental ratio but continued complete specialization in the single commodity. As accumulation continues, the rental on capital continues declining until it is profitable to produce the next-highest-numbered commodity. After production of that commodity has started, continued capital accumulation results in shifting the composition of output toward the more capital-intensive commodity. At some point, production of the commodity initially produced ceases. During the period of producing both goods, the wage/rental ratio is constant, since international prices are given. When production becomes concentrated on the next-higher commodity, the wage/rental ratio starts rising again and continues until it is profitable to produce the next commodity.[8]

There is, then, a two-phase progression up the commodity chain.[9] In the phase when only one commodity is produced, the wage/rental ratio increases with capital accumulation, but the pattern of production remains unchanged. In the phase of producing two goods, the wage/rental ratio is constant, but the structure of production is shifting among commodities. It is easy to see that starting from the initial position described in case 2 does not essentially alter the argument: initially, the composition of production would shift until the time when continued production of the more labor-intensive commodity was inconsistent with full employment at the existing wage/rental ratio; the wage/rental ratio would then start increasing, and production techniques would become more capital using.

Finally, there is case 3—that of factor rental equalization. Starting in such a position, output of the capital-intensive commodity would increase relatively faster than capital accumulated until production of the labor-intensive commodity ceased, and the story would then be the same as for cases 1 and 2.[10] In all three cases, as the country accumulating capital shifts its production structure to more capital-using goods, it must "meet" and "pass" some other countries along the way. During times when it begins producing new goods, there may be a period when factor rentals equal those of the country whose factor endowment is next most capital intensive to the country in question. Once that country is passed, specialization can rule again, but at some point the next country must also be met and passed. Indeed, in the context introduced above, with one country accumulating capital and all other countries unchanged, the accumulating country would eventually become the most capital abundant and would specialize in the production of one or more of the most capital-intensive commodities.

The two-stage progression here has strong implications for the pattern of trade and its changes over time that would be observed for a rapidly growing country: exports of labor-intensive commodities would gradually be replaced by exports of more capital-intensive commodities as the changing factor endowment altered the country's comparative advantage. Whether a commodity was an export or an import substitute would depend on the factor endowment and the demand pattern, and there is no prediction about relative factor intensity at a point in time.

4.1.4 An Agricultural Sector

Although the *n*-commodity model spelled out above may be a useful first approximation for trade in manufactured commodities, it is surely unsatisfactory for agricultural and other primary commodities, especially in the context of a discussion of developing countries' comparative advantage. Moreover, everyone knows that one of the key features of countries with low per capita income is the very high proportion of national income, and even higher proportion of population, in the agricultural sector.

Jones (1971b) has developed a two-good, three-factor model of trade that can be adapted to take into account this aspect of reality. To avoid confusion later, it is useful to refer to sectoral outputs as being "goods," in contrast to the n "commodities" produced within the manufacturing sector. One of Jones's goods will be regarded as food, the only output of the agricultural sector, and the other will be the n-commodity output of the manufacturing sector. The distinctive feature of Jones's model is that each good requires only two factors of production as inputs: one factor is specific to each sector, and one factor is mobile between the two sectors. For present purposes, labor is regarded as the mobile factor, employed in both manufacturing and agriculture, land is treated as the factor employed only in agricultural production, and capital is the factor specific to manufacturing.

Consider first the case with only one manufacturing commodity. For given (international) prices of the manufacture and food, an equilibrium is described by the following conditions: (1) equality of the wage between the two sectors; (2) full employment of all three factors of production, with the services of capital and land valued at their marginal products; and (3) competition among cost-minimizing firms within each sector. Unlike the two-by-two HOS model, factor rewards are not independent of factor endowments: for a given labor force, the wage, which is uniform, will be higher the greater the endowment of either capital or land, holding the other specific factor constant. For a given stock of land, the fraction of the labor force in agriculture will be greater the smaller the stock of capital. These results follow from the assumption of labor mobility and competitive factor rewards: if the stock of either land or capital increases, the marginal product of labor in that sector must rise. Maintenance of wage equality between sectors therefore implies that some labor must migrate from the other sector, which, with a given amount of the specific factor, implies a higher marginal product of labor in that sector, as well as reduced output.

Now consider what happens over time to a country faced with fixed international prices, still retaining the assumption of only one manufactured commodity. It is simplest to start by assuming an initial equilibrium with a zero capital stock and to investigate what happens if capital accumulation begins with a constant stock of land and an unchanging labor force.

In this initial no-capital-stock equilibrium, the wage will be determined by the land/labor ratio. The greater the labor force relative to the land, the lower will be the marginal product of labor. Presumably, some agricultural output would be exported in return for imports of manufactures. If a small amount of saving takes place, some labor must move from agriculture to manufacturing in order to maintain wage equality between the sectors. The wage must rise from its initial equilibrium as the labor/land ratio falls with the shift of workers to the manufacturing sector. Note that if two different countries started capital accumulation with very different man/land ratios, the initial choice of techniques in their manufacturing sectors would differ, with the country that has the more favorable endowment of land using, even initially, techniques that require more capital per worker. That, in turn, implies that the increment of manufacturing output per unit of capital would initially be smaller in the land-rich country.

Once a manufacturing sector is started, further increases in the capital stock imply a rising wage/rental ratio, an increasing marginal product of labor in agriculture, and reduced agricultural output as the same quantity of land is combined with fewer workers. In the two-sector model the country would initially be a food exporter and a manufactures importer, regardless of the land/man ratio. With capital accumulation, there would inevitably (at constant world prices) come a point where the country shifted from being a net exporter of food to being a net exporter of manufactures.[11] The higher the initial land/man endowment, the greater would be the capital accumulation necessary to reach the crossover point and the higher would be the wage at which such a point was reached. For present purposes, however, the precise location of the crossover is largely irrelevant: the pattern of production within manufacturing will be independent of whether the country is a net exporter of food or of manufactures.

This can be seen by joining the basic two-sector, three-factor model to the *n*-commodity, two-factor model outlined above. In particular, let there be *n* manufacturing production functions, each of which uses labor and capital with constant returns to scale and diminishing marginal products to either factor, while the agricultural sector produces food, using labor and land in its production process, again with constant returns to scale and diminishing returns to either factor. World prices are again given, equality of the wage between industry and agriculture is assumed, and all factors are fully employed.

Diminishing marginal product of labor in agriculture implies that more labor will be supplied to the manufacturing (urban) sector the higher the urban wage. To see the properties (and comparative statics) of an equilibrium, let the urban capital stock be given and consider the conditions under which the country would produce manufactured commodities 1 and 2; the wage/rental ratio is implied by the relative prices of the two manufactured commodities (given by world prices). If, at that wage, the quantity of labor supplied from the agricultural sector is such that the urban capital/labor ratio lies between the factor proportions associated with the wage/rental ratios in the first and second industries, both commodities will be produced. By construction of the ordering of commodities, the country's labor/capital proportions within manufacturing will be relatively high, and the country will have relatively low wages.

We now have a situation in which there is a capital/labor ratio for the country as a whole *and* a capital/labor ratio for the manufacturing sector. One might find two countries with comparable overall labor/capital ratios but very different wage/rental ratios, if one country was considerably more land abundant per man. The land-abundant country would have a higher capital/labor ratio in the manufacturing sector and a higher wage/rental ratio than the land-poor country. Conversely, identical wage/rental ratios might be observed if one country's overall capital/labor ratio was greater and its land/labor ratio less than the other's. In that case similar commodities would be produced by the two countries despite the diversity in their overall factor endowments. Paradoxically, for any given countrywide capital/labor endowment, the manufacturing sector's capital/labor ratio depends on the country's land/man ratio: the more land there is, the higher will be the wage for any given capital stock.

Suppose now that the wage/rental ratio implied by prices of manufacturing commodities 1 and 2 elicited an urban labor supply such that the overall manufacturing labor/capital ratio (given the fixed capital stock) exceeded the factor proportions that would be used in the first industry at that wage/rental ratio. It is clear that there would be an excess supply of urban labor. The equilibrium wage would therefore be below that associated with positive production levels for commodities 1 and 2. That would result in somewhat less labor being supplied to the first industry, but, even more important, it would imply that the commodity 1 is the only manufacture produced.

Consider, then, an equilibrium with wage equality between the urban and rural sectors, and manufacturing production specialized in the first commodity. The quantity produced might be insufficient to supply the domestic market, in which case it would be an import substitute (and the economy would necessarily export food), or it might exceed domestic demand, in which case it would be an export. Either way, it would be labor intensive relative to other manufactured commodities, which would be imported and not produced domestically.

Now examine what would happen if, from that initial equilibrium, an increment of capital were acquired. Capital deepening in the first industry would occur, thereby tending to raise the wage (inducing more workers to migrate to the urban area) and lower the rental on capital. The net effect would always be some degree of capital deepening within the first industry, because additional workers would migrate only at a higher wage. Thus capital accumulation would necessarily increase both the urban and the rural wage and lower the return on capital (and on land).

If capital accumulation continued, a point would be reached at which the wage/rental ratio rendered profitable the production of the second, as well as the first, commodity. At that point continued capital accumulation would result in increased output of the second commodity and reduced output of the first commodity, following the Rybczynski theorem, and constant factor prices (with a constant urban labor force, also). At some point the capital/labor ratio would reach that found in the second commodity's production, specialization would be complete in the second commodity, and the wage/rental ratio would once again start increasing as further capital accumulation occurred.

In a world of constant prices with one country accumulating capital, one can readily extend the model to show that the country could "progress" from specialization in agriculture with no manufacturing activity to a situation in which the most capital-intensive manufactured commodities were produced. Note that the production of some food would continue throughout the process, although, as stated, the model implies decreasing food output throughout the capital-accumulation process (and, perhaps, a shift from food exports to food imports).[12]

It is also simple to consider the situation in which the marginal product of labor in agriculture is high enough so that, instead, specialization is somewhere further up the commodity ordering: even at an early stage of development, comparative advantage within manufacturing need not lie in labor-intensive commodities.

Several points should be noted. First, the distinction between poor and underdeveloped countries emerges clearly from the model. A "poor" country is one with an unfavorable land/man endowment. An underdeveloped country is one with a relatively small endowment of capital per person. An underdeveloped country, however, could conceivably have a higher per capita income and real wage than a "more developed" but poorer country. Second, a country abundantly endowed with land and therefore with a relatively high wage would not necessarily have a comparative advantage in labor-intensive manufactures even in its early stages of capital accumulation: the real wage at which persons would leave agriculture might be too high. In such an instance, the capital/labor ratio in manufacturing would be higher in the early stages of development than in a poorer country, while output per unit of capital and the rate of return on capital would be lower than in a lower-wage country. The apparent paradox of a high-wage, land-rich underdeveloped country or a land-poor, low-wage developed country may thus be explained: Carlos Díaz-Alejandro suggested in correspondence that Argentina and Japan in the 1920s may be prototypes.

Third, the supply of labor to the urban sector (quite aside from the issue of population growth, which can readily be incorporated into the growth implications of the model) will be relatively more elastic the smaller is the urban sector relative to the rural sector and the more elastic is the output of the agricultural sector with respect to labor.[13] Thus one would expect comparative advantage to shift slowly in the early stages of growth, since small changes in the small manufacturing wage would elicit a relatively large change in labor supply from the large agricultural sector. For a constant rate of capital accumulation, therefore, one would expect to observe an increasing rate of increase in the urban real wage (and a commensurate change in the rate of change in the return on capital) and a decreasing rate of increase in the rate of growth of manufacturing output. An increasing rate of capital accumulation resulting from higher incomes would reinforce the tendency. "Early" development would therefore consist of the growth of the manufacturing sector, with relatively slow changes in the composition of output and the wage/rental ratio. "Later" development would witness a much slower rate of transfer of labor to the urban sector but more rapid changes in the wage/rental ratio and in the composition of manufacturing output.

4.1.5   Transport Costs and Home Goods

Despite the many appealing features of the model spelled out above, a troublesome aspect is that it forecasts the production of relatively few manufacturing commodities at each stage of development. That may, of course, be an accurate prediction. How many constitute "few" depends on the number of commodities relative to the number of countries. If there are two hundred countries and five thousand commodities, failure of production patterns to overlap might still imply the production of a sizable number of individual manufacturing commodities in each country.

Incorporating transport costs into the model provides a partial basis for believing that a somewhat greater overlapping of production patterns is possible without factor rental equalization than is implied by the basic model. It also suggests that the process of growth will entail continuous shifting of output compositions and an increasing wage/rental ratio, rather than the two-phase progression spelled out above.

Assume that transport costs are a constant percentage of international price for all manufactured commodities. Domestic prices of exportables would be less than their international prices by the percentage that transport costs constitute of international price, while the domestic price of imports and domestically produced import-competing commodities would be an equal percentage above the international price.[14]

When domestic price can vary at a constant world price—within a range, of course—two things change. First, it is no longer necessary that production be concentrated in one or two manufacturing commodities only, and an import substituting sector becomes much more likely. The factor intensity of domestic production of import-competing goods will still be similar to that of exportables: for the country with the lowest manufacturing capital/labor ratio, import-substituting production will generally be more capital intensive than export production, and conversely for the most capital-abundant country. For countries in the center of the endowment range, however, import-substituting industries' factor proportions are likely to lie on each side of that of the export industries.

Second, when domestic prices can vary within the range set by transport costs, there will be a slight change in the way the pattern of production will alter with increases in the capital stock. In particular, the prices of commodities will be free to change somewhat as capital accumulates. To see this, return to the example given in the last section, where it was assumed that a country with a low land/labor ratio (and therefore a low wage) began accumulating capital. It was asserted that such a country would initially produce commodity 1, the most labor-intensive manufacture, and that the wage rate would increase as capital accumulation continued until it became profitable to produce commodity 2. While that analysis remains correct, there would be an additional aspect to the process of capital accumulation: initially, the domestic price of commodity 1 could exceed the world price by the margin of natural protection afforded by transport costs. With capital accumulation, the wage would rise relative to the rental, but in addition the price of the commodity would decrease. Moreover, import-substituting production of the second manufactured commodity could start relatively sooner than was implied by the cycle of rising real wages followed by constant wages as production shifted between industries. This is because the domestic price of the second commodity could exceed its world levels. Thus the phase pattern described above would not be quite so pronounced; instead, relative price changes of domestically produced goods could absorb some of the alterations resulting from changed factor endowments in the urban sector.

With proportionate transport costs for all manufactured commodities, there is likely to be a range of commodities, on each side of the factor intensity of the country's exports (except where the country itself is in an extreme position), for which it would be profitable to produce for domestic consumption. Thus a moderately labor-abundant country exporting a commodity or commodities in the middle of the factor intensity range might produce import substitutes on both sides of the factor intensity of its export. It remains the case, however, that the goods it did not produce would require more extreme factor proportions than those it did produce.

If transport costs differ significantly among commodities, of course, the preceding analysis no longer holds. Some possibilities can, however, be dealt with. Suppose, for example, that labor-intensive commodities have higher transport costs as a percentage of international price than do capital-intensive goods. The following ought then to be the case: (1) for commodities more labor intensive than those exported by any particular country, the height of transport costs (as a percentage of international price) should be correlated with the labor/capital ratio in the industry; (2) one would expect to observe relatively less specialization in countries with capital-abundant manufacturing sectors than in countries with labor-abundant manufacturing, since the former would tend to have more import-substituting activity; and (3) world exports would constitute a greater proportion of the world supply of capital-intensive commodities than of labor-intensive commodities.

Of course, if transport costs are sufficiently high, a commodity can become a "home good," since international trade is virtually ruled out in all but exceptional cases. Many services, such as haircuts, medical care, and retail delivery of commodities, are generally thought to be labor intensive. However, there are other items, such as financial services, communications, and the like, that are probably equally location-tied and that seem to be capital intensive. The existence of home goods does not basically alter the propositions set forth above except in the ways it affects the basic two-commodity-model predictions.[15] If home goods factor proportions are at the world average for all commodities, home goods would tend to be capital intensive in labor-abundant countries and labor intensive in capital-abundant countries. When home goods are present, price-output responses of traded goods could become perverse, and thus some of the comparative-statics propositions set forth above would not necessarily hold. Propositions about the comparative advantage of a country within manufacturing industries would still be valid, however, for any allocation of labor and capital to the production of traded goods.[16]

4.1.5.1   Implications for Empirical Work

The model above served as a theoretical basis for much of the empirical work undertaken by country authors. Several implications should be noted that are important in examining labor coefficients associated with HOS goods: (1) as was already mentioned, natural resource based trade should be excluded from the computation; (2) there is no presumption whatever, except for the countries at each end of the manufacturing-endowment spectrum or in the presence of protection, that the factor intensities of import-competing and export production will have any systematic relationship; (3) judgment of a country's factor proportions should be based on its manufacturing capital/labor ratio and not on its overall endowment; (4) for countries not at either extreme of the manufacturing capital/labor range, any empirical evaluation of the pattern of trade must be based on a partitioning of that trade into the portion that is with countries higher up the endowment ordering and the portion that is with countries lower down.

The hypothesis emanating from the $n + 1$-commodity, m-country, three-factor HOS model, in other words, is that differences in factor endowments will show up in patterns of specialization: it is the capital-intensive equipment that is imported and *not* domestically produced that reflects a very labor-abundant manufacturing sector's comparative advantage. It is this result that led to the distinction between import-competing goods and noncompeting imports.

On the basis of the model developed above, several tests of the generalized HOS explanation are possible: (1) if one knows the country's overall relative capital/labor ratio in manufacturing, the hypothesis is that the commodities it produces domestically will be ones that require inputs in approximately those proportions: commodities imported and not domestically produced will have factor proportions further away from the country's manufacturing endowment; (2) the pattern of trade, including exports, may well differ between countries on the two sides of the country's manufacturing endowment, especially when the presence of transport costs is taken into account; and (3) insofar as transport costs permit a wide range of domestic production, transport costs as a percentage of world price will have to be higher, the further the commodity is from the country's factor endowment within manufacturing.

Consider each of these tests in the case of a country with a relatively labor-abundant manufacturing sector. The HOS model then predicts several things: (1) That country will import commodities whose production functions are more capital intensive from countries with higher capital/labor ratios in their manufacturing sectors and commodities that are extremely labor intensive from the few countries with lower capital/labor ratios in their manufacturing sectors. Testing this proposition would require partitioning the country's imports into those from more labor-abundant areas and those from more capital-rich areas, and then applying to them the capital/labor ratios of any country that produces all commodities (the United States? Japan?). (2) Insofar as the country's manufacturing exports differ between the two groups of destinations, the capital intensity of exports will be greater to the more labor-abundant area, and conversely.[17] (3) The capital intensity of production of import-competing commodities will be positively associated with the level of transport costs (and, as will be seen below, tariffs) for commodities competing with imports from countries with higher capital/labor ratios in manufacturing, and conversely.

4.2   The Effect of Commodity and Factor Market Distortions upon the Commodity Composition of Trade

Thus far, attention has been centered upon the factor proportions explanation of trade as a hypothesis about the determinants of the production pattern for goods not based on natural resources under efficient resource allocation. If resource allocation were always efficient, the task would be accomplished. The model developed above could be elaborated in numerous directions, but the basic propositions have emerged and empirical tests of it could be undertaken.

In some countries there is reason to believe that markets function fairly efficiently and that the model can therefore be tested along the lines sketched above.[18] Given that it was believed that distortions in the commodity and factor market might significantly affect the commodity composition of trade, however, an important question remains: How can one interpret the outcome of any examination of that pattern? To illustrate the difficulty, assume that, for a particular country where distortions are believed to be important, a pattern of trade in manufacturing emerges that does not conform to the specialization patterns set forth above. How can one distinguish between the possibility that the HOS model does not apply and the hypothesis that distortions so alter the trade pattern as to produce the observed result?

Research to date has thrown considerable light on what would happen if particular distortions were, in fact, observed. In this section those results are reviewed.

The procedure is as follows. It is assumed that the model developed in section 4.1 holds for a particular country.[19] To make exposition simple, it will be assumed that this country would, under efficient resource allocation, produce food and the first several manufacturing commodities: it is thus the country with the lowest capital/labor endowment in manufacturing and would, under an efficient allocation of resources, be a low-wage country. The question then is: Given particular distortions, what would be the observed pattern of production, and how would that pattern differ from the efficient one? In most cases the reader can readily generalize the results to cover countries elsewhere in the capital/labor endowment ranking. When application to countries in the middle of the endowment range may not be obvious, a note gives the relevant line of argument.

The questions now under consideration are the effect upon the structure of production of (1) distortions in the goods market so that domestic prices diverge from international prices by more than transport costs, and (2) distortions in the factor market so that domestic factor prices do not reflect the opportunity cost of employing those factors.

4.2.1   Goods Market Distortions

The effects of goods market distortions are well known and can be spelled out briefly.[20] In general, one can readily devise testable hypotheses about the systematic relation between those distortions and the shifts in patterns of production that will result if factor markets function efficiently.

The production structure that would result from efficient resource allocation can be altered by tariffs or subsidies to industries that would otherwise be unprofitable domestically.[21] When taxes and subsidies are used, it is possible not only to distort the structure of production, but to distort it so much that the "wrong" commodities are exported. This must sometimes occur in countries with large import substitution sectors built up under high levels of protection in circumstances where "export subsidies" are accorded only to new industries. In such cases industries that would be exporting under an efficient allocation may not produce at all, while others that might be not operating at all may be exporting.[22]

If all the incentives and market imperfections that result in distortions and inefficient production patterns are concentrated within the goods market, it still seems possible to devise a test to determine whether the HOS model of *efficient* production is valid: the net protection equivalents of all the various incentives, disincentives, and market imperfections should be positively correlated with the capital/labor ratios of the protected industries.[23] This is because, for the most labor-abundant country, which is the one on which the discussion is centered, the HOS model predicts that higher rates of protection will be needed to render domestic production possible, the higher the capital intensity of the industry. That the "wrong mix" of industries was producing would of course alter the equilibrium wage/rental ratio, but production of commodities that were too capital intensive for an efficient pattern of production would result in a decline in the equilibrium wage/rental ratio, thereby rendering the cost disadvantage of capital-intensive industries even greater than they would be at the wage/rental ratio associated with an optimal allocation of resources.[24]

When tariffs (and tariff equivalents) are the only distortion in the system, the correlation between protection and factor intensity should still hold. However, reversal of commodities is not possible, and thus the predictions of the HOS model would be observable. Under tariff protection, some industries would be producing that would not produce under an efficient allocation. It is not possible, however, to turn an industry that would be an exporter under an efficient allocation into a nonproducing industry. Protection can cause some resources to be used in import substitution that would otherwise have been employed in producing the commodities for export. However, the most that production can be diverted is to the point of autarky: tariffs can raise the internal price of commodities and thereby render their production for the domestic market profitable, but they cannot induce exports of those commodities at the lower world prices.

As long as exporting industries do not receive subsidies, trade patterns could not be reversed while factor markets continued to function efficiently. One could therefore still test the HOS model: the factor intensity of nonproduced commodities would be contrasted with the factor intensity of exportables and import substitutes not receiving protection. One would observe the manufacturing sector of the labor-abundant country producing the most labor-intensive commodities for export. In addition, of course, one could test for the relationship between the capital intensity of industries and the height of protection.[25] In the event that the labor-abundant country was not exporting labor-intensive manufactures, one could reject the factor proportions explanation of trade even though tariffs were used to protect domestic industry. Likewise, if the height of protection necessary to induce domestic production was not positively correlated with the capital intensity of the protected industries, that again would constitute grounds for rejecting the HOS model.[26] Of course, with subsidies to particular exports (or, as in some countries, requirements that firms export certain portions of their output in return for import licenses), comparison of the factor intensity of a country's exports with that of nonproduced commodities might reveal that either exports or nonproduced commodities were more capital intensive. However, the correlation between the height of the protective equivalents and the capital intensities of the various industries should still be positive, and one should be able to test the HOS model directly against observable data within the country.

4.2.2   Factor Market Distortions

The more difficult case is the one in which commodity prices are undistorted, that is, equal to world prices, while the prices of factor services differ from those that would prevail under perfect competition in factor markets.[27] The case is the precise opposite of that for commodity market distortions: when the distortions in factor markets are firm- or industry-specific, as with credit rationing, bureaucratic allocation of licenses for importing capital goods, and case-by-case decision-making on tax exemptions and subsidies, it is usually not possible to infer anything about the efficient pattern of trade from direct observation of the data. Firm- or industry-specific variations in factor prices are equivalent to subsidies and taxes; when such specificity occurs, the observed pattern of trade need not bear any relation to an efficient one.[28]

However, when the factor market distortion can be characterized in some systematic way, in some circumstances inferences can be drawn that make it possible to ascertain how the observed pattern of trade is related to an efficient one. By "systematic characterization" is meant departure from only one of the efficiency conditions for the allocation of factors of production among alternative uses. For example, if payment to one factor is uniform across all activities, while there are two different returns to the other factor with one subset of all activities paying a higher return than the other subset, the effects of that differential on resource allocation can be analyzed. Another systematic type of distortion occurs if the return to one factor is pegged above the level that would prevail under competitive conditions, with the result that the factor is not fully employed.

Since, within the manufacturing sector, only the wage/rental ratio affects resource allocation, the effects of the capital and labor market distortions can be analyzed as an increase in the wage/rental ratio above its efficiency level.

Factor market distortions may significantly affect observed patterns of trade. When certain types of systematic factor market distortions are present, a finding that production and exports are concentrated in a capital-intensive industry or group of industries by a labor-abundant country is no longer prima facie cause to reject the factor proportions explanation of trade. Nor, for that matter, is a finding of a labor-intensive pattern of production sufficient cause to accept it. Indeed, in the context of the standard two-commodity, two-factor HOS model, it has been shown that a difference in the wage/rental ratio paid by two industries may bring about any of the following results: (1) the "right" commodity will be produced and exported with the "right" factor intensity; (2) the "right" commodity will be produced and exported with the "wrong" factor intensity; (3) the "wrong" commodity will be exported with the "wrong" factor intensity; (4) the "wrong" commodity will be exported with the "right" factor intensity. Suppose one observed a production and export bundle of highly capital-intensive commodities in a labor-abundant country in which factor market distortions were thought important. One could not determine without further investigation whether this pattern was observed because capital/labor substitution had occurred in the export industry, causing it to be more capital intensive than it would be at a common wage/rental ratio with other sectors; because import-competing industries or nonproducing industries were the ones that should be exporting under an efficient allocation; or because the HOS model was inappropriate.

One of the interesting lessons of this distortion literature is that it is not enough to say "distortion": three separate types of distortion have so far been analyzed. Each case has been developed in the context of a two-commodity model, since the authors have had in mind an urban and a rural sector, and application of these analyses to the model of section 4.1 requires identification of the source of the distortion. In the first case, an exogenously imposed real minimum wage applies over the entire economy (with open unemployment when the real minimum wage is binding). This case readily extends to the n-commodity model by assuming a wage floor across the entire economy.[29] In the second case, based upon the Todaro (1969) and Harris-Todaro (1970) model of labor markets, the urban wage is above the rural wage, and the unemployment rate clears the labor market; in effect, the expected urban wage (equal to the actual urban wage times the probability of finding work, adjusted for the length of time it takes to do so) is equal to the rural wage. In applying this distortion model to the n-commodity, two-sector case, the natural interpretation is that there is a minimum real wage in the urban sector and thus a variable differential in the wage between the rural and urban sectors, with open unemployment. In the third, and probably most thoroughly explored, case, a two-commodity, two-factor economy with full employment has a wage/rental ratio in one industry that differs by a constant multiplicative factor from the wage/rental ratio in the other industry. Two alternative interpretations of this case are possible: (1) the wage differential in question can be between the urban and rural sectors; or (2) there may be an organized, large-scale sector within manufacturing in which wages are equal to those in the rural sector. This latter interpretation would correspond somewhat to the notion of a "modern" and a "traditional" sector within manufacturing.[30]

The task at hand is to apply results obtained in the literature for the two-commodity, two-factor case to the two-sector, n-manufacturing industries, three-factor model for a single country.

4.2.2.1 An Economywide Real Wage Floor

It is simplest to start with the case in which there is an economywide wage/rental ratio above that which would prevail under competition and perfect factor markets.[31] It is immaterial whether the distortion results from minimum wage legislation, union behavior, or other causes. Brecher (1974) has explored this case in the two-by-two context in terms of a real minimum wage, a practice that is followed here. The analysis holds equally, however, should the rental on capital somehow be pegged above its equilibrium level.

In the Brecher model, the locus of competitive outputs (LCO) coincides with the transformation curve until the point at which the wage implied by the relative price of the two commodities equals the real minimum wage; it then becomes a Rybczynski line from that point to complete specialization in the capital-intensive commodity; finally, it moves back toward the transformation curve as output of the capital-intensive commodity increases. Naturally, employment decreases from the point at which the locus of competitive outputs deviates from the transformation curve until the point of specialization in the capital-intensive commodity, then increases until full employment is reached at the point at which the transformation curve and the locus of competitive outputs coincide with specialization in the capital-intensive good.

The situation is depicted in figure 4.2a. The set of efficient production possibilities is the transformation curve AD. If an initial, efficient free-trade equilibrium is at point B, where production is concentrated in X, the labor-intensive commodity, the set of other outputs that can be

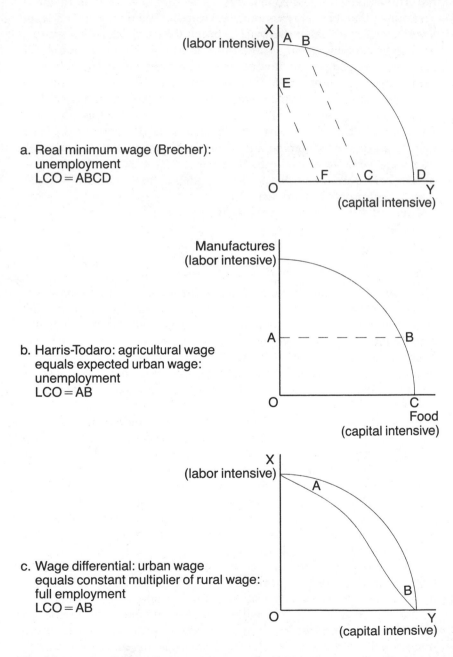

a. Real minimum wage (Brecher): unemployment LCO = ABCD

b. Harris-Todaro: agricultural wage equals expected urban wage: unemployment LCO = AB

c. Wage differential: urban wage equals constant multiplier of rural wage: full employment LCO = AB

Fig. 4.2   Locus of competitive outputs (LCO) under differing assumptions about the nature of distortions.

produced under profit-maximizing behavior by firms with the commodity prices implied by the slope of the tangent to point B (not drawn) is the line BC. Along BC, both commodities are produced, and employment declines as the output of the labor-intensive commodity decreases. At point C there is complete specialization in the capital-intensive commodity, Y. Curiously enough, as production of Y increases from C to D, employment is increasing and the production technique employed in Y is increasingly labor intensive.

To understand the Brecher model, it is useful to imagine that a minimum real wage law is passed, with the real wage denominated in terms of the labor-intensive good. The Rybczynski line must shift to the left. A sufficiently high real wage will make full employment with specialization in the labor-intensive commodity impossible. Such a situation is illustrated in figure 4.2a by the locus of competitive outputs described by EFD. That locus is associated with a higher real minimum wage than the locus described by $ABCD$. With the minimum real wage associated with EFC, full employment could be attained only with specialization in the capital-intensive commodity, and that could occur only if there were a sufficiently high price for the capital-intensive good to maintain the real wage in terms of the labor-intensive commodity. Of course, if the real minimum wage were increased without any change in commodity prices, production of the labor-intensive commodity would decrease, but the economy would not become specialized in producing the wrong commodity, and unemployment would simply increase as the real minimum wage was increased.

Three features of the model are especially relevant for present purposes: (1) within this model in its two-commodity form, it is possible that the "wrong" commodity will be produced and even that there will be specialization in it; (2) the higher the real wage, the greater is the likelihood of wrong specialization; and (3) at a sufficiently high real wage, full employment is possible only if the price of the capital-intensive good is sufficiently high *and* the real wage is fixed in terms of the labor-intensive commodity.[32]

Applying the Brecher model to the two-sector, three-factor manufacturing commodities model developed in section 4.1.1.1 is relatively straightforward. If there is an economywide real wage and the stock of capital is independent of the level of real output, a higher real wage will be associated unequivocally with a smaller level of urban employment *and* a lower level of agricultural employment.[33] At given international prices, a given capital stock and a real wage entirely determine the industry (or industries) in which it will pay to specialize. The higher the real wage, the more capital intensive the industries of specialization will be, and the lower will be the real return on capital.[34] From this it follows immediately that employment must be less than in the absence of the distortion.

Several consequences of the fixed-real-wage model are immediately apparent. First, since both agricultural output and manufactured output must fall with increases in the real wage, it is not clear what will happen to the agricultural/manufactures balance of trade: it could either increase or decrease. A country that might be a net importer of food under an efficient allocation of resources might become a net exporter, or conversely. There is no a priori basis on which to assign likelihoods to either outcome. Within manufacturing, however, it is clear that the higher the real wage, the more capital intensive will be the industries within which production will take place, and as long as relative prices of manufactures remain at free-trade levels, the more capital intensive will be the techniques of production used within those industries. It is not possible for the factor intensities of produced commodities to reverse; that is, it is not possible that an industry that would be labor intensive under an efficient allocation could become capital intensive with a higher minimum wage.

It would thus appear that when the entire economy is operating subject to a minimum real wage constraint, there is no possibility of industries reversing factor intensities. Therefore, if the most labor-abundant country was found to be exporting the most labor-intensive goods when it was subject to a minimum wage constraint, one could be confident that the same outcome would apply under an efficient allocation. If that country was exporting manufactured commodities that were not the most labor intensive, however, there would be a question whether the distortion changed the pattern of production or whether the HOS model did not describe an efficient allocation. One could not ascertain whether the failure to hold of the factor proportions hypothesis called into question the validity of the model or was due to the real minimum wage, and direct observation of data would not provide a means to distinguish between hypotheses. Simulation of optimal allocations, examination of changes in production patterns before the imposition of the real-wage constraint, or other means would have to be devised to test whether the HOS theorems would hold under optimal resource allocation.

4.2.2.2 Fixed Urban Real Wages

The second model, with a fixed real wage in the industrial sector above that in the rural sector, can have the same effects within the manufacturing sector as the economywide fixed real wage. The production pattern actually observed might be one in which the manufacturing sector was specialized in the wrong commodities. The higher the fixed urban wage, the more the production structure would shift toward more capital-intensive commodities, given international prices. As with the uniform wage, however, commodities that were capital intensive under the real wage constraint would also be capital intensive at free trade.

However, the fact that the Harris-Todaro model posits a difference in the wage/rental ratio between the urban (manufacturing) and rural sector adds a twist to the model: it is possible that the labor intensity of agriculture and manufacturing might be reversed. Suppose, for example, that industry were labor intensive at free trade.[35] As the real minimum wage applying to the manufacturing (urban) sector rose, the quantity of labor employed in the urban sector would decline. At some critical wage, the labor intensity of the manufacturing sector would equal that in the rural sector.[36] How soon this occurred would depend on what happened to rural employment as the urban wage rose. If total workers in the city, employed plus unemployed, increased as the wage increased, then the "crossover" would be relatively slow in coming; agriculture, as well as industry, would become less labor intensive with increases in the real wage. If, however, urban employment fell sharply with increases in the real wage, it is possible that agricultural employment would increase as urban employment fell. In such a case agriculture would become more labor intensive while manufacturing was shifting to production of more capital-intensive commodities (and substituting capital for labor within each producing industry), and the point at which the two labor intensities crossed would be attained more quickly.

The locus of competitive outputs under an urban wage constraint is illustrated in figure 4.2b. There it is assumed that manufacturing would be labor intensive in the absence of a real wage constraint, but that the fixing of the real wage sets the manufacturing output level at OA. The locus of possible output points is therefore the line AB, and the point B would be infeasible unless the real wage in agriculture happened to equal that in industry there. An increase in the urban real wage would shift the line AB downward. Thus the Harris-Todaro model differs from the fixed-real-wage model in its implications for the possibility of reversing factor intensities between agriculture and manufacturing. That may be of considerable importance in a number of contexts if it is believed that the Harris-Todaro description of labor-market conditions is valid. Even if it is appropriate, however, the analysis of comparative advantage and the effects of the distortion within the manufacturing sector can be carried out as in the Brecher model: a manufacturing wage rate above that under an efficient allocation would easily lead to concentration of production in commodities that were more capital intensive than the country's situation would render optimal. Such a circumstance could not, however, lead to a reversal of factor intensities, and if the country's production and trade appeared to conform to the HOS model, this would confirm the HOS hypotheses.

4.2.2.3   Wage Differential within Manufacturing

The most analytically interesting of the three cases of distortions is the two-commodity, two-factor model in which the wage/rental ratio in one industry is a constant multiple of that in the other, while full employment of both factors always prevails. For application to the n-manufacturing-industries model, the case is of interest if one subset of the n industries has the same wage as the agricultural sector while the other subset pays a different, presumably higher, wage.[37] If, for example, the chemical, basic metal, and machinery industries are favored, then the constant-wage-differential model developed by Johnson (1965), Jones (1971a), Herberg and Kemp (1971), and others would apply.[38]

The locus of competitive outputs in the two-commodity, two-factor model is represented in figure 4.2c by the line AB, which must everywhere, except at the two complete specialization points, lie inside the production-possibility curve. This follows immediately from the fact that the marginal rate of substitution among the two factors of production is different in the two industries, and it would therefore be possible to attain more of both outputs by reallocating factors between them at any point at which both commodities are produced.

The problem, in the full-employment, constant-differential case, is that it is no longer possible, with such a distortion, to identify the direction of the change in output that will result from a change in relative prices of the two commodities. It is possible, for example, that the price of one commodity might increase, and that the competitive response would be for output of that commodity to decrease and output of the other commodity (whose relative price had fallen) to increase.

The reason for this can be most easily understood with the aid of figure 4.3.[39] The Edgeworth box drawn there is based on the production possibilities between two commodities, 1 and 2, with a constant stock of labor and capital. In the absence of wage differentials (i.e., under conditions of efficient production), commodity 1 is assumed to be labor intensive. The locus of efficient output points (the curved line) lies below the diagonal representing equal factor proportions in both industries. Every point in the Edgeworth box corresponds to a particular set of input combinations and outputs. Moving to the east and to the north represents greater output of 1, and there is a given real income associated with each output point. For the sake of exposition, assume that demand patterns associated with those output points and real income levels mean that commodity 1 will be exported to the right of the mm line and will be imported to the left of the mm line.

Two distinct cases must be analyzed. In the first, the labor-intensive industry must pay higher wages than the capital-intensive industry. In the second, the lower wage/rental rate applies to the labor-intensive industry. Taking the first case, start with wage/rental equality and then introduce a differential. The labor intensity of industry 1 will diminish and that of industry 2 will increase. As the differential increases and commodity prices adjust, at some point, industry 1 will become capital intensive in the physical sense; that is, it will employ more capital per worker than industry 2. At that point the physical factor intensities are reversed, so

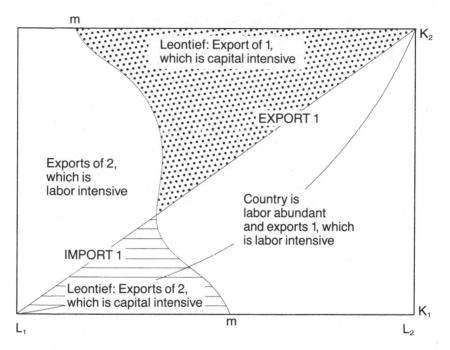

Fig. 4.3   Production possibilities between two commodities with a constant stock of labor and capital.

that production will take place somewhere above the diagonal representing equal factor proportions.[40]

There are now four possibilities:

1. The wage differential might not be sufficient to reduce production below consumption or to reverse factor intensities, so that the country might be operating below the diagonal and to the right of the *mm* line. In that case the differential would not be sufficient to alter production and trade patterns away from "true" comparative advantage. This corresponds to the white area below the diagonal in figure 4.3.

2. The wage differential might not be sufficient to reverse factor intensities, but it might result in an increase in production of commodity 2 and a reduction in production of commodity 1, to a point to the left of the *mm* line. In that case the country's production would have altered enough so that commodity 2 became the export commodity. Inspection of the factor proportions of the two industries would reveal that the capital-intensive commodity was the export. The finding of Leontief paradox would result. This is the case where the country exports the "wrong"

commodity with the "right" factor proportions. It is the horizontally striped area of figure 4.3.

3. The wage differential and accompanying price changes could be sufficient to move the country across the diagonal but leave production to the right of the *mm* line. In that case commodity 1 would be exported, but empirical estimation would show that commodity 1 was the capital-intensive commodity, and thus the "perverse" factor intensity of exports would be found—another Leontief-paradox area—in which the "right" commodity is exported with the "wrong" factor proportions.[41] This is the case illustrated by the shaded area of figure 4.3.

4. The distortion could be sufficient to render commodity 1 capital intensive and to reduce output sufficiently so that commodity 2 was exported and labor intensive. In this final case one would find that exports were indeed labor intensive and thus confirm the HOS comparative-advantage model! It corresponds to the unshaded area above the diagonal in figure 4.3. Here the "wrong" commodity is exported with the "wrong" factor proportions.

It thus appears that, in the two-commodity, two-factor model with full employment and a constant differential in factor rewards, anything can happen. The question, of course, is how these results can be extended to the *n*-manufacturing-commodities, two-sector model of efficient production developed in section 4.1. As already noted, the differential must lie within the manufacturing sector, so that some manufacturing industries are confronted with a higher wage/rental ratio than the rest. If that is the situation, few conclusions are possible unless the factor market distortion is somehow systematically related to the factor intensity ordering of the manufacturing industries. If it is, two cases can be analyzed.

1. Suppose that capital-intensive industries pay a higher wage/rental ratio than labor-intensive industries.[42] Then, if a country's comparative advantage under an efficient allocation lay in production of commodities in the middle of the factor intensity ordering, say commodity 5, one should observe specialization of production in commodities with disparate factor proportions on each side of the "natural" specialization point. It might be, for example, that the lower wage/rental ratio that would result for labor-intensive industries would enable industry 3 to become more profitable than 5, while the lower rental/wage ratio confronting capital-intensive industries caused industry 7 to bid resources away from industry 5. Thus, one would expect to observe a production pattern where industries of dissimilar factor intensities were profitable.

2. Suppose that labor-intensive industries pay a higher wage/rental ratio than capital-intensive industries.[43] If countries specialized in the commodities forecast by the HOS model, one could accept that as verification of the model: this is the case in which reversals could lead to the Leontief-paradox results even when the HOS model was correct, but

in which specialization in production of the "right" commodities could not result from distortion if the HOS model was valid.

Beyond these cases little can be said, although one can hope that examining specific distortion patterns that did not conform to either of those two cases might provide ways of testing the HOS model.

4.2.3   Summary

What emerges from consideration of the literature on distortions is an entirely new set of possibilities that must be evaluated when examining the employment implications of alternative trade strategies: the empirical measures appropriate under efficient allocation cannot be uncritically accepted in the presence of distortions. It is probably a valid first approximation that most industrialized countries' factor markets may not be sufficiently distorted to significantly affect production and trade patterns and factor proportions. The same may or may not be true for the developing countries.

The presence of tariff interventions and export taxes does not create fundamental difficulties for testing the factor proportions model. Indeed, some testable hypotheses about the relationship between factor proportions and the height of protection emerge to provide yet another way of testing the factor proportions explanation of trade. Subsidies to exports can influence the trade pattern in any conceivable direction and thus prevent testing. When factor market distortions are significant, all sorts of possibilities arise: a labor-abundant country, which would be exporting labor-intensive commodities under an efficient allocation, might in fact export commodities whose capital intensity was substantially higher than that. Other patterns, also at variance with the efficiency model, are possible, too.

In general, when there is a distortion between the manufacturing and rural sectors, some means of testing for the separate effects of distortion and efficiency influences on trade patterns are available. When the factor market distortion is within the manufacturing sector, however, no single set of observations can enable identification of the separate contributions of each factor. The important lesson is that, in the presence of factor market distortions that are thought to affect resource allocation significantly, one cannot draw any inferences about the efficient commodity composition of production and trade and its factor proportions solely from observing the actual pattern of production and trade.

5 Labor Coefficients in Trade: Results from the Country Studies

The theory presented in the preceding chapter, and the fact that alternative trade strategies induce significant differences in the commodity composition of output and trade, strongly suggests the need for a categorization of commodities beyond the usual importable/exportable dichotomy as a first step in ascertaining differences in factor proportions among activities. That is the task of section 5.1. Section 5.2 presents the labor coefficients for these categories with respect to domestic value added. Chapter 6 gives particulars pertaining to skills, direction of trade, international value added, and other salient features.

5.1 Categories of Commodities, Industries, and Sectors

In theory there are n commodities, each readily identified and associated with particular producing firms. Again in theory, whether a commodity is exported or imported is ascertained simply by examining trade statistics; each is either exported or imported. Moreover, an analytical classification of items into those whose comparative advantage is based upon "land" or "natural resources" availability and those based upon labor and capital endowment is made by assumption.

For empirical work, each of these three assumptions presents difficulties and challenges. The task of assembling and organizing data in a way corresponding to the theory is formidable for a large number of interrelated reasons. First, the classifications employed in trade statistics and in production and employment statistics often do not correspond and must be reconciled. Reconciliation itself can be done in a number of ways, and it is desirable to choose among alternatives in accord with the precepts emanating from theory, though an element of judgment must inevitably enter in. The task is complicated by the fact that the content of individual items is not completely homogeneous, particularly in the case of manufactures. Second, at any feasible level of disaggregation of the data, it is almost certain (partly for the reason just cited) that there will be cross-flows recorded in the trade statistics—that is, that both exports and imports will appear. Classification of items among the various trade categories must then be made. Finally, there are empirically and analytically difficult problems concerning the appropriate units of measure and weights to be attached to different items in a category. For this last, answers differ depending upon the questions being asked.

Sorting out these issues was one of the major tasks of the project. This section describes how they were resolved, and why, which is useful for interpreting the data reported below and judging the extent to which they are comparable across countries. Naturally, it is also hoped that the lessons learned during the course of the project will be valuable for future research efforts.

5.1.1 The Questions

For purposes of evaluating the implications of alternative trade strategies for the demand of labor, a first and essential task is to identify the commodities whose output would expand or contract significantly in response to alterations in incentives. Consider the problem that would have confronted a researcher or policymaker in South Korea in the late 1950s. The economy was heavily oriented toward import substitution, with a greatly overvalued exchange rate. Its trade deficit was significantly larger than its exports, and such exports as there were consisted 88 percent of primary commodities and 12 percent of manufactures. Even those processed goods that were exported were primarily items arising from temporary excess capacity in individual import substitution industries: the hallmarks of the trade statistics for manufactured items in the 1950s were that exports fluctuated and that there were no commodity categories that exhibited anything like sustained growth.

If researchers in the late 1950s attempted to estimate the probable effect on the demand for labor in South Korea of an alteration in trade strategy, they would have been badly misled had they projected an across-the-board expansion of all exports. Their major challenge, in fact, would have been to identify the commodities whose export would expand rapidly under the export promotion drive.

For the two countries, Brazil and Colombia, for which data were available covering the transition from import substitution to export promotion, authors tried to identify differences in the characteristics of the export bundle under the two regimes. That effort is reported upon below. Here a first task is to try to indicate the alternative measures that might be used to identify different aspects of the relationship between trade strategy and commodity composition of trade.

Consider the following questions:
1. What is the net factor content of a country's total trade?
2. What are the implications for factor markets of
   a. an expansion of exportable production and an offsetting contraction of import-competing production to leave the trade balance unaltered?
   b. an expansion of HOS-exportable production and an offsetting contraction of HOS-importable production to leave the trade balance unaltered?
3. What the the implications for the country's trade balance of
   a. an expansion of exportable production and an offsetting contraction of import-competing production to leave domestic employment unaltered? Or to leave demand for domestic capital services unaltered?
   b. an expansion of HOS-exportable production and an offsetting contraction of HOS-importable production to leave domestic employment unaltered? Or to leave demand for domestic capital services unaltered?

Under some conditions information to answer each of these questions would be much the same; but under other conditions it may be different. Understanding why is important for explaining many of the decisions made about data procedures in the course of the research.

There are three problems: categorization of commodities; choosing weights to find the relevant aggregates; and defining the appropriate units. Each of these is discussed in turn.

5.1.2   Categories of Commodities

The theory outlined in chapter 4, and knowledge that countries' exports of manufactures grow even more rapidly than exports of primary commodities, both motivated a delineation of traded commodities into "HOS goods" and primary commodities. Authors were first asked to use their judgment in deciding which commodities were primary (NRB, or natural resource based). All others were then classified as HOS. Within the HOS classification, however, there were some processing activities where authors judged that the country's ability to process the good economically hinged in large part on the domestic availability of the primary commodity. In those instances authors then formed a subcategory within the HOS classification, called PCB (primary commodity based) HOS goods.

The next step, and one of the most troublesome, was to identify for each country which industries and activities produce "exportables" and which are "import-competing." One means is to use the existing trade pattern and weights derived from it. The difficulties with this procedure are several: (1) to the extent that import substitution regimes have provided prohibitive protection to industries, use of, recorded trade figures completely omits an important component of import competing activities—a serious problem if consideration is being given to what might happen under a switch in trade policies; (2) in many import substitution regimes, there are very few manufactured (HOS) exports, and there is a problem of identifying which sectors and activities might have a comparative advantage if trade strategies were shifted; and (3) as already mentioned, there are grounds for believing that traditional exports would not expand as rapidly as nontraditional ones upon alteration of trade strategies. The experience of Brazil, Colombia, and South Korea in their export drives certainly lends credence to this view.

Using net trade figures simplifies the problem of identifying particular commodities as importable or exportable, but for purposes of the project the disadvantages were judged to outweigh the advantages. Instead an alternative procedure was chosen. Define a statistic, T_i as:

$$(1) \qquad T_i = \frac{C_i - P_i}{C_i},$$

where C_i = domestic utilization and P_i = domestic production. Each commodity or sector was classified as:

> exportable if $T_i < X_0$;
>
> import-competing if $X_0 \leq T_i < X_1$; and
>
> noncompeting if $X_1 \leq T_i \leq X_2$,

where the X's were chosen by the country authors.[1] T_is were then used by country authors to classify commodities. It was not deemed desirable or sensible to have common cutoff points: the range of T_is within countries varied substantially with the degree of disaggregation of the available production and trade statistics; the higher the level of aggregation, the more crossflows are likely to be recorded in a particular category.[2]

Data limitations precluded the use of comparable categories of commodities or levels of aggregation across countries. Moreover, there were inevitably sectors where authors' knowledge of policies and other factors led them to reclassify particular sectors despite the criterion set out above. It should be recalled, therefore, in all that follows that the present state of knowledge and data availability prevented the delineation of comparable categories across countries and that such comparisons as are made are subject to these qualifications.

Several substantive points about the T_is should be noted. First, and perhaps most interesting, T_is alter over time with the changing nature of the trade and payments regime. Thoumi carefully analyzed the ways in which the commodity composition of trade was changing for Colombia over the period 1970–73 period as firms had time to respond to altered incentives. Some changes were associated with specific events, such as changing world commodity prices of some of Colombia's exports. Over- all, however, sectors that were subject to low rates of effective protection were far more likely to switch to exporting than were sectors with higher rates of effective protection (Thoumi 1981, p. 159). Thus four industries that appeared to be import-competing in 1970 had an average rate of effective protection of 11 percent; they turned into exporting industries by 1973. Conversely, four industries that had been classified as exporters in 1970 had changed to the import-competing classification by 1973. Their average effective protection level was 16 percent. For import-competing industries that remain in the same classification, the average rate was 18 percent.[3]

Second, an alternative to classification by a trade statistic such as the T_is would have been to classify commodities according to their effective rates of protection, classifying those with the lowest rates as the potential exporting industries. As will be seen, some authors did this. Difficulties with this procedure are several: in some countries there is systematic discrimination between effective protection granted for sale in the home market and the protection given to exports of identical commodities.[4] A second difficulty arises because effective rate of protection estimates are generally available only at the level of aggregation of the input-output table. This was not available for the appropriate period in the case of Uruguay, and it was fairly aggregated in some other countries. Use of the T_i statistics permitted greater disaggregation than would otherwise have been possible.

Finally, effective rates of protection reflect two things: on one hand, they reflect excess of production costs over international value added; on the other hand, they may also reflect elements of monopoly profit accruing to producers who are enabled to sell their output behind a wall of protection without significant competition. Nonetheless, in some countries authors judged a classification according to the level of effective protection to be meaningful and included it in their analysis (see table 8.1 below).

We thus have the following categories for exportables: HOS-PCB, HOS-other, and NRB. Deciding which category each exportable be- longed to was left in part to the judgment of country authors. In particu- lar, there is a fine line between HOS-PCB manufacturing industries and other HOS industries. South Korea, for example, has imported lumber (primarily from Indonesia) and developed a sizable plywood industry for export. It is evident that the industry is not, in South Korea, based upon any cost advantage derived from raw material availability, and it should be regarded as an HOS-other exportable. If Indonesia developed such an industry, the question would naturally arise, Does its presence derive from the cost advantage associated with the raw material, or is it an industry whose comparative advantage stems from other factors of production? There is no easy answer to these questions, and country authors were asked to use their judgment in dividing industries between the two groups: in cases where they believed there was considerable margin for doubt, estimates were often presented including and excluding the questioned activities.

For imports, there are items for which there is no domestic competing production (noncompeting imports), and there are imports that compete with domestic production. Among both noncompeting imports and import-competing industries, there are primary commodities and HOS goods. However, a further breakdown is called for, especially among HOS goods. There are industries that would be import-competing even under free trade, and there are industries whose existence depends upon sufficiently high levels of protection.[5] Thus, HOS import-competing goods were further broken down into "natural" import-competing industries and "protected" import-competing industries.

5.1.3   Weights and Units

Returning to the questions posed in section 5.1.1, we now have identified commodity categories. For purposes of estimating the influence on the demand for labor of a shift in trade strategies (at constant factor input prices), it is probably HOS exportables and HOS import-competing goods that are of primary concern.

Indentifying which commodities and industries belong to each trade category is only the beginning of an answer to the problem posed in section 5.1.1. It is also necessary, once data are available for individual components of the various categories, to find meaningful ways of aggregating them into an average for the classification as a whole. And, just as trade weights (subject to a qualification discussed in section 5.1.3.2) are appropriate for estimating the net factor content of trade while the T_i statistic may be more suitable for classifying commodities to estimate the probable magnitude of the effect of a shift in trade strategies, so too the question of appropriate classification and weights may have a different answer depending upon the problem at hand, and even upon the situation pertaining in individual countries.

5.1.3.1   Trade or Production Weights?

It is evident that if one is considering the question of how the demand for labor might shift with a reallocation of resources into exportable production from import-competing production, one would ideally like to know not only which industries would expand and contract, but by how much. As a first approximation to that question, and subject to the caution suggested by the Colombian and South Korean experience cited above, it seems reasonable to take the bundle of commodities identified as HOS exportables by the T_i statistic as an indication of the ones that would expand with a switch in trade strategy. For weighting the various items, trade weights would then appear appropriate.

For the contraction of import-competing activities, however, it does not seem reasonable to use trade weights, especially when imports consist primarily of goods that are no longer domestically produced. Instead, production weights across existing import-competing HOS industries are more appropriate.

By contrast, if one were considering the effects of switching from an outer-oriented trade strategy to an import substitution one, it would be reasonable to use trade weights for both HOS import-competing and exportable goods, since further import substitution would imply the development of industries where demand was currently met primarily with imports.[6]

Thus, whereas trade weights seem to be appropriate for exports for evaluating all the questions posed at the outset, production weights may be more suitable for import-competing goods if contraction of the import-competing sector is under consideration.

5.1.3.2 Units: Value Added

There are several reasons why value added, rather than output, is the appropriate unit for weighting and for measurement. First, intermediate goods can be traded, and evaluation of the labor coefficients attaching to a shift in trade strategy will accurately reflect probable outcomes if use is made of value added as the unit under consideration, especially if the shift in question is toward an export orientation.

There is a second reason, however, that was equally important in some of the project countries and was relevant because trade was initially imbalanced. If interest was in the net factor content of trade, in the presence of initially balanced trade, output could be the unit of measure. Aggregation could be performed with weights corresponding to the shares of individual exports and imports in their respective totals. Taking domestic coefficients for labor and capital employed per unit of output in each industry, L_i and K_i, one could then simply perform the aggregations

$$(2) \qquad L_x = \sum_i e_i L_i \qquad K_x = \sum_i e_i K_i \qquad i = 1, \ldots, n$$

$$(3) \qquad L_m = \sum_i m_i L_i \qquad K_m = \sum_i m_i K_i, \qquad i = n+1, \ldots, s$$

where commodities 1 to n were exports, $n+1$ to s were imports, e_i is the share of the ith exportable in total exports ($= E_i / \Sigma E_i$), and m_i is the share of the ith importable in total imports. L_x, L_m, K_x, and K_m would represent the average input of labor and capital in import-competing and export industries. The net factor content of trade would then be defined by subtracting L_m and K_m from L_x and K_x: one could conclude that the country was a net exporter of labor if $L_x - L_m > 0$, and a net importer of capital if $K_r - K_m < 0$. The model set forth in chapter 4 predicts that a labor-abundant, capital- and land-scarce country would be a net exporter of labor and a net importer of capital.

Consider now the situation in which trade was not initially balanced (for any of a variety of reasons including the existence of capital inflows or debt-servicing obligations, the effect of weather fluctuations on the quantity of agricultural exports and imports, or the stage of the business cycle in world markets). In the presence of imbalance, several alternative procedures are possible. One could replace the e_is and m_is with E_is and M_is in equations (2) and (3). If this were done, a sufficiently large trade imbalance in either direction might result in a finding that the country was a net importer (in the case of a trade deficit) or exporter (with a trade surplus) of *both* labor and capital.[7] While it is well known that a current account imbalance is the way resources move between countries, it is not obvious what economic interest attaches to the "net factor content of trade" when computed in this particular manner.

Consider instead the implications of the first procedure in the presence of trade imbalance. It is tantamount to scaling down all exports (in the case of trade surplus) or imports (in deficit) by the same proportion. *If* exports and import-competing goods were produced only with primary domestic factors of production and without intermediate goods, such a procedure would appear to present a satisfactory solution to the problem. When intermediate goods are employed in production processes, however, $1 million of output of exports may represent a very different amount of net domestic product than $1 million of imports.

If production of all exports were reduced (increased) by a given amount, imports of intermediate goods would decline (increase). Thus the net trade balance would change by a smaller amount than the change in exports. Thus, to assume increasing exports and imports initially by a like amount, without taking into account changes in trade in intermediate goods, would not be appropriate.

To state the matter the other way around, under the conditions stated a $1 increase (decrease) in exports would lead to improvement (deterioration) of less than $1 in the trade balance, since value added in the export industry was less than the value of output. In the presence of balanced trade, this phenomenon creates no difficulties,[8] but with imbalanced trade when exportables and import-competing industries have markedly different ratios of value added to output, the problem is of some importance.

There remains the question of what value-added concept should be used. There is, after all, value added by a firm, by an industry, and within a country. Total domestic value added in producing steel, for example, can vary depending on whether imported or domestic ore is used: output from two steel plants might have different total domestic value added because one imported its raw materials and the other obtained them from domestic suppliers.

Under import substitution regimes, firms are very often required to obtain their inputs domestically whenever possible, and actual domestic value added includes value added not only by the firm but also by domestic producers of intermediate goods supplied to the firm. In a perfectly closed economy, of course, inputs—direct plus indirect—equal the value of output, and one is back in the position where no harm is done by taking coefficients per unit of output, direct plus indirect.

Experience has shown, however, that an export strategy requires that firms with export potential be enabled to obtain their inputs from the cheapest possible source, domestic or international. In terms of domestic value added, all that is relevant is the value added by the firm (direct) and the purchase by the firm of home goods that, by their very nature, cannot be obtained from abroad. If firms choose to purchase intermediate goods from other domestic firms, it is presumably because those other firms have at least enough comparative advantage so that they can compete with imports.

For the country studies, therefore, authors were asked to compute direct input requirements per unit of direct value added, and also direct-plus-home-goods-indirect requirements per unit of direct-plus-home-goods value added.[9] Some authors, in addition, computed total direct plus indirect inputs for various categories of goods in addition to home goods. Such calculations can be useful for indicating what is in fact happening under an import substitution regime (and might even be realistic for purposes of evaluating what would happen under that regime if output in that sector were to expand), but they do not help in indicating the probable effects of an alteration in trade strategy: very often it is the fact that domestic producers are required to purchase high-priced domestic inputs that precludes their ability to export profitably under import substitution.

Deciding that units of value added, rather than of output, are appropriate still leaves one final issue unresolved: whether value added should be evaluated in terms of domestic prices or international prices. It is at this juncture that there is a difference in the answer, depending on whether question 2 or question 3, posed at the outset, is at issue. Recall that question 2 pertained to the implications for factor markets, whereas question 3 related to the trade balance. To see what is involved, it is helpful to put aside the problem of value added for the moment and examine directly the implications of divergences between domestic and foreign prices. Naturally, if there were free trade and if domestic factor markets functioned perfectly, it would be unnecessary to pose the two questions separately, because international and domestic prices would be equal, and an expansion of output (or value added) of one currency unit's worth of exportables or contraction of one currency unit's worth of importables would be the same regardless of whether domestic or foreign prices were used in the valuation.

However, if significant protection is accorded to domestic import-competing industries, contraction of a unit of import-competing output evaluated at domestic prices will be greater than the same contraction evaluated at international prices. Thus, to effect a contraction of import-competing activities and an expansion of exportables by an amount to keep the trade balance constant will generally free some domestic resources: valued at domestic prices, more resources will be released in the import substitution activity than will be absorbed in the export activity to maintain balanced trade.

As will be seen below (section 6.1), this problem is of considerable importance empirically: using international prices to value outputs (and value added), some country authors found that a dollar's worth of import-competing activity required more of all types of resources (labor, capital, and even skills) than did a dollar's worth of export activity.

As the preceding discussion indicates, answers to question 2—implications for factor markets—require the use of domestic prices in evaluating various baskets of goods. In particular, when value added is used as the basis for evaluation, as it should be when intermediate goods are important, domestic value added (DVA) is the appropriate unit of measure. The basic question pertains to employment of the country's resources, and for purposes of analyzing domestic factor markets, domestic prices (of value added and of factors) are the appropriate unit of measure.[10]

For answering question 3, however, international value added is the appropriate unit. This is because maintaining balanced trade would occur only when international value added in the expanding sector equaled that in the contracting sector.

For the data presented in section 5.2 and later chapters, therefore, value added is always used as a basis for weighting, and it is always indicated whether domestic or international value added is the unit and whether direct or direct-plus-home-goods-indirect value added is the basis. Classification of commodities into trade categories was made in accordance with the T_i statistic except as otherwise noted. Finally, the weights are generally trade weights, except in those instances where further import substitution was considered the relevant alternative.

5.2   Labor Coefficients by Trade Categories

5.2.1   Direct Labor Coefficients

For reasons indicated in chapters 2, 3 and 4, observed labor coefficients are the joint outcome of underlying comparative advantage, the incentives accorded by the trade regime, and conditions in domestic factor markets. Nonetheless, they are of interest in their own right and are presented here and in chapter 6. It remains for chapters 7 and 8 to undertake an analysis of the reasons for the findings and the ways trade strategies and factor market imperfections influenced the observations.

Table 5.1 gives estimates of labor inputs per unit of DVA in various exportable trade categories expressed as a ratio of the labor per unit of DVA in HOS import-competing industries. For Brazil, for example, the average labor input per unit of DVA in HOS exportables was 2.07 times as much as the labor input per unit of DVA in import-competing HOS activities.

The first two columns give comparable estimates, again as a ratio to the figure for import-competing industries, for non-primary-commodity-based HOS exportables and PCB-HOS exportables separately.[11] A final

Table 5.1 Direct Labor Coefficients per Unit of DVA (Ratio of Coefficients in Designated Trade Category to Coefficients in HOS Import-Competing Activities)

| Country | Period | HOS Exports | | | NRB Exports |
		Manufactures Not PCB	PCB Manufactures	Total	
Argentina	1963	n.a.	n.a.	1.24	n.a.
	1973	n.a.	n.a.	1.30	n.a.
Brazil	1970	n.a.	n.a.	2.07	2.02
Chile	1966–68	1.50	n.a.	.80	n.a.
Colombia	1973	n.a.	n.a.	1.88	n.a.
Indonesia	1971	1.58	n.a.	2.09	n.a.
Ivory Coast	1972				
Modern sector		n.a.	n.a.	1.35	2.28
Total		n.a.	n.a.	1.16	9.04
Pakistan	1969–70	1.23	1.69	1.42	n.a.
Thailand	1973	3.20	1.58	2.07	n.a.
Tunisia	1972	2.08	.79	1.28	3.31
Uruguay	1968	n.a.	n.a.	1.53	1.45

Notes:
Ivory Coast: Modern sector ratios are relative to modern sector employment in modern sector HOS importables; total employment (including artisans) is relative to employment in all HOS importables.

Tunisia: Crude and refined oil are excluded from the individual exportable estimates; manufactured consumer goods were used for protected imports; import-competing sectors exclude those with negative IVA.

Uruguay: Data are for total workers per DVA (Bension and Caumont 1981, table 11.12).

column gives estimates, for those countries for which they are available, of the labor coefficients for NRB exportables. The Ivorian estimates provide an indication of some of the complexities of attempting to associate particular groups of industries with alternative trade strategies. In that country, natural resource based exports have predominated. For those commodities, "artisanal" labor is employed, and expansion of NRB exports (and NRB import-competing production) would entail increased demand for artisanal labor (some of which comes from immigration from neighboring countries). Artisanal labor is naturally unskilled, and most NRB export activities are highly labor intensive. Contrasting the labor coefficients for NRB exports with that for total labor in all HOS import-competing activities shows that NRB exports require more than nine times as much labor per unit of domestic value added. It is also true that labor per unit of DVA in NRB imports is higher, though not as high as that for NRB exports.

However, consider the case when attention turns to the modern sector in the Ivory Coast. HOS exportables produced in that sector are about one-third more labor intensive than are HOS import-competing goods produced in the moden sector, while modern NRB exportables are more than twice as labor intensive as HOS importables Thus, expansion of either NRB exports or HOS exportables would entail a greater demand for labor, given existing factor proportions, than would expansion entailing the same increase in DVA in the corresponding import-competing activities. If, however, expansion of DVA in the modern sector were to come about by pulling resources out of the traditional sector (and assuming that average and marginal coefficients are equal), it appears that the total demand for labor would decline. To be sure, this raises many of the problems discussed earlier, and in particular the question whether marginal labor requirements, especially in the traditional sector, can be approximated by average labor coefficients.[12] Nonetheless, it seems clear that an export-oriented strategy that encourages both types of exportable activities will lead to a greater increment in the demand for labor under Ivorian conditions than would an import substitution strategy.

It is of interest that, in all countries except Chile, total HOS exports had labor coefficients per DVA that exceeded those in the corresponding import-competing sectors. In the Chilean case, pulp and paper is a significant component of HOS exports;[13] when pulp and paper was treated as a PCB industry, Chilean HOS-other manufactures required 1.5 times as much labor as Chilean import-competing HOS activities. The differences between labor coefficients for total HOS exports and HOS import-competing industries are sizable for many of the countries, exceeding a factor of two for Brazil, Indonesia, and Thailand, and also exceeding that number in Tunisia when PCB-based manufacturing is excluded.

It is perhaps somewhat more surprising that, in those cases for which data were available, NRB exports turned out to be more labor-using per unit of DVA than were HOS import-competing industries.[14] In most cases this result is simply a reflection of the fact that most NRB exports originate from the agriculture sector, in which output per worker is very low and techniques of production are very labor intensive. As was discussed in chapter 2, there are important and unresolved questions about the functioning of rural labor markets and the interpretations of the observed labor coefficients. The predominance of NRB, labor-intensive exports in the total export bundle is yet another reason why labor coefficients should be estimated separately for NRB and HOS goods.

The reader will have observed that data for South Korea were not included in table 5.1. The reason for this omission is that estimates of the factor content of South Korea's trade have been made in terms of labor and capital inputs per unit of output rather than per unit of DVA. Hong's estimates for South Korea are for total trade, including both NRB and other trade in one category. A major difficulty with this is that the Westphal-Kim estimates[15] show the primary industries are generally considerably more labor intensive than manufacturing, as was true of the other countries. However, import-competing primary activities (which in the case of South Korea includes some major food grains) were about twice as labor intensive as were exporting primary activities.[16] Table 5.2 therefore reproduces the Westphal-Kim estimates for manufacturing sectors only. In light of South Korea's lack of raw materials, it is likely that there are few manufacturing sectors deriving their comparative advantage from raw material availability, so that the figures can be taken as representative of HOS categories.

As can be seen, South Korea's manufactured exports were on average less labor-intensive than her manufactures sold in the domestic market in 1960, although they were about one-third more labor-intensive than import-competing manufacturing. That year marked the start of the South Korean export promotion drive. By 1963 exports had increased their labor intensity relative to import-competing goods, and also relative to domestic output. By 1968 the labor/capital ratio in exporting had increased to 3.55, while that in import-competing industries was 2.33: all

Table 5.2   **Manufacturing Factor Proportions in South Korea, 1960–68 (Labor/Capital Ratios)**

	1960	1963	1966	1968
Domestic output	2.97	2.89	2.67	2.64
Exportables	2.72	3.02	3.24	3.55
Import-competing production	2.09	1.93	1.98	2.33

Source: Westphal and Kim 1977, table 7.10.

manufacturing except that destined for the domestic market had increased its labor/capital ratio over the course of the shift to export promotion.[17]

Data for Hong Kong are also of interest and are presented in table 5.3. Hong Kong has virtually no raw materials, so all exports can be regarded as HOS goods. Sung (1979) based his data on value of trade but made adjustments for differences in value-added ratios between exports and import-competing goods. It is of interest that in Hong Kong, as in South Korea, the domestic value added/output ratio was substantially higher in import-competing than in export industries. In the South Korean case this is in part a reflection of the fact that the authorities were very liberal in permitting exporters to import needed raw materials, but much more restrictive in their treatment of producers of goods destined for sale on the home market. In part, however, it may also reflect the fact that both South Korea and Hong Kong, situated at considerable distances from their major markets, have tended to find production for export most profitable in lines in which they could import raw materials without heavy transport costs. For activities where high transport costs precluded importing raw materials and intermediate goods, reliance upon domestic sources probably led to a competitive disadvantage in their trade.

Overall, the descriptive statistics—labor input per unit of domestic value added—tend to support the notion that HOS exportables, at least in the countries covered in the project, tend to be more labor-using than HOS import-competing production. This conclusion holds regardless of the influences of policy measures and other phenomena upon factor proportions and the commodity composition of trade. To be sure, these

Table 5.3   Factor Proportions in Hong Kong's Trade (per Million Hong Kong Dollars Value Added of Trade, Current Prices)

	1962		1973	
	Exports	Import-Competing	Exports	Import-Competing
Direct				
Depreciation (HK $000)	34	49	55	71
Profits (HK $000)	303	290	223	315
Labor (man-years)	265	279	74	60
Professional labor (man-years)	.87	1.98	.56	1.10
Direct Plus Home Goods				
Depreciation (HK $000)	34	47	60	74
Profits (HK $000)	301	290	263	346
Labor (man-years)	244	256	68	56
Professional labor (man-years)	1.44	2.59	.85	1.36

Source: Sung 1979.

statistics provide only a glimpse into the possible orders of magnitude of the potential impact on employment of a shift in trade strategy. Certainly, however, they suggest that a shift toward an outer-oriented trade strategy would generally not be inconsistent with the goal of increasing employment opportunities.

5.2.2 Direct-Plus-Home-Goods-Indirect Labor Coefficients

The pattern of factor demand implied by alternative trade strategies appears in general to be little affected by whether direct or direct-plus-home-goods-indirect coefficients are used. Data for Hong Kong were reported on both bases in table 5.3 above; as can be seen, all orders of magnitude are much the same except for the professional category, which will be discussed below. For the project countries, data on labor coefficients when home goods demands are taken into account are summarized in table 5.4.[18]

As can be seen, exportable HOS activities are more labor-using per unit of domestic value added than are the import-competing sectors. In most countries, inclusion of direct and home-goods-indirect inputs tends to result in a somewhat smaller differential between HOS exportable and import-competing sectors. This is only to be expected: unless there are underutilized factors of production or an NRB sector with extreme factor proportions, a country's overall capital/labor ratio will be a weighted average of the ratios in each sector. Only if the home goods ratio lies outside the ratio in either exporting or import-competing goods (as it apparently did in South Korea in 1960) could inclusion of labor utilized indirectly in home goods for production of exportables or import substitutes accentuate differences in direct labor coefficients.

5.2.3 Coefficients for Noncompeting Imports

As we saw in chapter 4, there are good analytical grounds for expecting that large differences between the factor intensity of a particular industry and a country's factor endowment are likely to be reflected in patterns of specialization in production. In the absence of protection, one would observe only "competitive" import-competing production, which would generally be expected to consist largely of goods whose factor intensities were not too "far away" from the country's factor endowments. Exceptions would be primarily among goods with relatively high transport costs per unit of value added. With protection of some import-competing industries, this association would be less strong; nonetheless, one would still anticipate that, by and large, the greater the divergence between the country's factor endowment and the factor intensity of a commodity, the less inclined the authorities would be to grant adequate protection to make the industry profitable domestically.

Table 5.4   **Direct-Plus-Home-Goods-Indirect Labor Coefficients per Unit of DVA (Ratio of Coefficients in Designated Category to Coefficients in IIOS Import-Competing Activity)**

| Country | Period | HOS Exports | | | NRB Exports |
		Manufacturing Not PCB	PCB Manufacturing	Total	
Argentina	1973	n.a.	n.a.	1.15	n.a.
Brazil	1970	n.a.	n.a.	1.65	1.97
Chile	1966–68	n.a.	n.a.	1.64	n.a.
Indonesia	1971	1.58	n.a.	1.92	n.a.
Ivory Coast	1972				
Modern		n.a.	n.a.	1.35	2.21
Total		n.a.	n.a.	1.17	8.54
Pakistan	1969–70	1.30	1.57	1.41	3.86
South Korea	1968	n.a.	n.a.	1.09	n.a.
Thailand	1973	1.88	1.32	1.53	n.a.
Tunisia	1972	1.67	.93	1.24	2.41
Uruguay	1968	n.a.	n.a.	1.13	1.10

Notes:
Argentina: Data from Nogues, 1980, chap. 2, table 2.8.
Chile: IIOS exports to developed countries.
Colombia: No data are available.
Ivory Coast: See note to table 5.1.
South Korea: Hong correspondence—data are per unit of output.
Uruguay: Ratios are for the wage bill per million dollars of DVA in table 5.1. See Bension and Caumont 1981, table 11.12.

A major problem arises, therefore, in attempting to estimate the factor proportions for producing commodities that do not have domestic production counterparts. Where data permitted, country authors were encouraged to attempt such an estimate by locating an input-output table or census of manufactures for a country producing some goods in common but also producing goods that were noncompeting imports within the country. Taking the ratio of inputs in the industries observed in common, it was recommended that authors scale their estimates of what factor requirements would be for the industries where domestic production was classified as noncompeting.

Sung's results for Hong Kong illustrate the procedure and also the order of magnitude of observed differences in factor proportions. He took spinning, weaving, and dyeing as the most established industry in Hong Kong and computed factor proportions in Hong Kong for 1973 and in the United States for 1947 per million dollars of output. The coefficients in the United States and Hong Kong (in 1973 prices) were as follows:[19]

	Depreciation (HK $000)	Man-Years	Depreciation/ Labor Ratio (HK $000 per man-year)
United States 1947	451	24	18.6
Hong Kong 1973	91	39	2.3

Sung then took the United States coefficients for 1947 for Hong Kong's noncompeting imports and scaled them in the same proportion as the spinning, weaving, and dyeing sector to arrive at an estimate of what the factor intensity might have been. Taking a bundle of HK $1 million of representative noncompeting imports, he was then able to calculate what it would have required for Hong Kong to produce the bundle. His estimates are that, for 1973, the depreciation/labor intensity in Hong Kong that would have been required to produce a bundle of noncompeting imports that would have been 3,227, compared with 1,038 for exports and 1,336 for import-competing production.[20] For Hong Kong, which has free trade with almost no exceptions, the difference between factor intensities of exportable and import-competing production is relatively small compared with that between either of those categories and noncompeting imports. This is, of course, the forecast that was made initially.

Wontack Hong provided a similar estimate for South Korea. His estimate for 1970 of the capital/labor ratio for all exports was $1,478 and that for all (HOS and NRB) import-competing products was $1,554.[21] He then used four different sets of coefficients (all at 1970 prices) to estimate the factor intensity of noncompeting imports: the United States coefficients for 1947 and 1958 and the Japanese coefficients for 1965 and 1970. Using United States coefficients, he derived estimates of $20,551 for factor intensity based upon 1947 coefficients and $22,630 based upon 1958 coefficients. By contrast, the Japanese coefficients were $4,075 and $4,795. Hong concluded, as did Sung, that "the largest difference in factor intensities lies not between exports and import-competing goods but between both of these categories and non-competing imports" (Hong 1981, p. 34).

Nabli was able to make a comparable calculation for Tunisia, using the French input-output table to estimate coefficients. According to his computations, Tunisia's noncompeting imports would have had an L/DVA ratio about 64 percent that of HOS exportables and 82 percent that of import-competing goods. These differences are in the predicted direction but are far smaller than the differences computed for South Korea and Hong Kong. In part this may reflect the fact that Tunisia's economy has been heavily oriented toward import substitution and use of fairly capital-intensive techniques (see chap. 6 below for discussion of DVA/IVA discrepancies).[22]

A similar result was obtained for Argentina. Nogues noted that the bulk of Argentine noncompeting imports comes from developed countries. He then computed labor intensity from the 1972 United States Census of Manufactures. The weighted average labor intensity was then scaled up according to the differential labor intensity of Argentina's most important exportable industries in relation to similar industries in the United States. These industries are slaughtering, preparing, and preserving meat; dairy products; fats and oils; and grain-mill products. Nogues concluded that labor intensity of exportable industries was 11 percent higher than what noncompeting imports would require if they were to be produced domestically.

The difficulties with computing input coefficients for comparable sectors are sufficiently great that other country authors were not able to obtain estimates of the factor proportions that would be associated with domestic production of the goods currently imported without domestic competition. The data from Argentina, Hong Kong, South Korea, and Tunisia may be taken as suggestive. The findings are certainly not inconsistent with the hypothesis that patterns of specialization, rather than factor proportions between import-competing and exportable industries, reflect differences in factor endowments.

It remains to chapters 7 and 8 to explore the reasons for the results and to study the determinants of the orders of magnitude involved. Before that, however, chapter 6 surveys some of the more detailed statistics emanating from the country studies that shed light on some of the hypotheses set forth in chapter 4.

6 Evidence with Regard to Skills, Direction of Trade, Capital Intensity, and International Value Added Coefficients

The data presented in chapter 5 already indicate that the countries covered in the projects have, at least in the "revealed" sense, their comparative advantage in the industrial sector in relatively labor-intensive industries. Those data provide, however, only a first and descriptive approximation to the link between alternative trade strategies and employment.

In this chapter we proceed further by examining the available data on various characteristics of factor inputs and trade that shed more light on the relationship between trade strategies and employment. At this stage the spirit continues to be "descriptive," in the sense that the coefficients are taken as given, without analysis of the underlying influences shaping them.

6.1 Skilled and Unskilled Labor Inputs

One of the empirical regularities that emerge in studies of developed countries' trade is the significance of indicators of skills as determinants of comparative advantage, however defined (see Branson and Monoyios 1977; Baldwin 1979). The theory developed in chapter 4 did not essentially distinguish between skilled and unskilled labor, but it makes more sense to regard the skills as a component of capital or as a separate factor of production than to regard all labor as homogeneous.[1]

It was indicated in chapter 2 that not all labor is homogeneous and that, in particular, education, training, experience, and other factors influence the productivity of a worker or groups of workers. Despite the desirability of attempting uniform estimates across countries of the skill composition of employment in different industries, we recognized from the outset of the project that the problems involved would be insuperable. It is difficult enough to obtain data within a country that contains enough information on worker attributes to permit estimation of their human capital or other measures of skills and training; across countries, any attempt to estimate skills comparably would be impossible not only because categories differ but also because it is not clear that units of measurement, such as years of schooling, have similar economic meanings. Country authors were therefore asked to use their judgment in seeking indicators of skills. In some cases, such as Thailand, they were severely constrained by the absence of data. In other cases considerable analysis was possible.

In this section the results of the individual authors' analyses are reviewed. The reader should be cautioned, however, that interpretation of the results is incomplete until the labor market has been analyzed, especially with regard to the determinants of wage structure and other factors that influence the choice of factor intensity, including the use of skilled or unskilled workers. Here focus is simply upon the differentials that exist, without regard to how much greater or less those differentials might have been had the trade regime or factor market structure been altered.

The country authors' estimates of the separate coefficients for skilled, unskilled, and managerial labor inputs are reported in table 6.1. There appear to be large and systematic differences between skill coefficients for HOS exportable and HOS import-competing industries. They are more pronounced than differences in overall labor coefficients. These differences prevail despite a variety of factors, discussed in chapter 7 below, that tend to keep them below the level they might assume in the absence of factor market distortions. They are confirmed not only by the individual country studies, but also by results reported in *Trade and Employment in Developing Countries,* vol. 2, *Factor Supply and Substitution* (Krueger 1982) in the papers by Henderson and by Corbo and Meller.[2]

It should be recognized that the definition of skills differed from country to country, depending on data availability. Since coefficients generally pertained to urban-sector production in HOS exporting and import-competing industries, it is a reasonable conjecture that in most cases the term "unskilled" labor refers to individuals without any training beyond primary school. In many countries, however, some degree of literacy is a prerequisite for factory employment, and the unskilled labor coefficients reported here may in fact reflect the number of persons in the least educated or trained category eligible for employment in any modern-sector activity.

There were only four countries—Brazil, Chile, the Ivory Coast, and Tunisia—for which authors had sufficient data to compute direct-plus-home-goods-indirect labor coefficients. In all cases the pattern was very similar to that shown in table 6.1.

Table 6.1		Ratio of Direct Coefficients of HOS Exportable to HOS Import-Competing Industries per DVA, Managerial, Skilled, and Unskilled Labor		
Country	Period	Unskilled	Skilled	Managerial
Brazil	1959	n.a.	.954	n.a.
	1971	n.a.	.978	n.a.
Chile	1966–68	n.a.	.842	n.a.
Colombia	1973	2.174	.519	1.231
Indonesia	1971	2.273	.810	1.100
Ivory Coast	1972	1.510	.960	.835
Tunisia	1972	1.582	.810	n.a.
Uruguay	1968	1.404	.939	n.a.

Notes:
Colombia: Unskilled worker ratio refers to blue-collar workers.
Indonesia: "Unskilled" is sum of "male operative"and "female operative" man-days.
Ivory Coast: Modern sector HOS coefficients from Monson 1981, table 6.13: averages for exportables and import-competing industries were used.
Uruguay: Skilled workers are "white-collar" workers.

For most of the countries with results reported in table 6.1 authors were forced, through lack of adequate data, to use some sort of weighting system for various categories of labor. In some instances these categories were simple counts of the work force by category assigned in the census or labor force survey. In Tunisia, for example, data were available for seven categories of labor: seasonal employees, apprentices, unskilled labor, semiskilled and skilled labor, supervisory personnel, white-collar employees, and management and engineers. To estimate skill content of different activities, Nabli formed skill indexes by taking the average wage in the ith skill category relative to the average wage for unskilled labor, w_i, and using those ratios as weights. He then formed an index, SK_j, of the skill content of the jth industry

(1) $$SK_j = \frac{\Sigma w_i S_{ij}}{L_j},$$

where S_{ij} is the number of persons with skill level i in industry j and L_j is the total numbers of workers in industry j.

Weights ranged from 0.36 for apprentices to 6.77 for management and engineers. For unskilled labor, he added man-years of seasonal employees, apprentices, unskilled labor, and half of the skilled and semiskilled category. Because they are indexes, they are sensitive to choice of weights and, in particular, to average wages by skill category. The ratios for skilled and unskilled workers for Tunisia given in table 6.1 are based on those calculations.

In an effort to avoid use of arbitrary weights (which are especially flawed if there is reason to believe that the sorts of labor market distortions discussed in chapter 7 influence relative wages), Carvalho and Haddad followed an alternative procedure.[3] They had the advantage of having previous work by Senna (1975), who has estimated an earnings function for Brazil. He had estimated the equation.

(2) $$1nW_i = \alpha_0 + \beta_1 S_i + \beta_2 J_i + \beta_3 J_i^2 + u_i,$$

where S_i is the number of full years of formal school attendance and J_i is number of years in the labor force for the ith worker. Carvalho and Haddad had data on the characteristics of the Brazilian labor force in individual industries and used Senna's regression estimates of the earnings function to estimate the "human capital content" of the labor force in industry. Using those estimates, they calculated the average skill intensities for expanding exportable and import-competing production and transformed those into an index by setting 100 equal to the average manufacturing wage in 1970.

The range of skill intensity over the twenty-two industries in their computation was from 89.4 (construction) to 165.4 (oil and derivatives). However, seventeen of their twenty-two observations fell within 10 percent of the mean. For 1959, as can be seen from table 6.1, the average skill content of exportable industries was below that for import-competing industries: for import-competing industries the figure was 100.3 percent, while for exports it was 95.7. By 1971 both import-competing and export industries had wages above the average, perhaps reflecting the fact that in Brazil home goods are intensive in the use of unskilled labor. Carvalho and Haddad also compared their estimates for 1971 of skill intensity with those they would have obtained had they used a direct measure of the ratio of the industry's wages to the average industrial wage. For 1971 their index of skill intensity was 111.9 for import-competing activities and 109.5 for exportables, reflecting a difference of 2.1 percent (contrasted with the range of about 20 percent). Had they instead used average wages, they would have calculated an index of 130 for import-competing activities and 120 for exportables, giving a difference of about 8 percent. While one cannot rely too heavily upon a single instance, it is somewhat reassuring that the direction of difference in skill intensity and the general order of magnitude appears to be much the same regardless of which measure is used to reflect it.

Returning to the data in table 6.1, when man-days per unit of DVA are broken down into skilled man-days, unskilled man-days, and managerial man-days, the picture that emerges is that unskilled labor coefficients in HOS import-competing industries are even smaller relative to HOS exporting industries than are total labor coefficients. In each case for which a breakdown is available, the unskilled labor coefficient ratio for exportables exceeds that for total labor. Likewise, in all cases the skilled labor coefficient in import-competing industries exceeds that in exportable industries. Data from Hong Kong show a similar picture. Recall that the overall ratio of direct labor coefficients was 0.719 in 1973. By contrast, the ratio of professional labor in import-competing industries to that in exportable industries was 1.77. Nogues likewise estimated a higher skill coefficient of import-competing industries, by 27 percent when a skill classification was used. Use of average wages as a proxy for skills yielded much the same order of magnitude.

Thus, based on the evidence from the countries covered in the project, it appears that not only are the HOS exportables generally more labor-using than HOS import-competing goods, but their input of unskilled labor is greater than that of import-competing industries by an even wider margin, while import-competing industries place a greater demand on the skilled labor forces in those countries.

6.2   Patterns by Direction of Trade

We saw in chapter 4 that there are a priori grounds for expecting differences in factor intensity both between exports destined to developed (more capital-abundant) countries and those destined to other developing countries and between imports by source. This expectation was in general borne out by the results of the individual country authors.

Table 6.2 provides the basic data from the individual country studies and Hong Kong. In some instances, notably Indonesia and Hong Kong, a sufficiently large fraction of exports is destined for developed countries that it is difficult to attach significance to the separate coefficients. In other cases, however, the trade with other developing countries is sizable, and differences in factor proportions are considerable. For Chile, for example, about half of all HOS exports are destined to other LAFTA (Latin American Free Trade Area) countries. Chile's exports to developed countries have a labor coefficient of 61, contrasted with 29 for exports to the LAFTA region. Uruguay, likewise, has sizable exports to LAFTA and, again, these exports appear to be far less labor intensive than exports to developed countries. For Brazil, too, LAFTA exports are less labor intensive than other exports.

For the Ivory Coast and Pakistan there are also pronounced differences on the import-competing side: for those two countries, production competing with imports from other LDCs was far more labor intensive than was production competing with imports originating from developed countries.

Table 6.2   **Direct Labor Coefficients per Unit of**
DVA by Direction of Trade

| | | HOS Exportables | | | HOS Import-Competing | | |
Country	Period	DC	LDC	Total	DC	LDC	Total
Argentina	1973	164	147	n.a.	n.a.	n.a.	n.a.
Brazil	1959	115	141	115	n.a.	n.a.	128
	1970	89	79	87	n.a.	n.a.	71
	1972	109	78	87	n.a.	n.a.	71
Chile	1966–68	61	29	34	43	43	43
Colombia	1970	28	21	24	n.a.	n.a.	n.a.
	1973	32	24	29	n.a.	n.a.	n.a.
Hong Kong	1973	75	67	73	62	55	60
Indonesia	1971	2,176	2,149	2,175	994	1,117	1,038
Ivory Coast	1972	n.a.	n.a.	2,488	1,520	1,743	1,652
Pakistan	1969–70	90	88	88	70	120	71
Thailand	1973	22	20	22	11	22	11
Uruguay	1968	441	239	366	n.a.	n.a.	238

Notes:
Brazil: Data are from Carvalho and Haddad (1981), table 2.14, and represent total labor requirements per DVA. The numbers for developed countries are an unweighted average of EEC and United States and Canada coefficients, while the LDC numbers refer to LAFTA trade.

Colombia: DC figure is an unweighted average of "United States" and "other developed countries."

Indonesia: Total man-days from Pitt 1981, table 5.15.

Ivory Coast: Data (expressed in man-hours) taken from Monson 1981, table 6.11 and refer to modern HOS sectors. No breakdown of HOS exportable trade between DCs and LDCs was made owing to the unimportance of the latter.

Pakistan: Excludes PCB exports (Guisinger 1981, table 7.14).

Thailand: Data supplied by Akrasanee 1981 for HOS import-competing goods, exclusion of alcoholic beverages and tobacco gives twenty-one for DCs and total.

The orders of magnitude of difference in labor intensity according to export destination are in some cases as great as the differences between overall labor coefficients for HOS exportables and import-competing production. For Chile, for example, reducing one unit of DVA of exportable production for developed countries and replacing it with one unit of DVA of import-competing production would entail a net "loss" of eighteen jobs, or a reduction of 28 percent in employment. By contrast, contraction of a unit of DVA of HOS exportable production for other LDCs (almost entirely LAFTA) and replacement with a unit of DVA of domestic import-competing production would result in a change from twenty-nine jobs to forty-three jobs—an increase of almost 50 percent in employment. To be sure, the coefficients are not necessarily perfect indicators of what would happen with an alteration in trade strategy, but the orders of magnitude are sufficient to suggest that it matters not only which sectors—NRB or HOS—trade originates in, but also which countries are the trading partners. For Chile, an export promotion strategy based upon the LAFTA market would probably result in a shift toward less labor-using industries, while an export promotion strategy based upon trade with the developed countries would have the opposite result.

This finding is supportive of the observation made in chapter 3, namely that not all policies designated as "export promotion" really constitute an "export-oriented" trade strategy. Uruguay and Chile, among others, were heavily oriented toward import substitution: the exports that were destined for LAFTA were subject to special inducements and represented much more the outcome of the incentives for import substitution than any genuine export promotion orientation.[4] Thus the bias of the regime remained toward import substitution industries, so much so that there were incentives for some of those industries to export. This finding is of importance in considering the overall implications of alternative trade strategies for employment. I return to it in chapter 9 below.

6.3   Evidence with Respect to Capital Intensity

Because even graver difficulties surround the availability and reliability of data on capital stock than data on labor, primary focus in all country studies was on labor coefficients. In theory, of course, capital coefficients would be inversely related to labor coefficients in a two-factor model at free trade. Nonetheless, where the data permitted, authors were encouraged to provide information on capital inputs. The results are summarized in table 6.3. For the countries for which data are available, except Chile, the results are as expected: HOS exportables were less capital-using than import-competing activities. For Indonesia, where Pitt had four proxy variables with which to approximate capital utilization, all show wide divergences. Only in electricity utilization was the difference between HOS exportables and HOS import-competing industries less than two to one, and even in terms of electricity used the differential exceeded 50 percent. For Uruguay data were available separately for exports destined to DCs and to LDCs, and they are reported separately. As can be seen, kilowatts used per DVA in trade with developed countries were 21 percent less than those employed in import substitution industries (where all HOS import-competing industries were replacing imports from developed countries). For trade with other developing countries, primarily LAFTA, kilowatts per unit of DVA were 2,573, or

Table 6.3   Evidence with Regard to Capital Inputs per Unit of DVA

	HOS Exportables	IIOS Import-Competing Industries
Argentina		
Cost of energy	29.96	51.03
Chile		
Thousand escudos of fixed assets	1,643.00	852.00
Hong Kong		
Profits 1973	222.94	315.39
Depreciation 1973	55.46	70.71
Indonesia		
Electric motor horsepower	2.46	7.99
Total horsepower	7.23	17.66
Electricity used (kwh)	2,386.00	3,886.00
Energy consumed (Rp 000)	45.00	91.00
Prime-mover horsepower	4.77	9.67
South Korea	99.00[a]	115.00[a]
Uruguay		
Kilowatts trade with DCs	915.00 ⎤	1,163.00
Kilowatts trade with LDCs	2,573.00 ⎦	

[a]Per unit of output.

2.2 times as great as those for import-competing industries. The figures are, of course, even more extreme in terms of IVA. For Chile it will be recalled that pulp and paper exports to LAFTA were a sufficiently large component of Chile's HOS exports that they dominated the labor coefficients.

Overall, the available data reinforce the conclusions emerging from the labor coefficients: HOS exportables tend to use more labor and less capital per unit of domestic value added than do import-competing industries.

6.4   Coefficients per Unit of International Value Added by Trade Categories

As was shown in chapter 5, consideration of labor—or other input—coefficients per unit of domestic value added is appropriate if the question under analysis pertains to alternative uses of given bundles of domestic resources. If, instead, one wishes to evaluate the effect of alternative allocations while holding the trade balance constant, coefficients per unit of *international value added* should be employed. These coefficients are closer to an efficiency notion of factor utilization, while domestic coefficients come closer to some representation of a full-employment condition.

At free and balanced trade, of course, the industry-specific coefficients are the same regardless of whether domestic or international value added is used, and the relationship of L/DVA and L/IVA ratios is one to one. Moreover, if adequate data were available so that one could rely on capital/labor ratios, the ordering of factor intensity would be invariant with respect to use of domestic or international measures.

However, when tariffs or other protective devices leads to differentials in the domestic/foreign price ratios for different commodities or industries, the one-to-one relationship between IVA and DVA breaks down.[5] Even in a two-factor HOS world, it could happen that L/DVA and L/IVA rankings were reversed. Figure 6.1 illustrates this possibility. In figure 6.1, unit isoquants for commodities A and B are given by the aa and bb curves respectively. At a wage/rental ratio represented by minus the slope of w^0w^0, industry A is labor-intensive, using a combination of labor and capital inputs represented by the coordinates of a^0, while industry B is more capital-using, with inputs at b^0. At input prices represented by the slopes of w^1w^1 (which is reproduced as w^2w^2), industry A would employ the combination of inputs indicated at a^1, while industry B would employ that represented at b^1. Thus a country with factor prices w^0w^0 would be able, at free trade, to produce both commodities at a price ratio of one to one. A country with factor prices represented by w^1w^1 ($= w^2w^2$) would not be able to produce both commodities at the one-to-one price ratio. If the wage/rental ratio represented by w^0w^0 determined international prices of both commodities, a country with factor prices w^1w^1 could produce both commodities only with protection to industry B. With such protection (in the amount $w^1 - w^2$ divided by Ow^2), both industries could produce under competitive conditions. Industry A would always be labor intensive in that the labor/capital ratio in that industry would exceed that in industry B for all common wage/rental ratios. Moreover, L/DVA in industry A would exceed that in industry B. However, L/IVA in industry B would exceed that in industry A, since it would require *both* more labor and more capital per unit of output in B than in A at the factor prices represented by w^1w^1.

The reason for this can be more readily seen in figure 6.2, which is not consistent with an HOS world of incomplete specialization and identical production functions between countries.[6] In figure 6.2, isoquants for commodities A and B are drawn for a unit of output of each commodity evaluated in domestic prices. Given the domestic factor prices represented by the slope of the line $p_d p$, factor proportions a^0 and b^0 would be employed in the two industries. Industry A is again labor intensive. Suppose now that industry A is the export industry, and not subject to protection, while industry B is highly protected. If, for example, the

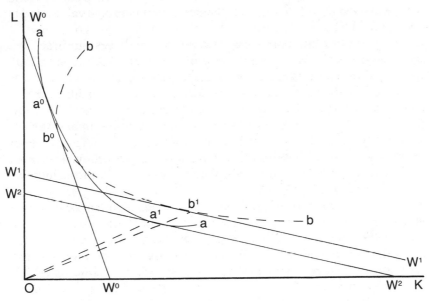

Fig. 6.1

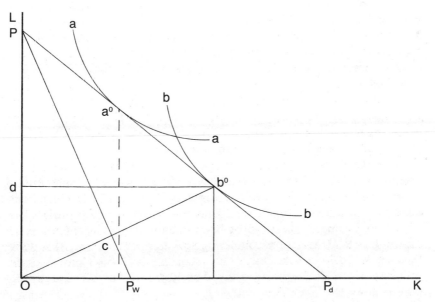

Fig. 6.2

world price ratio is pp_w, then labor per unit of international value added in industry B would be *od* times the ratio of domestic value added to international value added, or *ob/oc*. As can be seen, the proportionate difference between *ob* and *oc* is sufficient so that labor (and capital) per IVA in B exceeds that in A.

Regardless of which of the two underlying cases causes a reversal, it is apparent that a reversal of labor intensities between a DVA and an IVA basis represents a case paralleling "absolute inefficiency" in the engineering sense: when the ratios reverse, it would have been possible to achieve more international value added per unit of labor *and* of capital in the less protected industry. Stated otherwise, when a relatively labor-intensive commodity in a labor-abundant country uses more labor and more capital per unit of IVA (while using less labor per unit of DVA), there is no set of relative input prices at which it would be efficient to operate the industry *using existing factor proportions*.[7]

With that background in mind, the L/IVA coefficients from the country studies can be analyzed.[8] They are presented in table 6.4, in a format comparable to that of table 5.1 for purposes of comparison. Recall that all ratios are expressed relative to the labor per IVA in HOS import-competing activities. To transform estimates of labor per DVA into labor coefficients per unit of IVA, the L/DVA coefficients must be multiplied by the ratio of DVA to IVA (i.e., one plus the rate of effective protection). If ERPs for all exportables were zero, the L/DVA and L/IVA would be identical for exporting industries. If a regime were biased toward import substitution, so that ERPs for import-competing industries were positive, L/DVA would be less than L/IVA. This is what leads to the possibility of reversal, especially when there is negative effective protection for exportables (so that L/IVA is less than L/DVA) and positive effective protection for import substitutes (so that L/DVA is less than L/IVA).[9]

In practice, some exportable activities have positive levels of protection, and others have negative ones, so that the relationship between exporting and import substitution L/DVA and L/IVA ratios is not quite as straightforward as it at first sight appears.

Nonetheless, as can be seen from table 6.4, the ratio of labor coefficients in HOS exportable industries to those in import substitution activities is generally less when expressed for IVA than for DVA, reflecting the general bias of the trade regimes toward import substitution. For Chile, for example, the ratio of labor requirements overall for HOS exportables to HOS import-competing activities per DVA was 0.8, while the ratio is 0.47 for IVA. Only in Pakistan and the Ivory Coast does the ratio rise, since HOS exports received positive levels of effective protection in those two countries.

Table 6.4   Direct Labor Coefficients per Unit of IVA (Ratio of Direct
Coefficients in Designated Trade Category to Direct Requirements
per IVA in HOS Import-Competing Activities)

| | HOS Exports | | |
Country	Manufac- tures Not PCB	PCB Manufac- tures	Total
Argentina	n.a.	n.a.	.55
Chile	n.a.	n.a.	.47
Colombia	n.a.	n.a.	1.63
Indonesia	1.31[a]	n.a.	1.65[a]
Ivory Coast			
Modern sector	n.a.	n.a.	1.42[b]
Total	n.a.	n.a.	1.33
Pakistan	1.28[c]	n.a.	1.53[c]
Thailand	2.36	.85	1.23
Tunisia	n.a.	n.a.	.91
Uruguay	n.a.	n.a.	.66

[a]Direct-plus-home-goods-indirect labor per unit of IVA. For comparison, the comparable ratios for DVA are 1.46 for non-PCB manufactures and 1.92 for all HOS exports relative to import-competing HOS goods.
[b]See note to table 5.1 on Ivory Coast. Values refer to ratios of direct-plus-home-goods indirect labor per unit of IVA.
[c]Direct-plus-home-goods indirect labor per unit of IVA from Guisinger 1981, table 7.12. For comparison, the figures for DVA are 1.41 and 1.30.

There are three cases of reversals: Argentine, Tunisian, and Uru-guayan HOS exports. In those instances, labor coefficients for import-competing activities per IVA exceed those for exportable activities. The reasons are exactly those illustrated in figures 6.1 and 6.2: the ratio of DVA to IVA exceeds the proportionate difference in labor inputs. In Uruguay the difference is extremely large: HOS exportables took 50 percent more labor per unit of domestic value added than did import-competing goods, but only two-thirds as much labor per unit of international value added. This reflects the very high degree of protection accorded to import-competing industries (see table 7.1) in Uruguay.

The order of magnitude of the Uruguayan reversal can be seen from the following calculation. Suppose the direct capital employed in produc-ing one million dollars of IVA in import-competing industries in Uru-guay, as reflected in thousand kilowatts of energy consumption (4,576) had instead been allocated to HOS exporting industries. In import-competing industries, 934 workers were employed per million dollars of IVA; 4,576 thousand kilowatts would have been the capital coefficient for $3.1 million of IVA in HOS exportables to developed countries. The number of workers per million dollars IVA in HOS exportables was 707; it would therefore, at constant coefficients, have taken 2,191 workers, compared with the 934 in import substitution industries, to employ the same amount of capital (if energy consumption is an adequate proxy for capital inputs), and the international value of output could have been three times as great. To be sure, the estimates are imprecise, and in any event the Uruguayan economy could not for long have sustained such a shift in resources. Labor would undoubtedly have become scarcer, and factor proportions would have altered in response to an altered wage/rental ratio. Nonetheless, the numbers are large enough to indicate a sizable loss in potential welfare given the actual coefficients and trade strategy followed.

For most countries, of course, the numbers are not quite as extreme, though for both Chile and Tunisia the differences are significant. There is no single measure that accurately reflects the degree of bias toward import substitution in a country, but the evidence in the country studies suggests that the three countries with reversals were also among those with the greatest bias toward import substitution. Certainly the differentials between L/DVA and L/IVA ratios are much smaller in the Ivory Coast and Indonesia, where there is considerable evidence that the degree of protection to import-competing industries was substantially smaller (see table 8.1).

If one works only with capital/labor ratios, as seems reasonable given the underlying HOS model, the fact that L/DVA and L/IVA can reverse may be overlooked. Indeed, at the outset of the project we did not expect that such an outcome was possible: the reason for focusing upon labor coefficients rather than labor/capital ratios was that we believed data on numbers of workers, with or without adjustments for hours worked, skills, and experience, would be somewhat more reliable and generally available than data on capital stock employed. That L/DVA and L/IVA ratios diverge as much as they do points to the importance of examining capital and labor coefficients separately, even when reliable data are available for both, in the presence of significant variation in rates of effective protection.

6.5   Conclusions

Chapters 5 and 6 have been essentially descriptive, examining evidence on the labor coefficients for various categories of tradables and other data pertinent to analysis of the effect of alternative trade strategies on employment. Those coefficients are the outcome of market processes and government regulations in the countries covered by the project, and consideration of the determinants of the coefficients must take into account analysis of factor markets in chapters 7 and 8. Nonetheless, in light of the underlying theory suggesting that, in the presence of differentiated incentives and factor market imperfections, little systematic relationship can be expected between factor inputs and the commodity composition of trade, it is interesting that, in most of the countries covered by the project, production of HOS exportables was, by and large, considerably more labor intensive than production of import-competing goods. This picture emerges when considering employment coefficients per unit of DVA; if the size of the capital stock is the constraint upon the size of the manufacturing sector, then the clear implication is that employment could *expand* more under increases in HOS exportable production than under HOS import-competing production. This follows both because there would be more demand for labor in HOS exportable industries and because capital coefficients in those industries are generally lower, implying that total manufacturing value added could expand. In terms of IVA, the differential in employment coefficients is generally smaller, in large part because import-competing industries receive higher effective protection than do HOS exportables. As a consequence it can, and in some cases does, take *both* more labor and more capital per unit of IVA in import-competing industries than in exportables. This is more a reflection of the economic inefficiency of some of import-competing industries than an indication of employment potential: capital/labor ratios are not altered by changing from units of DVA to IVA.

When attention turns to the composition of employment, especially in its skill dimensions, once again the evidence is strong that HOS exportables use more unskilled labor and less skilled and managerial labor than import-competing industries. This result warrants careful analysis, especially in light of the determinants of wage structure in the project countries. Even at this juncture, however, the straightforward idea, emanating from the HOS model, that international trade enables developing countries to substitute their relatively abundant factor—unskilled labor—for their relatively scarce factor, seems to be borne out by the data despite whatever factor market imperfections may have influenced the results.

Finally, there is evidence that regional trading arrangements, especially LAFTA, induce a pattern of trade that uses factor proportions in exportables much more like those in import-competing industries than those in HOS exportables to developed countries. Such a result makes intuitive sense: if all LDCs have a comparative advantage in the world economy in a variety of goods that are relatively intensive in the use of unskilled labor, it is unlikely that they will be able to penetrate each other's markets significantly—transport cost differentials, combined with protection, presumably deter what trade might otherwise be profitable, and the HOS model in any event predicts that gains from trade will be large between countries with dissimilar factor endowments. It therefore seems plausible that, when tariff preferences are extended, they tend to encourage export of import substitution industries' output within the region. Whether this increases or reduces real incomes depends on whether the imports of capital-intensive goods from regional trading partners replace even higher-priced domestic output or whether instead they replace imports from developed countries. If it is the latter, there is clear evidence of trade diversion, with presumed attendant welfare losses from regional preferential arrangements, and very different employment implications for a given trade strategy depending on whether that strategy is global or regional in nature.

7   The Extent of Factor
      Market Distortions

Although theory suggests the possibility that sufficient factor market imperfections might result in a "reversal" of exports and imports, the evidence from the country studies indicates that in none of them did this occur for HOS trade, except in cases of regional trading arrangements. This finding is itself significant, in that it suggests that one can be fairly confident that adopting a genuinely export-oriented trade strategy will not lead to perverse results and that there is no potential conflict between employment and real output objectives involved in the choice of a trade strategy.

That reversals did not take place, however, does not imply that factor market imperfections are nonexistent or insignificant. Theory does not show that reversals must occur or even that they are likely; it does suggest that, in the presence of distortions, observed proportions and product mixes will differ from what they would be in their absence.

Important questions therefore remain: How sizable are factor market distortions? How great is their influence upon factor proportions within industries? What is the effect of product and factor market distortions upon the output mix? And to what extent would the employment implications of alternative trade strategies differ quantitatively in the absence of those imperfections? Would the potential for additional employment through choice of trade strategy greatly increase in the absence of imperfections? Or, on the contrary, are they either sufficiently small in magnitude or unimportant enough so that their removal would hardly affect the orders of magnitude reported in chapters 5 and 6? What sorts of policies to implement the choice of trade strategy are likely to increase the demand for labor or to adversely affect it? Are they integral parts of the trade regime or unnecessary appendages?

The questions are inherently difficult to tackle empirically. No "perfect market" has ever been observed. Information costs, frictions associated with the process of economic growth, transaction costs, and other phenomena are all reasons why complete uniformity of rates of return, wages, and prices will never be observed in all markets—nor should they be, in the presence of costs of adjustments. This implies that a first, and difficult, empirical task is to distinguish the components of observed differentials. More fundamentally, however, there are always market imperfections, and they differ only in scope and magnitude. A fundamental question is when those imperfections become sufficiently great so that they significantly affect the functioning of markets and the nature of responses to market signals.

Little is known about the probable orders of magnitude of factor market imperfections and their consequences. Given the complexity of the analysis, that is hardly surprising. We could not hope that the NBER project would result in definitive quantitative estimates as answers to these questions, in light of the paucity of data and prior analysis. Nonetheless, a number of pieces of evidence have emerged. It is the purpose of this chapter to evaluate the findings as to the orders of magnitude of distortions in the project countries.

Although the focus of the entire project was on employment creation, the fact that imperfections in both the labor and the capital markets can affect the relative profitability of alternative techniques implies that capital and labor market imperfections must both be examined in assessing distortions. In this chapter, therefore, the effects of both capital and labor market distortions are evaluated in terms of their effect upon relative costs of employing capital and labor. It remains to chapter 8 to evaluate the effects of those differentials and of product market distortions on labor coefficients.

Section 7.1 undertakes some necessary preliminary analysis, examining types of capital market distortions and their probable effects on costs of using capital and labor. Section 7.2 then provides evidence about the magnitude of factor cost distortions. Section 7.3 contains an estimate of the quantitative effects of these distortions on the wage/rental ratio. In section 7.4 these estimates are used to indicate the probable order of magnitude of the effect on the wage/rental ratio. It will remain for chapter 8 to consider the effect of these cost differences upon factor proportions, and their influence upon the implications of alternative trade strategies for employment.

7.1 Analysis of Capital Market Distortions

In addition to the possible effect of labor market distortions, discussed in chapter 2, on the relative costs of employing labor and capital, there are three avenues through which capital costs can be significantly affected, thereby affecting the relative attractiveness of different techniques and the relative costs of more and less capital-intensive industries. First, the trade regime itself may be administered in ways that affect the relative costs of capital equipment to different users. Second, there may be credit rationing that can affect the relative costs of labor and capital to different industries. Finally, the tax structure can affect the relative profitability of labor-intensive and capital-intensive techniques. Each of these three influences on the cost of capital is discussed in this section in turn.

7.1.1 Trade Regime and Costs of Capital Equipment

A variety of mechanisms have been identified, especially under import substitution regimes, through which the trade regimes may affect the cost of employing capital relative to the cost of employing labor,[1] and also the relative cost of capital to different activities.[2] Of these, the most visible is generally the preferential exchange rate generally granted to capital-equipment imports, especially under import substitution.

Many of the issues pertaining to capital market distortions can be analyzed in the context of one of the simplest mechanisms that can lead to a distortion: use of a different (and lower) effective exchange rate for imports of machinery and equipment than for other imports. Very often this arises in the context of currency overvaluation, when most imports are subject to high tariff rates while capital goods imports enter at low rates of duty or even duty-free. Consider first the case where all capital goods are imported and have no domestically produced substitutes. If capital goods imports are permitted at an overvalued exchange rate, while imports of other types of goods are either prohibited or else subject to a much higher effective price of foreign exchange, it is evident that purchasers of imported capital equipment will pay a lower price for that equipment than they would in the absence of the distortion.

Analysis of the effects of this policy, however, can be undertaken only after a mechanism is specified for determining the overall volume of imported capital equipment. To demonstrate this, it is sufficient to recognize that if all who wished to do so at the prevailing (subsidized) price were free to import capital equipment, the volume of imports of capital goods and equipment would be greater than it would have been at a nondistortionary price. The net effect would be a larger stock of capital equipment than would otherwise have been the case: presumably, domestic consumption would be smaller than it would have been in the absence of the distortion, while investment would be greater.[3] In this circumstance the effects of the distortion would be upon present relative to future consumption levels: a market-determined outcome would witness more present, and less future, consumption. There would not, however, be any distortion in domestic capital goods markets, in the sense that all users of imported machinery and equipment would face the same (distorted) price.

However, few observers of import regimes in developing countries believe that the volume of imports of capital goods is above optimal levels. When the exchange rate is overvalued and imports of capital goods are permitted at a lower EER than other commodities, the more usual situation is that the demand for foreign exchange for this and other purposes exceeds the supply. As a consequence, the authorities generally employ some sort of rationing mechanism to determine who is permitted to import how much at the implicitly subsidized rate. It is the rationing mechanism combined with the implicit subsidy received by those entitled to import that determines the precise nature of the distortion and its effects on capital costs as perceived by individual entrepreneurs.

A number of rationing mechanisms have been used, and their effects on capital costs differ. Among the prominent ones are: (1) designating "priority" industries and sectors eligible to import at the favored exchange rate; (2) determining which investment projects are to be permitted, subject to an overall budget constraint for imported capital goods; and (3) scaling down applications for licenses to import capital goods.

Where "priority" industries and sectors are permitted relatively free access to imports of capital goods, the cost of capital services to firms in those sectors is less than it is to firms in other sectors of the economy. Excluded firms confront higher capital costs than they would in the absence of distortion.

The way the second mechanism would work hinges crucially on how investment projects are screened for approval. On one hand, if individual businessmen perceive that the probability of approval of their applications for imports of capital goods is independent of the capital intensity of their projects, the net effect on resource allocation will be similar to that of the first mechanism: those projects approved and permitted to import capital goods will be more capital intensive than if a market-clearing price were to be charged (although, by hypothesis, the market-clearing price would presumably be above that which would prevail in the absence of exchange rate overvaluation, since total foreign exchange earnings would be less than with a higher, less overvalued, real EER). On the other hand, if applicants believe that the probability of approval of their applications hinges upon the capital intensity of the project, the outcome may differ. In the extreme case, if the authorities shadow price capital and labor correctly to ensure full employment and equate marginal rates of substitution of capital for labor in all lines, then the outcome with project evaluation should not differ from that of an efficient auction market for the available supply of foreign exchange, except that all recipients of licenses to import capital equipment implicitly receive subsidies equal to the value of their licenses, and the total volume of imports would, of course, be smaller than at full equilibrium.[4]

To be sure, this "perfect shadow pricing" mechanism is unlikely to be experienced in practice, but considering it points up the polar extreme from the first case and the fact that there are two distinct effects of exchange rate overvaluation upon capital costs and differentials in them. On one hand, because foreign exchange earnings are smaller, one would generally expect that imports of capital goods would be fewer and that the cost of capital perceived by the average firm would be higher than with greater foreign exchange availability. On the other hand, because licensing mechanisms for imports are necessarily imperfect, there is likely to be misallocation of the *given* capital stock. With "perfect shadow pricing," marginal rates of substitution would be equated across all activities, and importers of capital equipment would receive the equivalent of lump-sum subsidies, which would not affect their behavior. At the other extreme, the entire value of the implicit subsidies can be absorbed in the utilization of above-optimal capital intensity in the production process (or in producing very capital-intensive goods).

One particular form of allocating import rights has fairly readily identifiable effects on capital costs. That is, in their efforts to be "fair," the authorities establish criteria for import license allocation. Those criteria are often based on such phenomena as shares of existing capacity or shares of output that provide a formula for license allocation. Such formulas, when announced, differentially affect capital costs, since building new capacity or other actions in effect become part of the cost of obtaining import licenses.[5]

The third mechanism, scaling down applications for licenses to import capital goods, is in many regards a cross between the first two methods. However, the effects on costs depend upon how many firms, industries, and sectors are eligible to apply for importing machinery and equipment, and also upon applicants' expectations about the mechanism by which scaling down will be accomplished. If licenses are issued for value amounts of imported machinery and equipment, incentives will differ from those provided when licenses are issued for imports of specified types of machinery and equipment. In the former case, receipt of a license to import a specified value of capital goods imposes a budget constraint upon the recipient so that he may, if the license value represents less than the quantity desired at the prevailing exchange rate, choose labor-using and capital-saving techniques. If, on the other hand, the license is awarded for the importation of a specified type of automated loom or other capital-intensive equipment, the incentive to economize on use of imported capital goods is vastly different.

Under any of the three mechanisms, the effects of the implicit capital subsidy must be analyzed in two parts: (1) the effect of the rationing mechanism upon choice of technique in the sectors eligible for it, and (2) the effect on sectors that are utilizing less capital-intensive techniques than they would use under optimal resource allocation (given the existing pattern of output).

In Argentina and the project countries in which there seemed to be implicit or explicit subsidization of capital goods imports by means of an overvalued exchange rate—Chile, Pakistan, Thailand to a moderate extent, Tunisia, and Uruguay—the recipient sector seems to have been the large-scale urban industrial sector, which was also the sector encouraged by tariffs and trade barriers to produce import substitution goods.[6] The losing sectors of the economy appear to have been the informal, or small-scale, urban sector and the agricultural-rural sectors. The orders of magnitude of the implicit subsidy to imported capital equipment are discussed in section 7.2.

So far the discussion has been couched in terms of import substitution regimes in economies where all capital goods must be imported. In fact, construction is usually a home good,[7] and, in addition, in countries where import substitution has been adopted policy for a period of years, some types of capital goods are domestically produced. In those circumstances there is a secondary set of effects emanating from the trade regime: on one hand, implicit subsidization of capital goods imports encourages, as before, techniques of greater-than-optimal capital intensity among the recipients of import licenses; on the other hand, the authorities frequently prohibit the import of goods competing with domestic production.

This latter may offset in part the implicit subsidy to capital goods if import-license recipients are required to buy some parts of their plant and equipment from domestic suppliers. Since, by hypothesis of protection, domestic equipment is generally priced above world-market levels and accorded protection by the trade regime (in greater amount than the implicit negative protection associated with the overvalued exchange rate), the net effect on incentives to substitute capital for labor can be fairly complex. Whether the increased cost of domestically produced equipment exceeds or falls short of the reduced cost of the imported equipment will determine the net effect on the cost of investment goods. In this latter connection, there are significant questions about the degree of substitutability between imported and domestic capital equipment.[8] There are also questions about which kinds of investment are most affected, since the range of capital goods produced may be limited.[9]

For individuals and firms unable to obtain import licenses, the effect of protecting domestic capital goods producers probably tends, on net, to raise the relative cost of employing capital.[10] Whether the group denied import licenses coincides with the informal and rural sectors of the economy is not certain: it may also include firms within the organized sector.

In conclusion, implicit subsidization of imports of capital equipment can have different effects on the cost of using capital for those receiving import permits, depending on the allocation mechanism, the extent to which domestic capital goods industries are protected, the range of such goods, and the fraction of the investment package that domestic goods constitute. Implicit subsidization of import of capital goods for one group normally entails relatively high capital costs for those individuals and sectors of the economy denied access to imported capital goods. Import substitution regimes have in general tended through this mechanism to favor firms in the large-scale, organized sector of the economy. It may be that the implicit subsidy tends to offset the higher costs of production of those goods entailed by their comparative disadvantage. Nonetheless, it can constitute an implicit subsidy both for capital-using industries and for choice of capital-intensive techniques.

7.1.2   Credit Rationing and Domestic Capital Market Imperfections

In attempting to pinpoint markets in LDCs whose imperfect functioning may be empirically important in affecting resource allocation and growth, many observers have focused upon financial, credit, and equity markets.[11] An oversimplified characterization would entail the following ingredients: a fragmented or virtually nonexistent equity market so that most private firms are family enterprises; government restrictions upon the banking system, and in particular upon permissible interest rates, so that excess demand for loans prevails and financial institutions somehow ration credit among their customers; and the absence of a market for long-term borrowing and lending.

The combination of inadequate or nonexistent equity markets and nonavailability of long-term loans would, by itself, entail significant costs. For, even if the banking system were otherwise functioning smoothly with positive real rates of interest and loans available to all who applied,[12] entrepreneurs might be reluctant to resort to short-term borrowing for financing long-term investments. Conversely, if potential borrowers were constrained in their equity positions by the size of family assets, banks might well be reluctant to lend large amounts in the short term. Insofar as this combination of circumstances implies that each enterprise will expand at a rate dictated largely by its own available funds, in turn generated by its own resources, each firm has its own supply curve for capital and different costs of capital.

Governments in developing countries have responded to these phenomena in financial markets in a variety of ways: in some cases monetary reforms have been undertaken to liberalize the credit markets and induce financial institutions to provide equity capital and long-term loans. In other cases governments have used the absence of these markets as a rationale for introducing "selective credit allocation," under which government-owned or government-regulated institutions allocate credit, both short-term and long-term, according to various criteria.[13] In these circumstances the interest rate charged on loans is well below market-clearing levels and below what bank and other financial institutions would charge if unregulated. Often, rates are even considerably below the rate of inflation.

When this form of intervention is employed, the consequent credit rationing can have a significant effect upon individual firms' costs, depending on the ways loanable funds are allocated.

Two issues must be considered. First, there are a number of mechanisms within the domestic credit markets that can significantly affect the cost of capital among individual industries and firms. Second, governments have used credit-allocation mechanisms to channel resources into directions they deemed desirable. Those directions have often been closely associated with the choice of trade strategy, and the interaction of trade strategy and the domestic credit market in affecting the cost of using capital relative to labor may be substantial.

Turning first to domestic factors, the mechanisms for allocating credit, often with an implicit subsidy element at negative real interest rates, can have a significant and differential effect on capital/labor costs in different industries. This is especially the case in countries where government-owned or government-controlled institutions are the chief lenders. In countries where the preponderance of investment consists of imported capital goods, there is, or can be, considerable scope for choosing between credit mechanisms and import licensing mechanisms as a means of attempting to control the direction of investment. Because of this, the analysis of credit rationing and its effects on capital costs is very similar to the analysis of import licensing and its effects.

In particular, if credit applications are evaluated and decided upon without regard to the choice of techniques involved in a particular investment project, firms will view the prevailing interest rate as their cost of borrowing. If, on the other hand, all investors are entitled to some financing at subsidized rates but must obtain some financing at realistic curb rates, the effects may be quite different. In South Korea, for example, it appears that almost all enterprises are eligible to obtain a fixed fraction of their financing, at implicitly subsidized interest rates, well below the expected rate of inflation. They then resort to the curb market for the remaining portion of their financing, paying positive real rates of interest 5–15 percent above the rate of inflation. To the extent that the financing formula is known and invariant with respect to the size of the potential investment project, the "true" interest rate confronting would-be investors is a combination consisting of the fraction carried by subsidized interest loans times the borrowing rate and the remainder times the curb rate.

If, on the other hand, projects are divisible and precise expansion plans need not be submitted or carried out, the curb rate may truly be the marginal cost of borrowing. For in that circumstance much of the implicit subsidy entailed in receipt of a loan at below market-clearing rates is precisely that: choice of a more labor-intensive technique results in saving on borrowing at the curb rate of interest.

Figure 7.1 illustrates the various possibilities. In case I, the official borrowing rate is r_o, and all firms are eligible for two-thirds of their loan applications at that rate. Meanwhile, the curb rate of interset is r_c, and one-third of all borrowing is financed at curb rates. In that instance the actual lending rate firms face is r_a, equal to two-thirds times r_o and one-third times r_c. If firms all have access to the subsidized credit and know the proportions in which they will receive it, they will base their investment decisions on r_a. To the extent that all do so, no distortion results in the allocation of capital across potential borrowers, providing all are eligible to receive the same fraction at a subsidized rate.

In case II, r_o and r_c are as in case I, but the authorities finance some loan applications and not others. Thus there may be two classes of firms. Those with an investment schedule such as MEC_1 are ineligible for, or denied, subsidized loans. They therefore resort to curb financing entirely, borrowing ol_1 at interest rate r_c. Firms in the second group, represented by MEC_2, receive full financing of their projects at subsidized interest rates, in amount ol_2. In this case the distortion is obvious: there are opportunities for investment at rates of return above r_o that are not undertaken by firms in the first category, while the rate of return on investment is r_o for firms in the second category.

The third case is one in which firms receive loans in amounts ol_o but are then free to vary the amount they borrow in the curb market at rate of interest or_1. As drawn, curb market lending would be lo_1. In that instance the rectangular area r_1abr_o represents a pure lump-sum subsidy to the borrowers. If all borrowers receive such a subsidy and nonetheless borrow additional sums in the curb market, they all face the same marginal cost of capital on that account. Only if some borrowers do not find it profitable to resort to curb-market financing will capital costs differ between users.

In most countries, elements of all three cases undoubtedly arise. In South Korea the amount financed at official rates is sufficiently large (see section 7.2.8) that it seems probable that some borrowers are excluded from eligibility (as in case II) and that others regard the true cost of borrowing as in case I. In Thailand and Pakistan the large-scale enterprises were the main borrowers at official interest rates, so that case II seems to be a better characterization of the capital market effects of

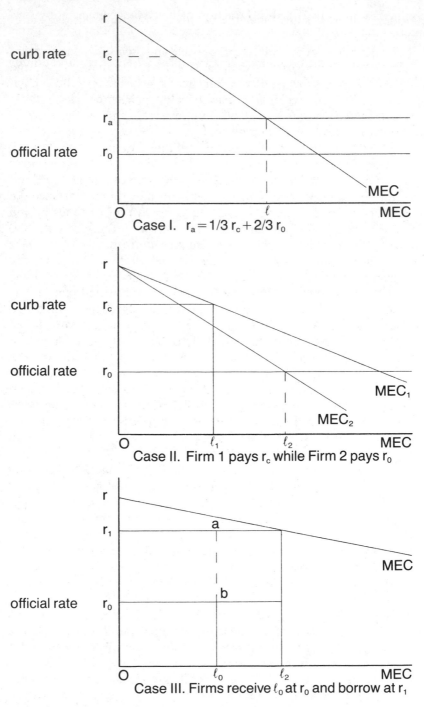

Case I. $r_a = 1/3\, r_c + 2/3\, r_0$

Case II. Firm 1 pays r_c while Firm 2 pays r_0

Case III. Firms receive ℓ_0 at r_0 and borrow at r_1

Fig. 7.1

credit rationing. In Brazil the fraction of investment financed by low-interest loans was sufficiently small (see section 7.2.2) that case III may be the best approximation.

There remains the question how any or all of the three credit rationing mechanisms interact with the choice of trade strategy. One obvious mechanism is when the designated priority industries eligible for subsidized credit are associated with choice of trade strategy. This has often been the case. In import substitution countries, the planning authorities have frequently drawn up lists of industries they wished to encourage, and available credit has been channeled to those industries. Even in export promotion countries, special financing facilities are often available to exporters. This mechanism was certainly an important feature of the South Korean export promotion strategy, and it is one Hong pinpoints as having led to resource misallocation and overly capital-intensive techniques within the Korean economy. In addition, the availability of low-cost capital services could, at least in principle, enable some relatively capital-intensive industries to export despite the absence of comparative advantage. The empirical importance of these elements is evaluated in section 7.2.

7.1.3   Taxes and Their Incentive Effect on Capital Costs

By and large, analysis of the effect of tax incentives on factor proportions is straightforward. The most frequently encountered set of taxes was upon labor: social security taxes and other measures substantially increased the costs of hiring labor. The evidence on this is reviewed below, and little needs to be said here except that, to the extent that taxes on labor are imposed on one sector of the economy only, the wage confronting that sector is higher than elsewhere, and incentives for use of techniques with greater capital intensity than would otherwise be the case will prevail for that sector.[14] In general this appears to have been true for many of the project countries.

Several other types of taxes (or tax exemptions to encourage certain activities) can also influence choice of techniques. Perhaps the most notable for the project countries concerns tax holidays granted to firms in designated (generally "priority") industries. Because tax holidays are granted to nonlabor returns only, these measures, which are generally intended to encourage the development of particular industries without regard to the choice of techniques within them, nonetheless increase incentives for use of capital-intensive techniques.[15]

By contrast, sales tax exemptions of the type used extensively by Brazil do not appear to have significant effects on factor proportions. Although the Brazilian tax structure discriminated in favor of sales in the foreign market, there appears to have been little bias introduced by it into the choice of techniques by individual firms.

7.2   Magnitude of Factor Cost Distortions

In this section the orders of magnitude of factor market distortions in the project countries are reviewed in light of the analysis of labor markets in chapter 2 and of capital costs in section 7.1.[16] As will be seen, the nature and extent of distortions differed considerably among the project countries. Hong Kong is not covered, since all the evidence indicates that the labor and capital markets are comparatively distortion-free.

7.2.1   Argentina

Argentina seems to have had all the types of differential capital costs discussed above and also to have had a number of factors raising the cost of employing labor.

The trade regime itself affected the cost of employing capital equipment, in that the exchange rate was overvalued and in that investors able to obtain licenses to import capital goods received an implicit subsidy of about 40 percent. Simultaneously, Argentina's import substitution had proceeded far enough so that, by the late 1960s, there was a substantial domestic industry producing capital goods. According to Nogues's estimates (1980), about 68 percent of investment in tradable capital goods was supplied from domestic sources. The domestic producers were protected with nominal rates of protection of 97 percent for machinery and 109 percent for transport equipment. Nogues was unable to estimate the differential allocation of licenses to import capital goods across industries, but he conjectured that public enterprises and firms in import substitution sectors currently being encouraged by industrial promotion laws received preferential access to licenses. On average, he estimated that the trade regime increased the price of capital goods about 8 percent above what it would be at free trade.

Domestic policies also influenced the cost of employing capital goods. Argentina encouraged the development of new import substitution industries by industrial promotion laws. Industries, enterprises, and regions benefiting from these laws were eligible for tax and tariff exemption and for credit at preferential interest rates. Tax holidays and deferrals (the latter being very valuable in a high-inflation country) were accorded to them. Nogues estimated that in the early 1970s eligible investors received a subsidy of about 40 percent of their capital costs through the fiscal mechanisms. Simultaneously, the subsidy of element implicit in negative real rates of interest was probably about 66 percent for a ten-year loan. Although only 14 percent of manufacturing investment was financed through these loans, the distribution among manufacturing sectors implied significant differences in costs of capital. On average, financial subsidies probably reduced capital costs in manufacturing by about 9 percent.

Government intervention in Argentine labor markets has also been an important influence on the relative costs of labor and capital. During the period Nogues covered, the government established a minimum wage for unskilled labor. These wages were probably binding for much of the large-scale manufacturing sector. In addition, charges for old-age retirement plans, a family allowance fund, and other legislated labor benefits undoubtedly contained a sizable element of tax. Nogues estimated that, on average, these taxes added about 15 percent to labor costs (above the effects of minimum wage legislation). The differential in labor costs between firms observing all government regulations and those evading all of them could have been as much as 40 percent.

7.2.2 Brazil

As was seen in table 3.3, Brazil's structure of effective protection discriminated in favor of capital goods during the import substitution period in the late 1950s. While the average effective rate of protection was 242 percent for consumer goods, it was 65 pecent for intermediate goods and 53 percent for capital goods. Since the exchange rate was considerably overvalued at that time, this probably led to a substantially greater incentive to use capital-intensive techniques than would have been optimal, especially since virtually all capital goods were imported during that period.

During the 1960s, the tariff reform substantially unified effective rates of protection, as is reflected in table 3.3. Thus, during the import substitution period, the structure of protection and the tendency to exempt capital goods imports from the restrictions surrounding other commodities probably resulted in a lower-than-optimal price of capital goods for those favored enough to be able to import. With the switch to an export promotion strategy, the discrimination in favor of capital afforded by the exchange rate largely disappeared, but it was partially replaced by the availability of implicitly subsidized credit.[17]

There were virtually no financial institutions providing access to medium- or long-term credit until 1964. At that time, the Banco Nacional de Desenvolvimento Econômico (BNDE) began lending for medium and long periods at fairly low rates of interest, usually under 5 percent in real terms. This compared with a real rate of return on capital during the period of about 12 percent annually. For 1965 to 1974, Carvalho and Haddad calculated that the implicit subsidy entailed in BNDE loans ranged from 10 to 50 percent of the value of the loan, with an average of about 20 percent depending on the time period of the loan and the repayment schedule. BNDE covered an average of about 60 to 70 percent of the cost of capital goods in projects they financed, the rest being financed through credit at market rates of interest. The implicit subsidy was thus about 12 percent of the cost of capital goods acquired under

BNDE loans. For recipients of such loans, therefore, the subsidy element was sizable. However, for most manufacturing sectors of the economy, the share of total investment financed by BNDE loans was relatively small: except for metal products, where 55 percent of investment was financed by BNDE loans, shares were less than 15 percent.

Although this suggests that the total value of the subsidy implicit in the BNDE loans was probably about 3–4 percent for the manufacturing sector as a whole, it is apparent that the ways credit was rationed led to different prices of capital to different users, and even to different capital costs of different projects for individual firms. Thus the discriminatory effects of credit rationing may have been marked.

It is perhaps noteworthy that the sectors financing the largest fraction of their investment from BNDE funds over the period 1967–69—metal products (55 percent), transport equipment (14 percent), and machinery and electrical equipment (12 percent)—were also among the sectors whose exports bulked large in the export drive of the late 1960s. In 1970, output of the metallurgy sector constituted 20 percent of manufactured exports, machinery and electrical equipment 14 percent, and transport equipment 4 percent. To what extent BNDE channeled its loanable funds toward export sectors or activities in support of the export promotion strategy is not known. What is clear is that the loans constituted a sizable subsidy to the recipients, and that their effects were clearly discriminatory within and between sectors.

There are also numerous phenomena in Brazil that affect labor costs. For example, provisions and restrictions concerning employee working conditions and compensation on night shifts have made multiple-shift operations more costly than they would otherwise be. There are also regulations affecting firms' ability to lay off or discharge workers. However, Carvalho and Haddad chose to focus upon two sets of government regulations in the labor market that are, in their judgment, potentially the largest source of labor market distortion.

First, they examined the effect of minimum wage regulations, which, if effective, would have had the largest influence upon employment of unskilled labor. In fact, examination of the data suggests that, over the late 1960s and early 1970s at any event, inflation was sufficiently rapid so that increases in the legal minimum wage were not effective: the real minimum wage was approximately constant over the period, while average real wages rose about 20 percent. Moreover, a very large fraction of workers earned considerably more than the minimum wage: in 1972, 44 percent of all workers earned more than 3.7 times the minimum wage, contrasted with only 14 percent in 1968. Although minimum wage legislation may have raised the cost of hiring unskilled workers in the mid-1960s, its effect had diminished sharply by the early 1970s.

However, a second form of distortion raising labor costs increased in importance during the 1960s and the 1970s: social security taxes. To be sure, if all firms are subject to the same rate of social security tax, then, in an otherwise perfectly functioning labor market, employee compensation would be relatively unaffected, with smaller take-home pay and higher fringe benefits (including, of course, the right to social security). Welfare losses would arise only to the extent that employees preferred greater pay in the present and less provision for retirement, or that the government was inefficient either in tax collection or in investment of the proceeds as contrasted with private firms offering pension rights. In fact, however, two circumstances served in Brazil to increase distortions: on one hand, not all firms were subject to the same legal rate of tax; on the other hand, there is a presumption that small-scale firms and activities in the informal sector (including self-employment) did not pay the tax.

The average rate of social security tax, as a proportion of wages, was 7.9 percent in 1945 and rose thereafter to a rate of 43.9 percent in 1971. It may have risen still further at later dates. In contrast to legal rates, the actual average paid for all manufacturing activities in 1970 was 27 percent, with some two-digit industries paying an effective rate of 22.8 percent and others paying as much as 29.7 percent.

The existence of the social security tax raised the cost of hiring labor to firms covered by it relative to the cost of labor to uncovered activities and also discriminated between manufacturing sectors on the basis of the rate of tax paid.

7.2.3 Chile

Corbo and Meller focused upon the effect of distortions introduced by the trade regime on the relative price of investment goods in Chile in the late 1960s. At that time, of course, the regime was oriented toward import substitution. However, there were no significant quantitative restrictions upon the import of investment goods, so that an estimate of the price distortion can be obtained by evaluating the degree to which the exchange rate was overvalued and to which the structure of protection favored import of capital equipment.

Using the estimated equilibrium exchange rate derived by Taylor and Bacha (1973), which was 30 percent above the official rate, and the ratio of the average effective exchange rate to that for capital goods (1.0543), Corbo and Meller estimated that with uniform pricing of all tradables the relative price of imported capital equipment would have been about 37 percent higher than it in fact was. Since importation was permitted without strict licensing, this estimate can be taken as indicative of the underpricing of (nonconstruction) investment goods attributable to the import substitution trade regime.

Corbo and Meller did not examine the effects, if any, of credit rationing, the tax structure, or labor market imperfections on the relative cost of using labor and capital.

7.2.4   Colombia

Thoumi's focus was on the early 1970s, by which time there was a crawling-peg exchange-rate system and overvaluation of the currency, if any, seems to have been fairly minimal. As was seen in table 3.3, the effective protection rate for imports of capital goods, 80 percent, was well above the 33 percent rate for consumer goods and the 15 percent rate for intermediate goods in 1969. It thus appears that, during the period on which Thoumi focused, Colombia's moderately export-oriented trade regime did not contain a significant identifiable distortion in the pricing of capital goods imports.[18]

Likewise, although there was strong minimum wage legislation and were fairly strict regulations on conditions under which workers could be laid off or terminated in the 1960s, by the 1970s the effect of the minimum wage legislation was much less, and other regulations had a considerably smaller effect on the labor market than was the case earlier. For Colombia, however, data on the characteristics of the labor force were not available with which to attempt to assess the remaining effects of these provisions.[19]

Thus, like Brazil, Colombia apparently had fairly strong incentives to use capital-intensive production methods in the 1960s, but these distortions were substantially reduced with the switch toward an export orientation in the 1970s.

7.2.5   Indonesia

There can be little doubt that, during the period of heavy emphasis on import substitution in the late 1950s and early 1960s, extreme overvaluation of the currency provided a strong incentive for using imported capital goods for those fortunate enough to obtain import licenses. With the reform of the trade regime in the late 1960s, however, this incentive was largely removed, both because the exchange rate was more realistically valued and because quantitative restrictions upon imports were largely removed. However, the structure of effective protection in Indonesia continued to provide a degree of discrimination in favor of imported capital equipment and against other imports. Pitt's estimates of ERPs for 1971 indicate that they were as low as 5.3 percent for nonelectrical machinery, 16.3 percent for electrical machinery, and 3.5 percent for railroad equipment. This compared with an average rate of 65 percent for all importables, and rates as high as 217 percent for radio, television, and communications equipment and 204 percent for motorcycles and bicycles. By the mid-1970s, outside the period covered by Pitt's work, credit subsidies, duty exemptions, and tax holidays for new investment further increased the attractiveness of capital-using techniques and industries.

Creation of new (productive) employment opportunities is an urgent policy problem in Indonesia because of the relatively rapid growth of the labor force. Until recently there have been few impediments to the functioning of the labor market. Minimum wage legislation was not enacted until 1975. Over the period covered by Pitt, he states that the available evidence indicates that "wage determination occurs in an undistorted labor market." (Pitt 1981, p. 193).

7.2.6   Ivory Coast

The Ivorian trade regime was generally outward-oriented and the exchange rate was fairly realistic during the period covered by Monson's data. The Ivorian case provides an interesting illustration of the ways the trade regime and other instruments of policy can be linked. A major instrument for encouraging economic activity, especially in the modern sector of the Ivorian economy, was the institution of a special legal status, priority firms, for activities so designated by the government. Firms with priority status were eligible for a number of special privileges that made the use of capital-intensive techniques cheaper than it would otherwise have been.

Significant interaction with the trade regime occurred in that (1) firms engaging in activities the government wished to encourage (exporting output from the modern sector, import substitution in consumer goods) were granted priority status, thereby using the domestic policy instrument to encourage favored trade activities; and (2) firms receiving priority status were generally granted greater protection by the trade regime than firms with common-law status. Thus, 78 percent of domestic value added in HOS exportable industries was produced by firms with priority status; 79 percent was the corresponding figure for import-competing HOS goods. The average rate of effective protection received by firms producing exportables with priority status was 58 percent, compared with only 9 percent received by common-law firms. Similarly, the average effective protection rate for priority import substitution firms was 105 percent, while common-law firms received an average of 62 percent.[20]

In addition to receiving greater protection, priority firms were generally subject to lower tax rates and also lower costs of borrowing. These circumstances were reflected in differences in costs for various categories of activities as reflected in the following ratios given by Monson:[21]

	Taxes to Gross Profits	Interest Payments to Debt
HOS exportables	.059	.049
HOS protected importables	.197	.067
All modern activities	.305	.038
Priority firms	.179	.038
All manufacturing firms	.307	.033

The real interest rate was not negative: inflation in the Ivory Coast averaged only about 3 percent annually in the 1960s and early 1970s. HOS-protected importables therefore paid an average real rate of interest of close to 4 percent, while the average manufacturing firm paid a real rate of interest of close to zero on borrowed funds. It appears that, for the Ivory Coast at least, differences in tax rates were probably quantitatively more important than differences in interest rates in determining after-tax profits.

One other aspect of the interaction between the trade regime and priority-firm privileges is of interest. That is, priority-firm status was used as an inducement to foreign investors. To some extent, greater capital intensity of foreign firms may be attributable, in the Ivorian situation, to the fact that their incentives to use capital-intensive techniques were greater than were the incentives offered to domestic firms.

The labor market also has a number of distinctive features that render an analysis of the degree of distortion particularly difficult. The Ivory Coast has higher real wages than neighboring countries, and it permits immigration from them. Simultaneously, many managerial and professional jobs are held by non-Africans, so that the wage structure at both the upper and lower ends of the wage and salary distribution is affected by supply conditions.

Monson identified the principal labor market distortion as arising from the system of minimum wages—separately established for different categories of workers—combined with the imposition of social insurance taxes equaling about 40 percent of base wages. For most categories of workers except the unskilled, actual wages were above the set minimum levels by a sufficient margin so that there is a strong presumption that the legislation was ineffective. For unskilled workers, however, the minimum wage plus social insurance charges on it exceeded the average wage (not subject to social insurance charges) in the informal sector by about 23 percent in the early 1970s. Since Ivorian workers in the unskilled categories had higher average wages than the migrant Africans in the same category, there is a presumption that, on one hand, the minimum wage legislation may have discouraged employment of African migrants and, on the other hand, that employers may have been able to hire those workers without paying social insurance charges. The average wage paid for unskilled migrant Africans was 8.7 thousand FCFA per month in 1971, compared with a minimum wage (not including the social insurance) of 10.1–11.5 thousand FCFA per month.

7.2.7   Pakistan

Guisinger's analysis of the effect of government policies upon capital costs pertains to the early to mid-1960s, a period during which policy was still heavily oriented toward import substitution. The Pakistani experience represents another example of interaction between the trade regime and domestic policies. On one hand, licenses to import capital goods carried a large scarcity premium and were allocated by the government to "priority" industries. These latter were generally large-scale manufacturing firms that generally were using more capital-intensive techniques than smaller firms within the same industries. Thus the scarcity premium emanating from an overvalued exchange rate was used as an instrument of policy to induce economic activity in desired lines. On the other hand, desiderata emanating from the trade status of various industries clearly influenced which industries and sectors were to receive priority designation. On average, it appears that firms engaged in import substitution activities were more likely to be accorded priority status than were their export-producing counterparts.

For the fiscal year 1959–60, Guisinger estimates that the equilibrium exchange rate was probably about Rs. 7.6 per dollar compared with an official rate of Rs 4.76. This amounted to about a 38 percent reduction in the cost of imported capital equipment as contrasted with a uniform rate. As can be seen from table 3.3, this discrimination through exchange-rate overvaluation was not significantly enhanced by low effective tariffs: in general, the effective tariffs on imported capital goods were relatively high, although exemptions and tariff reductions were once again accorded to priority firms, since each individual package was somewhat different from the others.

In addition to licensing of capital goods imports at an overvalued exchange rate, Pakistan had both tax measures and credit policies that further accentuated the degree to which users were faced with artificially low costs of capital equipment. Guisinger calculated the implicit value of these measures in 1959–60 to those fortunate enough to receive subsidized credit and tax privileges, on the simplifying assumption that interest payments were not subject to profits tax.[22] In Pakistan, firms able to secure loans were able to borrow at 5.74 percent. This contrasts with Guisinger's estimate that a realistic rate would have been about 15 percent. In the absence of any currency overvaluation, annual interest costs at 15 percent to finance an imported machine costing $21 abroad would have been Rs. 24. With a loan at 5.74 percent, this cost would have been reduced to Rs. 9.16. If, in addition, the importer could obtain the machine at the overvalued exchange rate, his carrying cost would decline to Rs. 5.7. Thus, overvaluation of the currency directly reduced user cost by 38 percent; artificially low interest charges alone would have reduced user costs by about 53 percent; the combination of overvaluation of the currency and low interest rates reduced user costs by 66 percent.

In addition, Guisinger calculated the value of accelerated depreciation provisions applied to taxes of favored firms in Pakistan. This measure was in large part a substitute for a tax holiday, frequently granted to starting firms. This is because accelerated depreciation provisions are worth nothing during the period of a tax holiday, and a tax holiday is worth less the higher the rate of permitted accelerated depreciation. Even so, had the exchange rate not been overvalued and had a realistic rate of interest been charged on borrowing, accelerated depreciation—permitting equipment to be written off over three years rather than over its economic life of sixteen years—would have reduced annual user cost by 45 percent. In the presence of credit rationing and overvaluation of the exchange rate, however, the incremental reduction in user cost was about 20 percent. Adding a tax holiday yielded a further small reduction in user cost. Taken all together, the subsidized exchange rate for capital goods imports, the availability of subsidized credit, provisions for tax holidays, and accelerated depreciation reduced annual user cost of imported capital equipment in Pakistan in 1959–60 by about 75 percent. Stated the other way around, eliminating these provisions would have increased the cost of capital virtually 300 percent. While these calculations represent orders of magnitude only, they are nonetheless indicative of the extent to which trade policies and domestic market interventions can interact to create large differentials between socially desirable policies and private incentives.

Guisinger proceeded to use estimates of the degree of currency overvaluation, interest rates, and tax schedules to estimate a time series of the ratio of the equilibrium rental rate on capital to the actual rate, where the equilibrium rate was defined as that which would have existed in the absence of those measures. According to his estimates, the ratio of the equilibrium rental to the market rental of capital stood at 3.62 in 1959–60 and rose as high as 4.34 in 1966–67. Thereafter it fell somewhat but still remained at 3.68 in 1971–72. With the Pakistani devaluation of 1972, the ratio dropped sharply to 1.27, where it remained until the end of his time series in 1974–75.

In Pakistan, large-scale firms generally had access to import licenses, credit at implicitly subsidized interest rates, and tax advantages. Small-scale firms were much more often forced to resort to the market, paying curb-market rates for their loans and buying domestic capital equipment or bonus vouchers to be able to import their equipment. Thus it appears that large-scale firms had an incentive to be substantially more capital-using than small-scale firms.

In contrast to the capital market until the 1970s, the Pakistani labor market appears to have been fairly distortion-free. Although a large informal sector coexisted side by side with large-scale industry and government employment, the available data, though fragmentary, do not suggest that workers with comparable characteristics had different earnings in the two sectors. Trade unions do not appear to have constituted a significant factor in wage determination, and real wages in the urban sector seem to have been influenced largely by shifts in supply (emanating partly from rising real wages in agriculture) and demand (reflecting in part the changing skill composition of the labor force), at least until the early 1970s.

In the early 1970s this situation may have begun to change, as the government began imposing minimum wage regulation and raising its own pay scales substantially. In 1971 and early 1972, for example, annual bonuses were made compulsory, and other fringe benefits (including profit sharing, life insurance, and medical benefits) were also mandated.

Thus, for the period covered by Guisinger's analysis of labor coefficients in various trade categories, Pakistan, like Indonesia (and South Korea), can probably best be regarded as having had fairly distortion-free labor markets. Whether the same conclusion would be valid at present is rather doubtful.

7.2.8 South Korea

Labor unions are not powerful in South Korea, and the government has not imposed any minimum wage or other regulations that significantly affected the determination of working conditions and remuneration during the course of the export-oriented strategy. To be sure, real wages rose dramatically, but this appears to have been the outcome of market forces with capital accumulation and rapidly rising demand for labor in the urban sector. Any distortions in the relative costs of using labor and capital lay in the capital market.

With her export orientation of the 1960s and 1970s, South Korea's exchange rate was fairly realistic, and there was little implicit subsidization of the use of capital goods through that route. However, a variety of policies designed to encourage exports had the side effect of rendering the purchase of imported capital goods relatively cheap for Korean exporters. Exporters were always permitted to import capital equipment duty-free for the production of exports. Over 70 percent of investment in machinery and equipment consisted of imported capital goods. The average rate of duties actually collected on imported machinery and equipment was generally about 5 percent, reflecting the predominance of exporters among investors and their tariff exemptions. Insofar as firms in a particular country are competing with firms overseas for international markets, it is arguable whether duties on capital equipment would or would not constitute a form of negative effective protection to the export industry. However, what is clear is that, compared with firms producing goods for the domestic market, exporters eligible for duty-free import of capital goods will have relatively lower cost of imported capital goods.[23] It should be noted that all foreign investment projects in South Korea were also eligible for duty-free import of capital goods after 1960.

Throughout the period of the export-oriented trade strategy (starting in 1960), exporters were always entitled to a higher depreciation allowance on their tax returns than were other firms. The magnitude of the increased allowance, and also its coverage, increased greatly in the 1970s.

Another major instrument used by the government to encourage exports was the allocation of credit, at below-market interest rates, to exporters. Hong estimates that the real rate of interest paid by those receiving credit allocations was 8 percent in 1962–66, 3 percent in 1967–71, and −6 percent in 1972–75.[24]

The majority of these credits were allocated to manufacturing firms producing for export. Hong estimates that the subsidy element implicit in these loans rose sharply after 1970, going from about 8 percent of net capital stock in 1969 to about 35 percent by 1975. In addition, the Bank of Korea allocated rights to domestic firms to borrow abroad. Since the international interest rate was below the domestic rate of inflation, a significant subsidy element was involved in those loans as well.[25] Hong estimates that the implicit subsidy entailed in foreign borrowing was about 6 percent of net capital stock in 1970 and rose to 11 percent in 1975.

Most of these implicit subsidies went to the manufacturing sector. Hong calculated the real rate of return to capital (including subsidy) for different sectors of the economy and found that for manufacturing it rose from about 12 percent in 1954–61 to 17 percent in the early 1960s, 26 percent in the late 1960s, and 27 percent in the early 1970s. This contrasted with a real economywide rate of return in all nonprimary sectors combined of about 15 percent for the period 1967–75. He concluded that "this striking increase implies that the use of large amounts of domestic and foreign borrowed capital at low interest rates has yielded extremely high rates of return on equity investment in Korean industries" (Hong 1981, p. 374).

Some puzzles remain with regard to the Korean case. The real wage rose rapidly during the period when low-interest loans were apparently an inducement to use capital-intensive techniques. Since there was relatively full employment, this implies that some other sector or sectors of the economy were facing higher capital costs than they otherwise would have incurred. But Hong's analysis does not extend into the question of which sectors were relatively capital-short. If there were such sectors, the argument must be made that under optimal capital pricing the real wage would have risen even faster than it in fact did during the early 1970s. That it already rose very rapidly lends some credence to the view that low capital costs may have constituted more a lump-sum subsidy, as discussed in section 7.1.2, than an incentive at the margin.

The point remains that, in the Korean case, and presumably in other instances where exchange rate overvaluation and import licensing cannot be used to confer protection upon industries the government wishes to encourage, domestic credit policies and credit rationing can have many of the same effects. To the extent that those means are used to encourage exporting industries, they are likely to reduce the costs for the exporting firms of employing capital-intensive techniques.

7.2.9 Thailand

Recall that the Thai economy's trade orientation was mildly toward import substitution in the early 1970s, although the exchange rate appears to have been set at a fairly realistic level. There were a number of domestic policies that influenced the cost of capital and rates of return to different firms, and these policies were undoubtedly directed toward firms in import substitution industries in lines deemed most desirable by the government. To that extent, domestic policies were utilized in support of the trade regime, although administrative decisions on these measures were taken largely ad hoc.

Within the trade regime itself, the fact that the exchange rate was fairly realistic removed any distortion arising from that source. However, duties on imported capital equipment were substantially lower than duties on other types of imports, and so on that account there was some discrimination in favor of the use of imported capital equipment. Akrasanee was unable to provide quantitative estimates of the magnitude of the differential in duties actually paid. However, he judged that, though some distortion was entailed, it was probably quantitatively rather small when contrasted to that in other countries.

Tax exemptions, and especially tax holidays for firms the government wished to encourage, appear to have been the largest single factor influencing the cost of capital in Thailand. Some industries, such as textiles, chemicals, iron and steel, and motor vehicles, were important recipients of these tax holidays in the early 1970s. The same firms that were eligible for duty-free import of capital goods were generally also entitled to the tax holiday privileges, again illustrating the link between domestic and trade policies.

Akrasanee did not provide any estimate of the quantitative importance of tax holidays or duty exemption. He did, however, note that credit rationing was not a significant factor in the Thai context. With relatively low rates of inflation, interest rates ranged from 10.5 percent for "big regular customers" to 14 percent for small-scale firms. He was unable to find any difference in bank treatment or loan terms according to industry or trade orientation.

No minimum wage legislation was introduced in Thailand until 1973, and there have been no other significant government interventions. Any labor market imperfections in the early 1970s therefore arose from the presence of unions or other private-sector phenomena.

Attempts to estimate earnings functions have been frustrated by the absence of data on the skill composition of the labor force in individual industries. Indeed, the only piece of information available that might be related to skill composition (aside from industry itself) was the male/female ratios among employees within each industry. Recognizing that the male/female variable might represent a proxy for skills, given the absence of any other variable, Akrasanee reported on work he and Chutikul had done in attempting to analyze wage determination in Thailand. They found considerable explanatory power in the male/female variable, and also in average firm size and unionization of the industry.

Because of data limitations, these results are suggestive only, and they indicate the need for further research. While the evidence suggests that unions and other factors may have had an influence on wage structure, that influence does not appear to be pronounced.

7.2.10 Tunisia

Tunisia's economy appears to have had as many factor market distortions as any other country covered in the project.[26] The cost of capital was affected by credit rationing, by other domestic measures, and by the trade regime. In general, capital goods imports were usually permitted, so that all who wished to import capital goods could do so at approximately the same price: there was no difference in price to different sectors.[27] The question then is: By how much was the exchange rate overvalued, and to what extent did the tariff differentiate between imports of capital goods and of other commodities? EERs for foods were estimated by Nabli to have been about 28 percent above those for industrial equipment, and consumer manufactures were subject to rates estimated to be about 18 percent higher. In addition, there were fewer quantitative restrictions on imports of capital equipment than there were for other categories.

Nabli estimated that the premium on import licenses for foods and manufactures of consumer goods was probably on the order of 25 percent. Combining these estimates with Blake's estimate, that currency overvaluation was on the order of 20–40 percent in 1969, Nabli concluded that 50 percent was probably the upper bound on the extent to which currency overvaluation and differential tariff (and licensing) treatment lowered the price of imported capital equipment. His own preferred estimate is that there was probably about a 30 percent implicit subsidy entailed in the price paid for imported capital equipment (Nabli 1981, pp. 467–68).

Interest rates in Tunisia were quite low, and Nabli estimates that the real interest rate paid by borrowers was never above 4 percent, compared with a "conservative" estimate that a realistic rate would have been at least 10 percent. Credit was therefore strictly rationed, and the details of the lending pattern clearly affected resource allocation and choice of capital intensity. Among the sectors that apparently had relatively favorable access to cheap loans in Tunisia, Nabli identified public-sector firms as the most favored recipients. Within the private sector, there was apparently considerable variability in access to credit, depending on "personal relations, nonmarket phenomena, and government policy" (Nabli 1981, p. 468). Nabli "conjectured" that large firms, on average, probably had somewhat better chances of obtaining loans than smaller firms.

Data on worker characteristics and earnings were better for Tunisia than for any other country covered by the project. Even here there were significant omissions, since no data on education, age, or experience variables were available. However, a breakdown was available of the labor force by industry, by skill category (skilled, unskilled, etc.), and by type of sector in which employed. Hoping that the skill categories would sufficiently reflect the "human capital" component of earnings, Nabli used regression analysis to assess the influence of other factors—size of employer, monopolistic versus nonmonopolistic sector, private versus public—on wages in Tunisia.

Here wage payments included a social insurance contribution, which constituted between 15 and 25 percent of compensation in the covered sectors. Two skill variables—the proportion of white-collar employees and the proportion of skilled and semiskilled workers—and a variable reflecting the proportion of female labor were used as explanatory variables, along with dummy variables reflecting structural characteristics of the industry. From the analysis, Nabli concluded that:

1. The skill composition of the labor force explains a significant part of interindustry wage differentials.

2. There is some evidence, though not very strong, that female labor is paid less than male labor, but it cannot be determined whether this is due to sex discrimination or male/female productivity and skill differences.

3. The labor market may be categorized in three ways.

a. The nonmonopolistic private component, exhibiting the smallest degree of distortions in the labor market, with the largest share of interindustry wage differentials explained by skill differentials.

b. The public sector, which exhibits a higher degree of wage variation that is not explainable by skills. The evidence is also that the public sector pays higher wages for unskilled labor.

c. The monopolistic private component, which exhibits a highly variable wage structure that is not explainable by skill differentials and that pays very high average wage rates. [Nabli 1981, pp. 466–67]

Thus, subject to the qualifications concerning data adequacy and reliability, the evidence for Tunisia suggests that the wage structure, although partly reflecting differences in workers' skills, also was significantly influenced by other factors. Industrial structure and the practices of the public sector appear to have been the most significant influence upon wage payments to workers, with unskilled workers receiving about 20 percent more than their earnings in the rest of the economy.

7.2.11   Uruguay

Uruguay's system of domestic and trade controls was so complex that quantifying the effect of their influence upon incentives for choice of capital intensity is impossible. It seems clear that the exchange rate was substantially overvalued, though the rate of inflation was so high that the degree of overvaluation differed from month to month. The situation appears to be similar to that in Argentina. Tariffs were exceptionally high for virtually all categories of imports, implying that capital goods imports were not permitted when domestically produced substitutes were available. Even for nonelectrical and electrical machinery, Bension and Caumont estimate that ERPs were 55 and 591 percent respectively. These figures, combined with knowledge about the degree of currency overvaluation, suggest that the effective price of capital goods to any given user depended very specifically on the extent to which the types of equipment he wished to purchase were produced domestically, the tariff rate to which he would be subject, and the date at which he wished to invest. Thus, while the trade regime undoubtedly affected the cost of capital equipment, no single quantitative characterization of it is possible.

Given the difficulty of collecting estimates of effective rates of protection and labor coefficients in Uruguay, it was not possible to analyze sources of differences in wage payments. A major difficulty was that, in the year for which data on nominal payments were available, 1968, the rate of inflation was over 60 percent. Consequently, a substantial part of differences in wage payments might have reflected nothing other than differences in timing of dates for nominal wage adjustments throughout the year.

7.3   Total Effect on Wage/Rental Ratios

It is always difficult to generalize from the experience of a limited number of countries, and it is more difficult here because several authors were unable to quantify some or all of the influences impinging upon labor and capital costs. Nonetheless, in light of the importance of the subject and the paucity of evidence available, it is worth attempting a preliminary assessment of the findings. The influence of the trade regime, domestic factors influencing capital costs, and labor market phenomena are considered in turn. Thereafter there is a preliminary assessment of their relative importance.

7.3.1   Trade Regime

Exchange rate overvaluation, coupled with the reluctance of policy-makers to tax imports of capital goods heavily, has been a significant factor in contributing to low capital costs under import substitution regimes. There are five countries where authors were able to estimate the order of magnitude involved under import substitution—Argentina, Brazil (in the 1950s), Chile, Pakistan, and Tunisia. In all cases the authors believed that currency overvaluation, combined with low rates of protection on imports of capital goods contrasted with tariffs on other commodities, led to significant undervaluation of imports of producer goods. In Chile and Tunisia, imports of capital goods appear to have been fairly freely permitted, whereas in Argentina and Pakistan licensing was an important component of the system. Interestingly enough, in all cases the authors' estimates of the order of magnitude of the subsidy from the trade regime implicit in the pricing of capital goods were in the range of 30–40 percent, by no means a negligible amount. It is likely that in Indonesia before 1965, and in Uruguay, orders of magnitude were no smaller, and they may have been larger. In the absence of controls over imports of capital goods through licensing procedures, the question remains of what sectors were discriminated against when importation of capital equipment was permitted at such overvalued exchange rates and low tariffs. It seems doubtful whether, in countries such as Chile and Tunisia, the ability to import capital goods at low prices was so frequently exercised that the volume of imported capital equipment exceeded what it would have been at a realistic exchange rate with uniform EERs for all transactions.

It seems reasonable to conclude, therefore, that overvalued exchange rates have, in many import substitution countries, provided greater-than-optimal incentives for importing capital goods. This result does not appear to have been an inevitable concomitant of the import substitution strategy. It came about because policymakers failed to impose sufficiently high duties on imports of capital equipment to offset the overvaluation of the currency. In that sense part of the low cost of capital equipment that has characterized import substitution regimes has not been an integral part of the strategy, but rather a by-product of the unwillingness or inability of the authorities to impose offsetting tariffs or other charges on importation of capital goods.

When it comes to export promotion, the picture is different. There the currency has been fairly realistically valued, so that little opportunity for undervaluation of capital goods has arisen. Rather, the experience has tended to be that domestic incentives, such as low-interest loans, are accorded to exporting industries.

7.3.2 Domestic Capital Costs

In contrast to trade regimes, under which import substitution countries have lowered costs of imported capital equipment more than export promotion countries, credit rationing, or at least provision of some low-interest loans, has been a feature of almost all.[28]

One or more forms of subsidy to the use of capital or imported capital equipment were found in all cases analyzed. The implicit subsidy involved appears to have been substantial, exceeding the estimated magnitude of cost reduction associated with currency overvaluation in some cases. Even in South Korea, interest subsidies appear to have become a distortionary element of some magnitude, especially in the late 1970s, after the period covered by Hong.

Two additional conclusions emerge. First, in many instances sizable reductions in the cost of using capital equipment were made for firms carrying out objectives associated with the trade regime. Thus the Ivory Coast's "priority industry" status, which did provide for access to loans at preferential rates and tax exemptions, was a means whereby the authorities could induce production of the types of commodities they wished. Likewise, Brazil's BNDE loans seem to have been destined largely for some of the sectors associated with her export promotion drive. These and other examples provide yet another strong indication that one cannot divorce analysis of the trade regime and its effects from consideration of conditions in domestic markets.

Second, low-interest loans and currency overvaluation are in many ways substitutes insofar as they affect the cost of using imported capital equipment. In some cases, such as in Pakistan, they interact to provide very large reductions in cost. In principle, however, either an overvalued exchange rate or availability of credit at below-market borrowing rates can provide strong incentives for use of capital-intensive techniques.

7.3.3 Labor Market Distortions

A first, and perhaps most important, conclusion to be drawn from evaluation of the individual country results is how little is known about conditions in labor markets in LDCs. In part this is because the data requirements for satisfactory analysis of these phenomena are inherently heavy, and definitive data sets are hard to come by. Nonetheless it is clear that further research on determinants of wage structure is called for, and that the results would substantially enhance our understanding of a number of important phenomena in developing countries.

A second conclusion, necessarily considerably more impressionistic than the first, also emerges. That is that the extent and magnitude of labor market distortions appears to be considerably smaller than might have been anticipated and that, in particular, mispricing of capital goods and capital services seems to be proportionately considerably larger than mispricing of labor and labor services.

The most frequently encountered intervention in labor markets that prevents competitive wage determination is the imposition of social insurance payments and other charges upon the employment of labor, which large firms in the formal sector are obliged to pay but those in the informal sector are able to avoid. That pattern appears to hold in Argentina, Brazil, Colombia, the Ivory Coast (in combination with minimum wage legislation), and perhaps Thailand. The same type of differential in unskilled wages arises in Tunisia between government enterprises and small-scale employers, in which the same factors play an important role.

At least until the early 1970s, the effect of these regulations appears to have been restricted to the formal sector and unskilled labor. If one is focusing upon the effect of alternative trade strategies upon employment, however, it is precisely the unskilled workers, and the ability of firms and industries using them intensively to compete on international markets, that must be the focus of analysis. It is perhaps noteworthy that both Brazil and Korea, during their periods of rapid export growth, had few interventions with wage determination and that, in the Brazilian case, those that existed appear to have diminished considerably in importance over the period. Likewise, the countries where there are sizable differences in labor coefficients according to trade categories—notably Indonesia, Pakistan, and Thailand to a lesser extent—are countries where there has not been, at least during the period covered by the analysis, any significant degree of intervention with wage determination for unskilled workers.

7.4   Conclusion: Total Size of Factor Cost Distortions

Again recalling that the estimates only indicate orders of magnitude and fail to convey the variability in costs across firms and industries, it is possible to attempt overall quantitative estimates. The evidence reviewed above can be assembled to provide estimates of the degree to which wage/rental ratios diverged from those that would have prevailed under well-functioning factor markets.

Table 7.1 provides the data, based on the preceding discussion. The numbers would have greater comparability if one could provide estimates of the variance of these cost-increasing and cost-reducing distortions, as well as their mean, but it is not possible to do so. The comparability across countries is therefore extremely limited. For example, Nogues estimated that the reduction in costs of capital owing to the trade regime in Argentina when all capital goods were imported was on the order of 40 percent—remarkably close to the estimates from Chile, Pakistan, and Tunisia (as well as Brazil in her import substitution period). However, for Argentine firms there was an offset in that domestically produced capital goods cost more than imported ones would have at equilibrium. Thus the average 8 percent figure calculated by Nogues represents what the net effect would be on a manufacturing firm employing imported and domestic capital goods in the proportions used by the sector as a whole. In reality there were undoubtedly firms importing almost all their capital equipment, and others relying almost entirely on domestic capital goods. Whether Argentina's 8 percent *average* increase in capital cost owing to the trade regime represents more or less of a distortion given the presence of the import substitution industries producing domestic capital goods than the 38 percent reduction in Pakistan, where almost all capital goods were imported (and where, therefore, the reduction was probably relatively uniform and across the board), is an open question.

Before we examine the data in table 7.1, one other preliminary comment is in order. That is, it is clear in theory that the presence of a distortion affects the wage/rental ratio in all sectors of the economy. If, for example, one sector has a tax imposed upon the utilization of a particular factor of production, the return to that factor of production and all others will be affected, both in the tax-affected sector and in the rest of the economy. It is well known that there are conditions under which raising the price of, for example, labor to a particular sector can lower the real wage to workers in both sectors.[29] In the empirical estimates that follow, no account is taken of this phenomenon, and it is assumed that the wage/rental ratio in the sectors not subject to any distortions is unaffected by their presence elsewhere in the economy. In a sense, the estimates of the magnitude of distortions presented here are really an estimate of the differential in relative factor prices between sectors subject to distortions and sectors not subject to distortions.

There are conditions under which such an estimate might also reflect the absolute deviation in the wage/rental ratio in the affected sectors contrasted to what the ratio would be in equilibrium, but those conditions are rather stringent. Suppose, for example, that capital were perfectly mobile internationally, so that the country under consideration faced a given rental rate for the use of capital services. If, further, there were an Arthur-Lewis-like perfectly elastic supply of labor for the affected industries (either because there were a large supply of rural workers willing to migrate to the cities or because the affected sectors were a small enough fraction of the entire economy), then the estimates would also reflect the degree to which distortions altered the wage/rental ratio for the affected sectors away from their general equilibrium level. In the context of the countries under study, those assumptions are undoubtedly too stringent. The degree to which the general equilibrium wage/rental ratio was affected by the distortions surely varied from country to country and over time.

Turning then to the data in table 7.1, it is apparent that labor market factors, the trade regime, credit rationing, and tax systems all contributed to raising the wage/rental ratio for firms subject to them. There is no single pattern of relative importance among these factors, however. Pakistan, which appears to have the highest degree of implicit subsidization to the use of capital-intensive techniques, has (or, more accurately, had) a relatively free labor market. Tunisia, by contrast, appears to have had factors leading to cost differentials of virtually all types, as did the Ivory Coast. Yet the rank order of the estimated magnitude of distortion seems to be independent of the number of different types of distortions identified. Thus Nogues was able to quantify labor market interventions of several types as well as trade regime and credit rationing influences upon capital costs. Yet his estimates for Argentina fall far below Nabli's estimates for Tunisia, where the same pattern of pervasive distortion seems to have existed.

What does seem clear, even from these impressionistic data, is that the exporting countries—Hong Kong, South Korea, Brazil, and to a lesser extent the Ivory Coast—had relatively lower levels of factor market distortions than did the import substitution countries, with the possible exception of Argentina. Even there, the Argentine data perhaps represent more of an average among highly subsidized and unsubsidized firms: Nogues estimated that, under certain assumptions, the wage/rental ratio in the modern sector might be as much as eight times that in the traditional sector.

A second conclusion probably not unrelated to the first is that currency overvaluation and favorable treatment of capital goods imports were potent sources of lowering the costs of capital utilization for firms eligible to import. For Argentina, Chile, Pakistan, and Tunisia, as well as Brazil in her import substitution days, this source of underpricing of capital goods was judged to be important.

Credit rationing at subsidized interest rates is estimated by Hong and Guisinger to have constituted a major source of underpricing of capital services. Finally, social insurance taxes have driven a wedge, again of about 20–30 percent, in the price of labor between firms and sectors subject to the taxes and other activities within the economy.

Each of these sources of pricing disparity between firms and sectors by itself could significantly have affected incentives, but together the effects may have been fairly powerful. All of them work in the same direction, to induce lower capital costs and higher labor costs than would be chosen at appropriate shadow prices.

Moreover, insofar as the factor proportions model of trade developed in chapter 4 explains comparative advantage, at least for HOS goods, one

Table 7.1   **Percentage Distortions in Labor and Capital Costs from Various Sources**

| Country | Period | Percentage Increase in Labor Costs | Percentage Reduction in Capital Costs Owing to | | | | Percentage Increase in Wage/Rental Ratio |
			Trade Regime	Credit Rationing	Other	Total	
Argentina	1973	15	8	9	n.a.	17	38
Brazil	1968	27	0	4	n.a.	4	31
Chile	1966–68	n.a.	37	n.a.	n.a.	n.a.	n.a.
Hong Kong	1973	0	0	0	0	0	0
Ivory Coast	1971	23	0	3[a]	12[a]	15	45
Pakistan	1961–64	0	38	53	10	76	316
South Korea	1969	0	0	8	2	10	11
Tunisia	1972	20	30	6	n.a.	36	87

Note: No quantitative estimates are available for Colombia, Indonesia, Thailand, or Uruguay.

[a]Estimates based on differentials given in Monson 1981, table 6.15 and are reproduced in section 7.2.6.

cannot help but question the extent to which distortions of the order of magnitude reported by the country authors may have "wiped out" whatever comparative advantage there may have been.

This, of course, raises a fundamental empirical question, about which there is little information to date. That is, How large are the differentials in "natural" wage/rental ratios that would be observed under an efficient allocation of world resources? If, in fact, Pakistan's optimal wage/rental ratio is one-fiftieth that of her major trading partners, then the circumstance that trade and domestic policies distorted that ratio by a factor of four need not have significantly adversely affected her potential pattern of commodity trade. If, on the other hand, the optimal wage/rental ratio in Pakistan were one-fifth that of her major trading partners, distortions of the order of magnitude estimated by Guisinger would have had a severe impact on the potential for gains from trade. Moreover, if there were "neighboring" countries in the chain of comparative advantage with fewer distortions in factor markets than Pakistan, one can again imagine that distortions within Pakistan could have adversely affected the scope for profitable (and economic) expansion of exports.

Of necessity, these questions must remain unanswered at this stage. One can estimate the extent to which distortions of the magnitude reported in the country studies might have affected factor proportions, and that is undertaken in chapter 8.

At this juncture two other observations are in order, although again qualifications must be made in view of the very limited data available. The first concerns the prevalence of "informal" markets and their relation to factor market imperfections, while the second focuses upon the link between wage distortions and the country authors' findings concerning the skill intensity of trade.

A frequent feature of developing countries' economies, as noted in chapter 2, is the presence of a sizable informal sector, which generally consists of small shopkeepers, service personnel, and even fabricating facilities that are generally de facto exempt from the social insurance taxes, sales taxes, and other regulations that govern economic activity among larger firms. Those small-scale activities are also generally less favored than large firms in access to low-interest loans and to import licenses, and factor proportions differ drastically between the two sectors of the economy within, as well as between, lines of economic activity. Evidence on the degree to which social insurance charges, and interventions in the capital and credit markets, can affect relative input costs certainly suggests that the sharp dichotomy between the behavior of the informal sector and that of the formal sector may itself be the outcome of distortions imposed by government policies. To the extent this is so, it would significantly affect analysis of developing countries and interpretation of observed factor price differentials.

The second conjecture—focusing upon skills—pertains to the frequency with which minimum wage legislation was observed but was deemed not to be effective, except perhaps for unskilled workers. In cases where minimum wage legislation is binding, there is likely to be a bias within the system toward hiring more highly skilled workers: if the wage must be paid anyway, and more-qualified workers are available, it will pay to substitute skill-using techniques for processes using unskilled labor. It may perhaps be coincidence, but the country findings regarding utilization of skilled labor seemed to yield much more pronounced differentials than did their results pertaining to unskilled labor. To the extent that wage determination for skilled workers was free of distortion, while that for unskilled workers was affected by minimum wage requirements, it is at least possible that the observed systematic differences between trade categories and skill intensity arose because of the clearer incentive signals confronting entrepreneurs in their choice of skill categories than in their intensity of utilization of unskilled labor. To the extent that wage differentials appropriately reflected the scarcity of skilled workers,[30] the comparative disadvantage of the project countries in skilled labor-intensive commodities might have been expected to show up more clearly than their comparative advantage in use of unskilled labor. While this must remain only a conjecture, it nonetheless suggests that minimum wage legislation may adversely affect employment of unskilled workers—precisely the group presumably being helped by it.

8   The Effect of Trade Strategies and Domestic Factor Market Distortions on Employment

The evidence presented in chapter 7 indicates that there are sizable factor market imperfections in some of the project countries. Knowledge that they are large, however, does in itself not tell us the effect these distortions have on labor coefficients and employment potential.

The task of this chapter is to analyze the influence of trade regime (product market) interventions and domestic factor market distortions on labor coefficients. The objective, of course, is to provide a rough estimate of the order of magnitude of the potential increase in the demand for labor, especially unskilled labor, that might arise under altered trade strategies and under altered factor market conditions.

8.1   Within-Strategy Inefficiencies

The labor coefficients for exporting and import-competing HOS industries reported in chapters 5 and 6 reflect the outcome of several influences: the "natural" factor intensity underlying comparative advantage; the domestic factor market incentives discussed in chapter 7; and the particular instruments chosen to promote the trade strategy in operation in each country.

Insofar as the trade strategy, through exchange rate overvaluation or other instruments, influences incentives to employ alternative techniques of production, that influence is reflected in the estimates provided in chapter 7. However, there is another route through which trade strategy influences labor coefficients: by affecting the composition of industries encouraged under a given regime. Empirically, the phenomenon is far

In revising this chapter, I benefited greatly from comments by members of the Workshop on Economic Development at the Center for Research on Economic Development at the University of Michigan.

more important under import substitution regimes than under export promotion: the height of protection accorded to different industries under import substitution varies considerably, and it is at least a plausible hypothesis that alternative structures of effective protection might result in labor coefficients associated with exporting and import-competing activities different from those reported in chapters 5 and 6.

In this section, concern is with the degree to which observed coefficients by trade category may have been influenced by elements of the protective structure. Two types of evidence are available: first, there are country authors' estimates of the association between the height of protection (both for exporting and import-competing industries) and the inferences that can be drawn from the variation in labor coefficients within trade categories as to the potential for greater labor utilization[1] within trade strategies; second, there is the evidence from countries that did alter their trade strategies as to the effect on observed coefficients of the change.

It should be noted first that there is a good basis for believing that any attempt to estimate the degree to which observed coefficients might be altered by improved resource allocation within existing trade regimes is likely to result in an underestimate of the "true" potential. To some extent this is indicated by the experience of countries that altered their trade strategies, discussed below. However, there are other reasons. To an unknown extent, choice and implementation of trade strategy and factor market distortions may interact to preclude the emergence of certain activities, and it is not possible to infer the potential of those "missing" activities. For example, Lipsey, Kravis, and Roldan's (1982) results demonstrate that the choice of location of activities by multinational corporations is influenced by the real wage rate prevailing in the host country. To the extent that some countries with relatively abundant labor nonetheless established and enforced high legal minimum wage levels, certain types of labor-intensive activities may not have been located in those countries, and instead developed elsewhere in the world, possibly even in countries with a higher capital/labor endowment but a lower real wage.

Likewise, Henderson's findings, discussed in more detail in section 8.3.2, show relatively broad-based comparative advantage for South Korea and Taiwan, contrasted with relatively narrowly based comparative advantage for some of the import substitution countries. What this suggests is that the coefficients and activities observed under import substitution may not at all reflect what would happen, either in import substitution or in exporting activities, under an alteration in trade strategy and domestic factor market structure. Stated in another way, using the existing HOS exportable activities observed under an import substitution regime as a guideline to indicate where comparative advantage lies for industrial exports may vastly understate the potential for improved efficiency of resource allocation among exportables. It is quite possible that some potential exportable activities do not even exist under an import substitution strategy, and that some activities that do export do so only because their major raison d'être is the incentives generated under an import substitution regime.

Bearing in mind that the estimates of within-regime inefficiencies probably understate the potential for gain through reallocation, we can turn to the evidence from the country studies. Focus is upon the potential effect upon average labor input coefficients for HOS exportables and import-competing industries that might have resulted under alternative incentives within existing trade strategies.

8.1.1 Variance in Levels of Protection

Data on the mean height of effective protection by the major categories of tradables are given in table 8.1.[2] As can be seen, not only was the level of protection different for import-competing and exportable activities, but there were sometimes large differences in rates of protection for different types of goods within the same category. For Indonesia, for example, the average level of effective protection for HOS import-competing goods was 66 percent, but it was 132 percent for those Pitt classified as protected, and − 14 percent for those deemed competitive.

The data in table 8.1 are only the beginning of the story. Within categories there was often wide variance, as was seen in chapter 3. For Chile, for example, Corbo and Meller calculated the range of ERPs for each category of tradables. For HOS exportables, the range of ERPs for export sale was − 23 to + 14 percent; for HOS import-competing goods sold domestically, it was − 15 to + 1,830 percent. Carvalho and Haddad estimated ERPs for Brazil for a variety of years. Among manufacturing industries in 1958, during the Brazilian import substitution period, ERPs ranged from 17 percent for pharmaceuticals and 22 percent for machinery to 281 for plastics and 387 percent for food products. In Tunisia, HOS exports had a mean rate of effective protection of 23 percent with a standard deviation of 44 percent, while HOS import-competing goods had a mean rate of protection of 300 percent and a standard deviation of 772 percent (Nabli 1981, table 10.6).[3] Uruguay's range was also large: even at a two-digit level, ERPs for goods produced for the domestic market ranged from 20 percent for leather and leather products to 689 percent for transport equipment and 1,014 percent for beverages, while for exports they ranged from 24 percent for leather products to 156 percent for primary metal products (Bension and Caumont 1981, table 11.7).

Table 8.1   Effective Rates of Protection by Trade Categories

Country	Year	Exportables			Importables		
		PCB-HOS	Other HOS	All HOS	Protected HOS	Competitive HOS	Total HOS
Argentina	1969	n.a.	−3	−3	n.a.	n.a.	130
Brazil		n.a.	n.a.	n.a.	n.a.	n.a.	n.a.
Chile	1967	n.a.	0	n.a.	n.a.	n.a.	267
Colombia	1969	n.a.	34	−17	n.a.	n.a.	n.a.
Indonesia	1971	n.a.	−11	n.a.	132	−13	66
Ivory Coast	1973	−40	35	−36	84	−21	13
Pakistan	1968	n.a.	n.a.	n.a.	n.a.	n.a.	n.a.
South Korea (manufacturing)		n.a.	5	n.a.	n.a.	n.a.	−9
Thailand	1973	−18	0	−10	69	25	53
Tunisia	1969	−13	−8	n.a.	n.a.	n.a.	90
Uruguay	1968	—	37	—	384	—	—

Sources: Argentina, Nogues 1980, table 2.3; all others, Krueger et al. 1981: Brazil, table 2.9; Chile, table 3.10; Colombia, table 4.4; Indonesia, table 5.11; Ivory Coast, table 6.10; South Korea, table 8.9; Thailand, table 9.9; Tunisia, table 10.6 (Blake's estimates); Uruguay, table 11.7.

8.1.2   Labor Coefficients by Level of Protection

A natural question therefore arises. Insofar as labor coefficients vary systematically with the level of protection and there existed opportunities within trade strategy to alter the mix of industries toward those with less protection, there presumably existed opportunities to increase international value added, employment, and real incomes for given levels of investment within the manufacturing sector by switching within a category to less-protected activities.

There were three countries for which authors provided estimates of the labor coefficients in their countries by height of protection.[4] The estimates are reproduced in table 8.2. As can be seen, in these cases there did appear to be a relationship. In Chile, exportables with ERPs above the median had average labor coefficients below those of import-competing industries. Within import-competing industries, less-protected activities had a labor coefficient about one-fourth larger than did activities with above-median levels of protection. For Indonesia the same pattern emerges for import-competing activities with below- and above-average levels of protection, although firms with average levels of protection had somewhat higher labor coefficients than firms with below average levels of protection. For the Ivory Coast, exportables' labor coefficients decreased as effective protection increased; for import-competing goods, however, below-average protection implied somewhat lower labor coefficients. This reflects in part the fact that part of the Ivory Coast's HOS import-competing industry is competing with other low-wage African countries. It is highly protected and, despite the labor coefficients, has a much higher capital/labor ratio than does production competing with imports from DCs. (See Monson 1981, pp. 266–67, and section 8.1.3.6 below.)

For Tunisia, Nabli attempted to evaluate the relationship between labor coefficients and ERPs by regression analysis. He computed a simple correlation coefficient between indicators of factor intensity and ERP estimates, excluding those with negative ERPs and those with ERPs over 400 percent. While there was no significant relationship for total labor inputs, there was evidence of negative association between unskilled labor intensity and the height of ERPs (Nabli 1981, p. 484). Reasoning that the weakness of the results might be attributable to the scaling procedure used, Nabli then classified activities into seven groups, according to their height of effective protection, and computed average labor employed per unit of DVA for each group. Again, results were stronger for unskilled labor: the average unskilled labor coefficient for the two groups with the lowest average effective protection (negative and less than 50 percent) was 37 percent greater than that for the two groups receiving the highest effective protection (Nabli 1981, pp. 460–61).

Table 8.2   Labor Coefficients by Level of Protection (Labor Units per Unit of DVA)

	Chile	Indo-nesia	Ivory Coast[b]
Exportables with ERPs			
Below median or average	91.98	—	2,695
Median or average	—	2,175	2,488
Above median or average	44.39	—	2,160
Import-competing industries with ERPs			
Below median or average	67.77	1,130	1,534
Median or average	—	1,326[a]	1,652
Above median or average	53.81	752	1,709

Sources: Krueger et al. 1981: Chile, table 3.17; Indonesia, table 5.19; Ivory Coast, table 6.13.

[a]This number refers to inputs with "medium" levels of protection.

[b]Numbers are total man-hours (management, skilled, unskilled, and artisanal) per million FCFAs, HOS activities only.

The same general pattern emerged in Thailand: Akrasanee regressed value added per employee (taken as a measure of capital intensity) on the rate of effective protection and found a significant positive association for direct, but not direct plus home goods, value added (Akrasanee 1981, p. 429).

8.1.3   Potential for Within-Strategy Gains

Thus there does appear to be evidence of a link between labor intensity and the height of effective protection within both exporting and import-competing industries among the countries covered. It remains to estimate how much potential there was for altering coefficients within strategy. This can best be done considering the evidence from each country in turn.

8.1.3.1   Argentina

Although there was considerable variation in ERPs and labor coefficients among import-competing industries, Nogues concluded that import substitution had proceeded so far in Argentina that there was little scope by the early 1970s for shifting activities within import-competing industries. On the export side, there was substantially greater potential, although the chief source of within-strategy variation appeared to be the labor intensity of exportables going to LAFTA, which was markedly less than that of exportables destined for developed countries. In general, Argentine HOS exports going to LAFTA originated from import-competing industries, and it did not appear that, given the strong protection accorded the domestic market, there was much potential for improved resource allocation and greater employment within the existing trade strategy.

8.1.3.2 Brazil

Data for Brazil are too aggregated to provide meaningful evidence on the within-strategy variance in labor coefficients. What is available and suggestive of the indiscriminate nature of incentives under the import substitution strategy is a comparison of trade levels and labor coefficients in 1959 and 1968–74. If one takes either 1959 or 1970 labor coefficients and applies them to actual HOS trade flows over the years, the results are striking. They are presented in table 8.3. The first two columns give the estimated average labor input per million cruzeiros of actual exports and imports on the basis of constant 1959 labor coefficients for each sector. The last two columns provide the same estimates based on 1970 labor coefficients. These data are based on the twenty-one-sector input-output table, and it is quite possible that further disaggregation might show somewhat different results. Nonetheless, the figures are instructive. Holding input coefficients constant, the changing composition of Brazilian exports over the period 1959–74 would have required a 70 percent increase in employment for the same value of exports, based on 1959 labor coefficients. Using 1970 coefficients, the estimate is even larger: about 83 percent. It will be recalled that the Brazilian government had begun altering trade strategies in the mid-1960s, and that the export boom began in 1968.

The data seem to indicate that the industrial composition of the import-competing industries (as reflected in the actual bundle of imports) changed little after the shift in trade strategies. The change in labor coefficients among exportables is sizable, and the estimated magnitude is

Table 8.3   **Brazilian Employment per Unit of Trade Implied by the 1959 and 1970 Labor Coefficients (1968 = 100)**

	1959 Labor Coefficients		1970 Labor Coefficients	
Year	Exports	Imports	Exports	Imports
1959	70.9	100.2	69.6	102.5
1968	100.0	100.0	100.0	100.0
1969	104.3	101.6	105.0	101.3
1970	106.2	102.2	107.5	101.9
1971	107.0	103.6	109.9	103.8
1972	112.8	104.8	117.4	105.7
1973	125.2	103.1	131.7	103.1
1974	120.4	90.0	127.3	90.6

Source: Data are from Carvalho and Haddad 1978, appendix tables A1, A5, A7, and A10.

remarkably similar regardless of whether 1959 or 1970 coefficients are used. This probably reflected a more rational allocation of resources among export industries, emanating from more uniform export incentives (as contrasted with the exporting from import substitution industries that had occurred earlier). With greater uniformity, there was a sizable increase in the labor intensity of exportables. If that interpretation is correct, it gives support to the suggestion offered above, that an observed difference at a point in time in labor-input coefficients between exportables and the import competing goods under import substitution regimes understates the potential difference.[5]

8.1.3.3   Chile

Chile is among the project countries whose trade regimes was biased toward import substitution throughout the period covered by Corbo and Meller. Differences in labor coefficients by level of protection were reported in table 8.2, and we saw that exportables with above-average protection were less labor-using than import-competing industries with below-average protection, thus attesting to the large variation within trade categories.

Further evidence comes from data that Corbo and Meller provide on labor coefficients per DVA for individual four-digit industries. These cover only the eight largest HOS exportable industries and the ten largest HOS import-competing industries. Even among HOS exportables, most either were directed to other LDCs (see Corbo and Meller 1981, table 3.12) or are related to resource availability, as with canning of fruits and vegetables, wine, sawmills, and pulp and paper. The range of labor coefficients among the eight HOS exportable industries is from 21.5 persons per million escudos of direct value added (for malt liquor and materials) to 121.2 persons for sawmills. For import-competing industries, the range is from 20.3 persons per direct DVA (motor vehicles) to 71.5 for structural metal products and 83 for repair of aircraft and aircraft parts (which is almost always an industry in which domestic production within the category does not correspond to imports).

The overlapping of these ranges is, of course, to be expected, and there is no strong suggestion of selectivity within either exports or import-competing HOS industries. This impression is reinforced by the results Corbo and Meller obtained when they regressed net imports for individual commodity groups at the four-digit ISIC levels against unskilled labor and capital coefficients. Although signs were as expected and the coefficients significant for skilled labor (positive) and unskilled labor (negative), the explanatory power of these variables was not high: R^2s ranged from .33 to .39 (see Corbo and Meller 1981, table 3.18), thus further suggesting high variance in factor proportions among both export and import-competing industries.

8.1.3.4   Colombia

Among the most convincing pieces of evidence about the wide variance in activities induced by an import substitution regime was Thoumi's careful examination of the industries that changed trade categories in Colombia between 1970 and 1973. Recall that Colombia switched trade strategies in the late 1960s, removing much of the bias for selling in the home market. There is reason to believe that in 1970 the pattern of output still largely reflected the earlier incentive structure and that, during the next several years, the composition of output and trade was shifting in line with comparative advantage as the new incentives induced producers to alter their production patterns. Excluding food and tobacco, there were six industries that had been import-competing and became exporting industries by 1973. The unweighted average labor coefficient for those six industries was 32.9. By contrast there were four industries that had been exporting in 1970 and were classified as import-competing by 1973. Their average labor coefficient was 11.3, although the number of industries was smaller and the reliability of that coefficient is open to question.

That examination of the 1970 trade pattern shows some import-competing industries with relatively high labor coefficients and others with very low ones, relative to what occurred with a realignment of incentives, is strong evidence that the Colombian import substitution strategy had encouraged import-competing industries without great selectivity. This suggests that, if it had been possible under import substitution to channel more resources into those relatively more labor-using industries, the employment implications of the import substitution strategy would have been less unfavorable than they in fact were. That such a move would also have improved resource allocation is suggested by Thoumi's examination of the effective protection rates associated with the industries that switched classifications: industries that became exports by 1973 had an effective protective rate of 11 percent (contrasted with 19 percent for all manufacturing), while industries that turned from exporting to import-competing had an average effective protective rate of 16 percent. It would be of great interest to trace Colombia's shifting pattern of trade after 1973 as her realigned trade strategy continued to pull resources in new directions. And, though the data do not permit a diagnosis of the extent to which the export strategy induced a greater uniformity in input coefficients across sectors, they strongly indicate that the pattern of trade induced under the import substitution regime had considerably greater variance in input coefficients than an alternate pattern might have had.

One can infer the resulting shift in the ratio of labor coefficients in exportable and import-competing industries from the following line of reasoning. Thoumi estimated that the number of workers per million 1970 pesos of direct value added for all HOS exports rose from 23.8 in

1970 to 29.1 in 1973, or 22 percent; if sugar, petrochemicals, and jewelry are excluded, the increase was from 28.6 to 35.5, or 24 percent. There is no indication of the corresponding change for import-competing goods. If the shift was of approximately the same order of magnitude (toward greater capital intensity of import-competing activities because the labor-using among them became exportable industries), there would have been a 25 percent increase in capital intensity in import-competing industries owing to their changing composition. The Brazilian evidence, however, suggests that the effect may be substantially smaller on the import side than on the export side, and so a figure of 10 percent seems more plausible. Using that estimate, the implied capital intensity of import-competing industries in 1970 would have been 14.00 (calculated by taking the 1973 ratio of labor coefficients, 1.88, to infer a 1973 coefficient for import-competing industries of 15.39 and multiplying that by 0.9). This estimate implies a labor coefficient for exportable industries in 1970 relative to that of import-competing industries of about 1.7, compared with 1.88 in 1973.

One further point should be stressed. Not only did Colombia's import substitution industries in 1970 consist of a mix of labor-intensive and capital-intensive activities, but those few industries that were exporting encompassed a similar range of factor uses. Thus, while it is possible to conclude that import substitution more discriminately carried out might have resulted in both more output (valued at international prices) and a greater demand for labor, it also follows that the same sort of rationalization might have occurred among the HOS exporting industries, as is evidenced by the realignment of industries traced by Thoumi over the next several years. What is not clear from Thoumi's data, or from other available evidence with regard to other countries, is the cause of the indiscriminate pattern that appears among exporting industries. It may have resulted from incentives within the trade regime or instead may have been a function of domestic policies that reduced the costs of using capital and thus made capital-intensive activities more profitable. It seems clear that both influences—especially currency overvaluation associated with the trade regime itself and domestic policies making credit available at implicitly subsidized interest rates—played a role. It is not, however, possible to evaluate their relative importance.

8.1.3.5   Indonesia

Pitt estimated that man-days per million rupiahs of DVA were 2,175 for HOS exportables and 1,038 for HOS import-competing activities (Pitt 1981, table 5.19). There was, however, sizable variance in labor coefficients according to the height of protection (see table 8.2). Skill and capital utilization per man-day were also higher among highly protected industries: skill-days per man-day for the import substitution group with relatively low protection were 1.08, while for the highly protected group the corresponding figure was 2.60. Energy expenditures per man-day showed a similar pattern: 72.43 rupiahs per man-day for import substitution activities with below-average protection and 120.8 per man-day with above-average protection (contrasted with 20.5 in exportable industries).

These data suggest that there was probably considerable scope for increasing value added (at international prices) and employment within the import substitution sector: if capital, as reflected in energy utilization, was the binding constraint upon the size of the import substitution sector, employment could have increased about 66 percent within import substitution industries if resources had all flowed into the less-protected sectors. If, instead, skill availability was the constraint, the potential increase would have been even larger. To be sure, a shift of resources toward exporting industries at the coefficients reported by Pitt could have generated an even larger increase in IVA and employment for the same capital or skill constraint. Nonetheless, it seems clear that there was scope for improved resource allocation within import substitution industries in Indonesia, which might have permitted substantially more rapid growth of employment within the urban sector than in fact occurred.

There was not much variability among Indonesian HOS exportables, however. It thus appears that in the Indonesian case rational resource allocation within import substitution sectors might have reduced the differential in the labor coefficients between exportable and import-competing industries.

8.1.3.6 Ivory Coast

Labor coefficients for firms with above- and below-average protection were reported in table 8.2. As can be seen, there appears to be somewhat less divergence within exportables and import-competing industries than in other countries. Monson concluded that this was largely because whatever incentives there were—priority firm status with the built-in bias toward capital-intensive techniques, low-interest loans, and the like— were provided to firms regardless of their trade status.

Monson uncovered one source of considerable variance in factor proportions among import substitution industries: import substitution industries competing with imports from other developing countries received higher protection than did imports competing with imports from developed countries and used markedly different factor proportions. Priority firms competing with imports from LDCs produced 89 percent of DVA in those activities and had a capital/labor ratio of 3,824 FCFA per man-hour contrasted with priority firms competing with imports from DCs, whose average capital/labor ratio was 1,522 (see Monson 1981, table 6.14).

Monson noted that policies to encourage import substitution in industries competing with LDC imports had really begun in the early 1970s, and that they therefore constituted a relatively small part of total domestic import substitution activities in 1972, the year covered in his study. Encouragement of industries competing with LDC imports within the import substitution sector would entail much higher costs, and reduced scope for additional employment, than would policies that tended to provide incentives for the relatively lower-cost import substitution activities. Indeed, if the incremental capital stock were the binding constraint upon expansion of value added and employment in Ivorian manufacturing sectors, and if Monson's estimates correctly reflect the disparity in the capital/labor ratios between the two sets of import-competing industries, encouragement of import-competing activities with LDCs would permit only 40 percent the expansion of employment, and about 57 percent the increase in international value added (calculated on the basis of effective protective rates given in Monson's table 6.13), that expansion activities competing with DC imports would provide. Although the size of the activities competing with imports from LDCs was not large in 1972, there is reason to believe that it may have grown since, and that the losses in employment (and foregone IVA) resulting from that policy may be sizable.[6]

8.1.3.7 Pakistan

The Pakistani economy provides an excellent illustration of how complex the interactions between domestic and trade variables can be. Table 8.4 presents data on labor coefficients within individual industries in relation to the import substitution strategy. The first column gives the effective rates of protection prevailing in 1970–71. The next three columns give the range of labor coefficients, including the mean, high, and low coefficients found in firms within the industry. The final three columns give the average labor coefficients within the industries depending on size of firm.

As can be seen, the strongest pattern that emerges is that small-scale firms have higher labor utilization rates than large firms, though there is wide variability among categories. For example, large and small firms in the basic metals sector have almost identical coefficients, while medium-sized firms have a labor coefficient only about one-eighth that of the other firms.[7] That small firms in Pakistan are significantly more labor-using probably reflects in substantial part the existence of the informal sector discussed in chapter 2.

For purposes of analyzing within-strategy inefficiencies, these data raise numerous troublesome questions. A trade strategy that encourages the expansion of small-scale firms would undoubtedly have a larger positive influence on the demand for labor than a trade strategy that encouraged expansion of large-scale firms in the same industry to create the same additional domestic value added. However, there is little hard evidence directly identifying the size of firms that would expand under

Table 8.4   Variability in Labor Coefficients in Pakistan by Industry Subgroups and Firm Size, 1969–70, and ERPs

| | | Man-Years per Million Rupees of DVA | | | | | |
| | | Range within Industry Subgroups | | | Labor Coefficient by Size of Establishment | | |
Industry	ERP 1970–71	Mean	High	Low	Small	Medium	Large
Food and beverages	130%	62	91	29	127	57	54
Cotton textiles	172	122	274	122	184	171	111
Footwear	n.a.	113	244	85	307	236	91
Paper and paper products	177	101	102	100	248	170	82
Printing and publishing	36	124	271	110	198	131	109
Leather and leather products	177	79	84	30	126	25	58
Rubber and rubber products	132	62	299	20	434	168	39
Industrial chemicals	106	63	95	15	229	64	31
Basic metals	220	119	240	117	124	17	126
Metal products	235	207	538	115	296	157	205
Electrical machinery	192	101	242	45	286	86	98
Nonelectrical machinery	188%	222	473	189	279	208	209

Source: Guisinger 1981, tables 7.9 and 7.11.
Note: ERP for food and beverages is that for edible oils.

either strategy. Import substitution firms may on average be of larger size than exporting firms within a country. An offsetting factor, however, would arise if exports originated in the larger firms within potential export industries.[8]

Given the wide variation in labor coefficients within industries, it is difficult to estimate the degree to which within-strategy efficiency gains (as reflected by shifting resources toward industries with lower ERPs) might be realized in Pakistan. There is not even a strong pattern of association between the height of effective protection and the degree of labor utilization.

8.1.3.8   South Korea

As seen in chapter 3, South Korea's pattern of protection after 1960 was based largely on a commodity's trade status: the same industry was subject to different levels of protection depending on whether the product was destined for export or for sale in the domestic market. Thus, encouragement appears to have been based upon prospective export performance, which meant that incentives for exporting were relatively uniform for different industries.

This incentive pattern appears to have resulted in improved efficiency of resource allocation. This can be seen from Henderson's results based on the Korean input-output tables for 1966, 1970, and 1973. The first year, 1966, was fairly early in South Korea's transition to an export-oriented economy, whereas by 1973 the export orientation of the economy was well established.

Henderson computed "g_j" coefficients for each activity, reflecting the degree to which international value added would be altered with expansion of the activity by one unit (a negative g_j therefore reflects the finding that the activity was, at the margin, uneconomic and that international value added would increase if the activity contracted and the resources were reallocated elsewhere). A rough measure of the efficiency of resource allocation can be taken to be the mean absolue value of the g_js.[9]

Henderson's results show that the developed countries had mean absolute g_js of about .1, whereas most of the developing countries included in his computations had g_js of more than .3. South Korea was an exception. The figure for 1966 was already .19, and by 1973 it had fallen still further, to .15. It is unfortunate that the comparable data are not available for Korea in the 1950s. If the efficiency of resource allocation under import substitution in that country was similar to that of the LDCs for which Henderson did have data, and the mean g_j was more than .3 in the earlier period, it would suggest a substantial improvement in resource allocation, within both exportable and import-competing industries, resulting from the alteration in trade strategy.[10]

Table 8.5   Labor Coefficients for Manufacturing Industries
within Trade Categories, Thailand 1973
(Direct Labor Inputs per Million Baht of DVA)

Trade Category	Lowest	Median	Highest
Protected import-competing	4.9	21.6	89.3
Competitive import-competing	5.3	41.9	118.2
Noncompeting imports	10.7	34.9	61.8
PCB-HOS exports	8.8	19.0	86.5
Other HOS exports	14.4	32.2	80.2

Source: Akrasanee 1981, table 9.12.

8.1.3.9 Thailand

Thailand appears to have had above-average variation in input proportions within trade categories. Table 8.5 provides data on the labor input per million baht of DVA according to trade categories, with industries recording the highest, lowest, and median labor inputs. As can be seen, the range within each category is enormous: the industry with the highest labor input had more than 22 times as high a coefficient as the lowest among protected import-competing industries, and for competitive import-competing industries the spread was almost as great. For PCB exports, the range was from 8.8 to 86.5, and even for HOS exports it was from 14.4 to 80.2. Thus, in Thailand's case, it appears that wide variation within sectors was at least as significant in affecting the growth of employment opportunities as was any overall bias of the regime. These differences were also reflected in wide ranges of effective protection rates within, as well as between, categories of tradables (see Akrasanee 1981, tables 9.8, 9.9, and 9.10). Clearly there was considerable scope for improving resource allocation within both exportable and import-competing industries.

8.1.3.10 Tunisia

The indiscriminate nature of import substitution in Tunisia prompted Nabli to estimate the order of magnitude of potential gains in employment and output, for the actual investment that took place, that might have been achieved under a more selective import substitution strategy. Nabli started by identifying relatively labor-intensive import substitution industries where imports were still entering the country. He then estimated the expansion in output that could have occurred at existing prices to replace imports and identified some capital-intensive industries that might have contracted. This would have released some capital, but the value of output at domestic prices would have been unaltered while employment would have increased. He then investigated the scope for additional import substitution in industries identified as relatively labor intensive in the rest of the world but for which Tunisia had very low levels of production or had not started the industry, and he examined the scale on which they could have operated with the capital released from the capital-intensive import substitution industries.

Nabli found that domestic value added in import-competing industries could have increased by about 40 percent, while total employment in those industries could have been augmented by 51.5 percent. The increase in employment of unskilled labor would have been even greater—58 percent.

8.1.3.11 Uruguay

The Uruguayan system was characterized by such detailed controls that wide variation was inevitable. This was reflected in a very wide range of ERPs for import-competing goods (import licenses were generally not issued for goods that could be produced domestically) and also for exportables. ERPs for products sold on the home market exceeded 500 percent for beverages, footwear, paper and paper products, rubber products, nonmetallic mineral products, electrical machinery, transport equipment, and miscellaneous manufacturing. By contrast, they were less than 100 percent for printing and publishing, leather and leather products, and nonelectrical machinery. For export, EERs exceeded 50 percent for beverages, footwear, wood and cork products, rubber products, primary metals, nonelectrical machinery, and miscellaneous manufacturing.

Such large divergences in rates of protection were reflected in wide variations in labor and capital coefficients. For export industries, the number of persons employed per million dollars of DVA ranged from 218 (tires) to 1,615 (for wool spinning and weaving), averaging 366. Differences in utilization of unskilled labor were even larger, ranging from 15 persons per million dollars of DVA in the tires sector to 472 in fish preserving. Similarly, electricity utilization per million dollars of DVA ranged from 469 (fish preserving) to 5,498 for cement, averaging 1,483 among the eleven largest HOS export industries. The range of capital/labor ratios (as reflected in electricity utilization per worker) was from 0.55 thousand kilowatts per worker (in wool spinning and weaving) to 26.06 thousand kilowatts per worker in cement production, with an average of 4.06 for the eleven major exportable HOS industries.

The range among Uruguayan import-competing industries was similar. Labor per million dollars of DVA ranged from 34 (tobacco products) to 373 in metal products, averaging 238. Capital utilization ranged from 86 in tobacco products to 5,150 in industrial chemicals, with a consequent range of thousands of kilowatts used per worker from 1.20 in pharmaceuticals to 22.0 in industrial chemicals, with an average of 4.88.[11]

Although the labor per unit of DVA was greater in exportables than in import-competing production on average, there are two of the ten ex-portable industries whose labor coefficients were below the average of the import-competing sectors, and one import-competing industry whose labor coefficient exceeded the average of the exportable sectors. More-over, if one sorts Uruguayan exportable industries by their destination (between DC and LDC), the difference in factor proportions is striking. Cement was the largest export to other LDCs and had the highest capital/labor ratio of any of the twenty major industries enumerated by Bension and Caumont. Wool spinning and weaving was the largest industry in terms of HOS exports to developed countries, and it had the lowest capital/labor ratio. Thus a switch of a million dollars of DVA from exporting to LDCs to DCs would have implied a reduction of 85 percent in electricity utilization, and an increase of more than sixfold in employ-ment per million dollars of DVA. Within import-competing industries, the same divergences existed. Without data on the size of the domestic market, it is impossible to ascertain the magnitude of reallocation of resource within import-competing sectors that would have been feasible within an export substitution strategy.

8.2 Substitution Possibilities

That the relative costs of employing the services of labor and capital diverged from their opportunity costs undoubtedly influenced choices of techniques and hence resulted in different labor coefficients than might have been observed under regimes with no factor market imperfections. The magnitude by which relative factor costs may have differed from their shadow prices was estimated in chapter 7. Here the purpose is to employ those estimates to indicate the order of magnitude by which labor coefficients might have been greater under alternative incentives.

For Argentina, Brazil, and Chile, country authors themselves esti-mated that extent to which factor market imperfections affected the choice of technique. For those countries, the authors' estimates are reviewed first. For other countries where there is an indication of the extent to which factor prices may have diverged from opportunity costs, the estimates of the magnitude of price differentials given in chapter 7 are employed, along with Behrman's estimates of the elasticity of substitu-tion, to indicate the extent to which techniques might have altered in the absence of factor market imperfections.

8.2.1 Argentina

Nogues (1980) first considered the effects of removing distortions introduced by interventions in the labor and financial markets, then estimated the effects of also eliminating the influence of the trade regime on the price of capital goods. His results are presented in table 8.6. The first column gives his estimates of the percentage increase in labor coef-

Table 8.6   Potential Effect of Removing Factor Market Distortions on
                   Labor/DVA Ratios in Argentine Manufacturing Industries

	Percentage Increase in L/DVA Resulting from Removal of Distortions in Labor and Financial[a] Markets under	
Industry Category	Protection	Free Trade
Exportables	25.1	18.9
Import-competing	18.5	10.0
With DC	20.8	11.4
With LDCs	23.0	12.1
Other import-competing	23.0	4.1
Total manufacturing	19.0	12.6

Source: Abridged from Nogues 1980, table 3.12.
[a]Assuming: (1) loans granted for ten years; (2) repayable in equal annual installments; (3) real interest rate of −9 percent and opportunity cost of 10 percent.

ficients that might result from removal of labor and financial distortions. As can be seen, for Argentine manufacturing production of tradable goods, Nogues estimated that the labor input per unit of value added might have increased 19 percent. He noted that removing these distortions would not have altered the ranking of industries by factor intensity. When Nogues assumed, in addition, that capital goods prices would be determined under free trade at an equilibrium exchange rate, the estimated total increase in labor utilization declines. This is because of the high proportion of (highly protected) capital goods that are domestically supplied, so that, at free trade, the price of capital goods would be relatively lower. Nonetheless, the combined effect of labor, financial, and trade market interventions has been to encourage the use of capital and discourage the use of labor-intensive techniques, as is reflected in Nogues's estimate that manufacturing employment might have increased 13 percent for the same composition of domestic value added, had firms maximized at prices more closely reflecting opportunity costs of factors of production. To be sure, it is questionable whether the supply of labor to the Argentine manufacturing sector is sufficiently elastic so that a 13 percent increase in demand for labor could be met without an increase in the real wage. The estimates serve to indicate, however, that the effect of factor market distortions may have been sizable.

8.2.2   Brazil

Carvalho and Haddad found that, even in the late 1960s, there was probably still a 30 percent differential between the relative cost of employing labor and capital in the organized sector and in the informal sector, which was not receiving BNDE loans or subject to social insurance taxes. Since these estimates make no allowance for differentials between sectors in severance pay provisions and other fringe benefits, or in minimum wage legislation,[12] it seems clear that even for the late 1960s they understated the amount by which incentives to employ capital were excessive at the height of the import substitution years.

Carvalho and Haddad used estimates of elasticities of substitution provided by earlier work of Macedo (1974) and combined those estimates with plausible values of supply elasticities for capital and labor to attempt to ascertain the effect on factor proportions. Table 8.7 summarizes their results. Column 1 gives the actual number of man-years of employment associated with a million cruzeiros of production in 1970 for each major manufacturing sector. Columns 2 and 3 then give estimates of the incremental employment per million cruzeiros that would have resulted if the social security taxes and the implicit subsidies to capital had been removed and if the elasticity of supply of labor had been infinite. In other words, the estimates of the second and third columns correspond to the case where manufacturing industries could have employed all the additional labor they demanded with no change in the wage (beyond that which would have arisen because of the removal of the social insurance charges). Column 4 then gives the total increments in man-years per million cruzeiros of output if both distortions had been removed. For all manufacturing industries, the unweighted average increase in the labor coefficient would have been about 15 percent on these assumptions.[13]

Carvalho and Haddad also provided estimates of what the effect would have been on employment if the true elasticities of the labor supply and of capital were as indicated above columns 6 and 7. To be sure, a less than perfectly elastic labor supply would have resulted in an increase in the wage in response to the removal of capital subsidies and social insurance taxes. Even after allowing for those phenomena, the increase in manufacturing employment in Brazil would have remained substantial: with an elasticity of the labor supply of unity, an elasticity of supply of capital of unity would have implied an increase in the average labor coefficient of about 8 percent, whereas an elasticity of capital supply of 2 would have implied an increase of about 6.4 percent. To be sure, the magnitude of the effects varies across sectors: tobacco products is estimated to have an increased labor coefficient (in the case of perfectly elastic labor supply) of about 30 percent, while pharmaceuticals has a 25 percent increase in labor input per unit of output. Rubber products, transport equipment, and metal products also show increases of more than 18 percent. By contrast, textiles' labor coefficient rises by 11 percent, and several other sectors also have increments well below 15 percent.

It should also be noted that a change in relative input prices would affect costs of labor and capital-intensive industries somewhat differently. If the social insurance taxes were removed, the relative cost of producing the more labor-intensive goods would fall. That being the case,

Table 8.7 **Effect of Social Insurance Taxes on Employment in Brazil (Direct and Indirect Man-Years per Million 1970 Cruzeiros of Output)**

| Sector | Actual in 1970 (1) | Increment with Elimination of | | | Total (1)+(4) (5) | Total with $\epsilon_L=\epsilon_K=1$ (6) | Total with $\epsilon_L=1,\epsilon_K=2$ (7) |
		Social Security (2)	Subsidies to Capital (3)	Both (2)+(3) (4)			
Nonmetallic minerals	67.5	8.1	.8	8.8	76.3	72.1	71.4
Metal products	29.1	3.8	1.6	5.4	34.5	32.5	32.2
Machinery	42.3	5.4	.5	5.9	48.2	45.4	44.9
Electrical machinery	33.5	4.6	.5	5.1	38.6	36.2	35.9
Transport equipment	28.8	4.7	.5	5.2	34.0	31.7	31.4
Wood products	89.6	11.5	.9	12.4	102.0	95.4	94.3
Furniture	81.6	8.0	.6	8.6	90.2	85.6	84.8
Paper products	35.0	4.7	.3	5.0	40.0	37.6	37.2
Rubber products	25.2	4.6	.4	5.0	30.2	27.9	27.5
Leather products	61.7	7.0	.6	7.6	69.3	65.6	64.9
Chemicals	12.0	1.5	.1	1.6	13.6	12.8	12.7
Pharmaceuticals	16.7	3.9	.3	4.2	20.9	19.2	18.8
Perfumery	18.4	3.2	.3	3.5	21.9	20.3	20.0
Plastics	18.7	3.7	.3	4.0	22.7	21.0	20.7
Textiles	52.7	5.5	.4	5.9	58.6	55.8	55.4
Clothing/footwear	89.9	11.9	.9	12.8	102.7	96.0	94.9
Food	26.5	4.7	.3	5.0	31.5	29.4	29.0
Beverages	36.5	6.8	.5	7.3	43.8	40.6	40.1
Tobacco	14.4	4.2	.3	4.5	18.9	17.1	16.8
Publishing	48.5	5.3	.4	5.7	54.2	51.0	50.4
Miscellaneous	48.5	5.4	.4	5.7	54.3	51.4	50.9
Average	41.8	5.6	.5	6.1	47.9	45.0	44.5

Source: Carvalho and Haddad 1981, tables 2.20, 2.22.   *Note:* Figures may not sum to totals shown owing to rounding.

the competitive position of some of the labor-intensive items might have improved. Thus the Carvalho-Haddad estimates probably represent something of a lower bound of the effect that distortions must have had on manufacturing employment, both because of the omissions noted above from the list of labor and capital market interventions, and because quantification of the average shift in labor coefficients fails to take into account the shifting composition of output that might result from realignment of relative factor prices.[14]

8.2.3   Chile

Corbo and Meller assessed the influence of the implicit subsidization of capital goods imports on the choice of techniques within various industries. Using their estimated production functions (see Corbo and Meller 1982), they simulated what would have happened had the exchange rate been at its equilibrium level (i.e., the relative price of tradable goods increased 30 percent with respect to home goods) and the favorable treatment of capital goods imports had been eliminated (i.e., had the relative price of capital goods imports contrasted with other tradables increased by 5 percent).[15] Their estimates are reproduced in table 8.8, based on the assumption that the commodity composition of trade would have been unaffected by the removal of the distortion in the pricing of capital goods imports. Hence the reversal of factor proportions in Chile's trade, discussed above, is assumed to persist.

Corbo and Meller estimated that, both for exportable and for import-competing products (both to DCs and to LDCs), employment would have increased about 6–7 percent if the price of capital goods imports had increased about 36 percent. Capital coefficients in both exportable and import-competing industries would have fallen by about 30 percent.[16]

8.2.4   Simulation for Other Countries

For other countries, the estimates from chapter 7 can be combined with Behrman's estimates of the elasticity of substitution to provide an estimate of the order of magnitude of the effect of factor market distortions on employment. It will be recalled that Behrman found that the elasticity of substitution in most of the industries for which he had data was very close to unity, and that a Cobb-Douglas formulation was a reasonable representation for most purposes (Behrman 1981, p. 186).

It is possible to use that result to estimate the proportion by which factor proportions might change. This can be seen as follows. The Cobb-Douglas production function is:

(1) $Q = A\,L^{\alpha}\,K^{1-\alpha},$

which can be rewritten as

Table 8.8   **Corbo-Meller Estimates of Effect of Distortions on Factor Proportions (Direct-Plus-Home-Goods-Indirect Coefficients)**

	Labor	Capital	Skills	Capital/Labor	Skills/Labor
Exportables					
Observed coefficients					
World	58.5	1,719	122	29.6	2.10
DCs	98.6	1,830	84	18.6	.85
LDCs	49.6	1,712	131	34.6	2.65
Simulated coefficients					
World	62.9	1,348	133	21.4	2.10
DCs	105.6	1,472	90	13.9	.86
LDCs	53.5	1,321	142	24.7	2.65
Import-Competing Products					
Observed coefficients					
World	60.1	983	146	16.4	2.42
DCs	60.0	910	148	15.2	2.46
LDCs	60.7	1,339	134	22.0	2.21
Simulated coefficients					
World	64.1	789	156	12.3	2.43
DCs	64.0	731	158	11.4	2.47
LDCs	64.9	1,072	144	16.5	2.22

Source: Corbo and Meller 1981, tables 3.15 and 3.19.

Note: Skills are in "skill units" and are not dimensionally comparable to labor coefficients, which are in man-years.

$$(2) \qquad q = Ak^{1-\alpha}, \text{ where } q = Q/L \text{ and } k = K/L.$$

Equation (2) can be solved for the capital/labor ratio as:

$$(3) \qquad k = q^{\frac{1}{1-\alpha}} \; A^{-\frac{1}{1-\alpha}}.$$

The first-order conditions for profit maximization are

$$(4) \qquad \frac{\partial Q/\partial L}{\partial Q/\partial K} = \frac{\alpha}{1-\alpha} k = w,$$

where $\qquad w = \dfrac{W}{R}.$

Let $w_s =$ a distortion-free wage/rental ratio and w_a, the actual wage/rental ratio, equal $w_s(1+d)$, where d is the proportionate distortion.

Combining equations (4) and (3), and letting $w_a = w_s(1+d)$,

$$(5) \qquad q_d = c \, w_s^{1-\alpha} (1+d)^{1-\alpha},$$

where $\qquad c = \left(\dfrac{1-\alpha}{\alpha}\right)^{1-\alpha} A, \text{ and}$

(6) $q_s = cws^{1-\alpha}$,

where q_d is the observed (inverse) labor coefficient and q_s is the one that would prevail in the absence of distortion. Combining equations (5) and (6),

(7) $\dfrac{q_s}{q_d} = (1+d)1-\alpha.$

Estimates of the d's are available from table 7.1. All that is not known is the average labor share. Table 8.9 presents estimates of the range of potential percentage increases in labor coefficients for plausible labor shares on the basis of the equation (7).[17] As can be seen, the more capital-intensive the industry, the greater the proportionate increase in the labor coefficient for a given distortion in the wage/rental ratio confronting profit-maximizing firms under the assumptions indicated.

Since the distortions listed in table 7.1 refer at least as much to import substitution as to exportable industries in the project countries, the estimated increases in coefficients in table 8.9 provide estimates of the degree to which all (modern sector) tradable manufacturing industries, both exportable and import-competing, may have substituted away from labor and toward capital as a consequence of distorted incentives. The estimates are indicative only of orders of magnitude involved. Nonetheless, in countries such as Tunisia and Pakistan, with large rural populations and rapid population growth, the estimates in table 8.9 suggest that switching to more appropriate incentives within the manufacturing sector might enable a sizable increase in output and employment for a given rate of investment, even within existing trade strategies.[18]

8.3 Relative Importance of Trade Strategy, Implementation, and Factor Market Distortions

We are now in a position to attempt to estimate the combined potential effect of choice of trade strategy, within-strategy inefficiencies, and factor market distortions on the increase of demand for labor in the project

Table 8.9   **Estimated Increases in Labor Coefficients by Country Assuming Elimination of Factor Market Distortions**

Country	Estimated d	Percentage Increase in Labor Coefficient If Labor Share Is			
		.1	.2	.3	.5
Ivory Coast	.38	33	29	25	17
Pakistan	3.16	360	312	271	203
South Korea	.11	10	9	8	5
Tunisia	.87	76	65	55	37

countries. Such estimates are, of course, based on a number of assumptions, not to mention imprecise data. They can best be interpreted as indicating possible orders of magnitude only. There are two bases for the estimates: data from the individual studies, and comparative analysis within a common model.

8.3.1   Individual Country Estimates

A first set of estimates is contained in table 8.10.[19] There the observed labor coefficients in HOS exportables and import-competing industries (with the labor coefficient in import-competing industries set equal to 100) are given in column 1. Columns 2 and 3 then indicate the percentage increase in the labor coefficient that might have been expected if there were no domestic factor market interventions, and no incentives associated with the trade strategy that lower the cost of using capital-intensive techniques of production (from the estimates in table 7.1). Column 4 then gives the best estimate of the extent to which the labor coefficient might increase by altering the commodity composition of output under the trade strategy indicated. Finally, Column 5 gives the coefficient that would be observed if all sources of distortion were removed.

As can be seen, the estimated increments in labor coefficients are sizable. For example, if the underlying assumptions and data are correct, Tunisia might have generated more than twice as many employment opportunities as in fact were generated under the import substitution strategy. By and large, the estimates suggest that there is more scope for improving the efficiency of resource allocation among import-competing industries than there is among HOS exportable industries. Only for Chile and Colombia do the estimates indicate opportunities for greater proportional potential increases in exportables. In both those instances this reflects the fact that exportables under the import substitution strategy in effect at the time of the estimates probably constituted in part a response to import substitution incentives. In the Chilean case, especially, it was the incentives under import substitution to export to LAFTA out of import substitution output that account for the sizable potential for increasing employment in exportables. This could have been realized simply by shifting toward greater emphasis on exports destined for developed countries.

Table 8.11 summarizes the findings from table 8.10 and in addition provides an estimate of the proportionate differences in labor coefficients under alternative trade strategies. For example, the estimates suggest that the Ivory Coast could have realized an increase in employment within HOS exportable industries of 25 percent, and within import-competing industries of about 40 percent. In addition, shifting a thousand FCFA of domestic value added from HOS import-competing to exportable production (within the modern sector) would have permitted a 21 percent increase in the demand for labor per unit of shift.

These numbers by no means indicate the extent or possibilities for a shift in the demand for labor. In particular, if substitution of labor for capital were encouraged by the dismantling of incentives for employing capital, there could presumably be additional investment in some tradable activities; the increment in the demand for labor that might arise from that source is not considered here, partly because the estimates are already conjectural enough and partly because the same "released capital" effect would occur regardless of which of the three sources of increased demand for labor evaluated in table 8.11 in fact took place. For the latter reason, there is some basis for believing that the magnitude of the numbers in table 8.11 already reflects the relative potential for increasing the demand for labor by working within existing trade strategies and also by altering trade strategies.

Comparisons across countries based on the data in table 8.11 should be made with care. In particular, the low estimated potential for South Korea is a misleading figure, given knowledge of the rapid expansion of manufacturing employment that occurred after that country's switch in trade strategy. Indeed, the evidence suggests that the South Korean emphasis on export promotion resulted in a fairly efficient pattern of production within import-competing as well as exportable industries, which had already been realigned by 1968. Thus, comparison of the Brazilian potential for increasing the demand for labor through shifting trade strategies (which was presumably largely realized during the late 1960s and early 1970s) with the South Korean potential is unwarranted.

Of greater interest is the extent to which inferences can be drawn from the comparative magnitudes within countries. For Tunisia, the greatest potential source of increase in the demand for labor appears to arise from rationalization of the import-competing sectors of the economy. For Pakistan, removing incentives for employing overly capital-intensive techniques appears to offer even greater promise of shifting the demand for labor upward than does a shift in trade strategy. To be sure, Pakistan could, by shifting trade strategies *and* removing incentives to employ capital-intensive techniques, realize an even greater upward shift in the demand for labor. That is, if the labor/value added ratio in Pakistani HOS exporting industries rose by 271 percent in response to the abandonment of capital-intensive techniques *and* Pakistan simultaneously shifted resources toward exportables, the scope for increased employment would be 1.41 times 1.71, or 3.82, since domestic factors of production allocated at the new factor proportions in exportables would result in a labor/value added ratio 2.41 times as high as the preexisting labor/value added ratio in HOS import-competing industries. For all the countries except possi-

Table 8.10   **Sources of Potential Increase in Labor Coefficients**

Country	Period	Observed Direct Labor Coefficient (1)	Increase (Percentage) with			Potential Coefficient (5)
			No Domestic Factor Market Intervention (2)	No Trade Strategy Distortion (3)	No Within-Strategy Inefficiency (4)	
		HOS Import-Competing Industries				
Argentina	1973	100	16	−6	0	110
Brazil	1970	100	15	n.a.	n.a.	115
Chile	1966–68	100	n.a.	7	n.a.	107
Colombia	1970	100	n.a.	n.a.	10	110
Indonesia	1971	100	n.a.	n.a.	66	166
Ivory Coast	1972	100	25	0	12	140
Pakistan	1969–70	100	271	0	n.a.	371
South Korea	1968	100	8	0	0	108
Tunisia	1972	100	17	38	51	243

		HOS Exportable Industries			
Argentina	1973	130	25	−6	0	149
Brazil	1970	207	15	n.a.	n.a.	238
Chile	1966–68	80	n.a.	7	68	144
Colombia	1970	170	n.a.	n.a.	24	210
Indonesia	1971	209	n.a.	n.a.	0	209
Ivory Coast	1972	135	25	0	0	169
Pakistan	1969–70	142	271	0	n.a.	384
South Korea	1968	100	8	0	0	108
Tunisia	1972	128	17	38	0	198

Sources: Column 1 from table 5.1; columns 2 and 3 derived from tables 7.1 and 8.9; column 4 from section 8.1 of text. Argentine data are from Nogues 1980, table 3.12.

Notes:

Ivorian estimates are for modern sectors only.

Corbo-Meller estimates for capital costs refer to direct plus home goods indirect (1981, table 8.8).

An estimated labor share of .3 was used from table 8.9.

For Chile, within-strategy inefficiency within exports taken to be LDC exports.

Table 8.11   Potential Sources of Increased Demand for Labor
(Percentage of Observed Labor Coefficient)

| Country | Period | Increase in Labor Coefficient at Constant Value Added | | Shift in Strategy |
		Exportable	Import-Competing	
Argentina	1973	19	10	30
Brazil	1970	15	15	107
Chile	1966–68	80	7	34
Colombia	1970	24	10	91
Indonesia	1971	n.a.	66	26
Ivory Coast	1972	25	40	21
Pakistan	1969–70	271	271	41
South Korea	1968	8	8	0
Tunisia	1972	55	143	23

bly South Korea in 1968, there clearly was sizable room for increasing the demand for labor consistent with improved resource allocation, generally through more than one avenue.

8.3.2   General Equilibrium Estimates

A complementary means of estimating the combined effect of distortions and trade strategies is to develop an optimizing model and employ properties of the solution to indicate the magnitude of divergences from optimality. Henderson did that for the project countries for which adequate data were available, as well as for some developed countries for comparative purposes.[20] His analysis is set forth in *Trade and Employment in Developing Countries,* vol. 2, Factor Supply and Substitution (Krueger 1982), and some results have been mentioned earlier. Here those features of the model that are pertinent for interpreting his estimated costs of trade strategies and distortion are discussed.

Henderson's model is a constrained optimizing model[21] subject to linear and nonlinear constraints. For countries with input-output tables and tariff data available, the model maximizes international value added in tradable-goods production subject to constraints on home-goods production (that it equal base-period domestic consumption levels plus intermediate uses as inputs to tradables) and on the total employment of labor and capital. In addition, there are constraints preventing output levels from lying outside a range of a specified percentage of their observed levels, 25 percent in the empirically implemented version.

These output constraints are useful for a variety of reasons. They prevent the model from driving to an extremely specialized solution.

They indicate feasible limits of change within medium-term time horizons. Also, the shadow prices attaching to the capacity constraints can be interpreted as indicating the extent of comparative advantage or disadvantage in particular activies, given the pattern of production.[22]

For present purposes, focus is upon the magnitude of the cost of distortions. Of the estimates emanating from Henderson's model, two are especially useful and interesting in this regard. On one hand, he estimated the attainable increase in IVA that could result from reallocation of resources (including factors of production, since substitution between capital and labor according to Cobb-Douglas production functions occurs in the model until the marginal rate of substitution is equated in all activities). This measure is an indicator of the loss in real income associated with the combined influence of the trade strategy and factor market distortions, although it has limited comparability across countries because of differing degrees of aggregation of input-output tables and because the output constraints limited the feasible extent of reallocation of factors between industries. Owing to the 25 percent reallocation limits, the model might show two countries achieving approximately equal proportionate increases in IVA, whereas an unconstrained optimizing model might show one country nearing an optimum within approximately a 25 percent band of output while another country might be shown to have much higher reallocation, with commensurately larger gains in IVA.[23] Also note that the ouput limits constrain the size of gains the model can generate.

The other measure is the average shadow price attaching to the capacity constraints. This number represents an estimate of the gain in IVA that might be had were those constraints relaxed. In that sense it provides some insight on the scope for gains from further reallocation beyond that permitted within the model. One should recall, however, that the problem of differing degrees of aggregation remains and that, for both sets of estimates, observed input coefficients are taken as indicating sectoral coefficients (subject to substitution possibilities) that would exist under either trade strategy. In fact, one suspects that alteration of the trade strategies may influence the coefficients themselves, as was reflected in the Brazilian and Colombian experience reported in section 8.1. It is also given credence by Henderson's findings of relatively broadly based comparative advantage across manufacturing industries for South Korea and Taiwan (and the developed countries) and much more narrowly confined areas of comparative advantage in the import substitution countries.

The estimates are given in table 8.12. The first column gives the year to which the data pertain, and the second column gives the number of sectors in the input-output table employed. The third column gives the average shadow price of the output constraints. This number represents an average, covering both sectors for which the shadow price is positive

Table 8.12 Estimated Costs of Trade Strategy and Factor Market Distortions, Henderson's Model (Percentage of Base-Period Values)

Country	Year (1)	Number of Sectors (2)	Shadow Price of Output Constraint — Average (3)	Average Absolute Value — Positive (4)	Average Absolute Value — Negative (5)	Increase in Tradables — IVA (6)	Increase in Tradables — DVA (7)
Chile	1962	54	8.9	37.5	26.4	3.6	-4.9
Indonesia	1971	168	-3.8	12.3	37.8	3.3	.1
Ivory Coast	1972	47	14.2	31.5	31.8	6.7	-1.0
South Korea	1966	118	-3.3	16.9	21.2	3.9	.7
	1970	118	-4.9	18.0	23.6	4.2	1.0
	1973	118	.7	12.6	16.9	2.8	.4
Tunisia	1972	68	-1.6	24.3	24.9	2.8	-1.4
Uruguay	1961	20	-8.9	9.7	43.8	8.9	-4.8
Belgium	1965	62	2.3	16.3	8.9	3.0	1.7
France	1965	62	6.9	20.8	7.3	2.7	.7
Germany	1965	62	5.9	14.1	6.7	6.8	5.2
Italy	1965	62	1.3	24.4	10.5	2.8	.4

Sources: Henderson 1982, tables 1.5, 1.6, appendix table 1.A.1.

and also those for which it is negative. Countries with a positive average shadow price associated with the output constraints generally show larger potential gains from expanding production for export than inefficiencies in import substitution sectors; countries with a negative shadow price are showing the opposite. This can be seen in more detail by examining the average absolute values of all positive—and all negative—shadow prices, given in columns 4 and 5. These absolute values represent unweighted averages of the individual activity coefficients for those activities with the shadow price of the sign indicated.

For example, for Uruguay, the unweighted average absolute attainable increase in international value added per unit of relaxation of capacity constraints across sectors with a positive shadow price was 9.7 percent. By contrast, the average gain by contracting import substitution sectors beyond the limits imposed by the model was 43.8 percent. For Uruguay, therefore, the costs of inefficiency on the import substitution side seem sizable. Chile's large average positive shadow price seems to reflect a comparative advantage in a variety of sectors that was underexploited in the import substitution regime. The Indonesian averages accord well with Pitt's findings that the export side of the economy seemed to be fairly efficient, but that there were sizable inefficiencies on the import substitution side.

The South Korean data are of interest, given that the number of sectors is standardized over the three years used and that the years covered are those during which the export promotion drive was in progress. In 1966 and 1970, South Korea appears to have had a legacy of import substitution industries, the average inefficiency of which was still fairly substantial. This is reflected in the negative average shadow price attaching to capacity constraints, which suggests that the gain in international value added to South Korea from contracting import substitution industries beyond the capacity limits would have exceeded the gain from expanding her exporting sectors even more than the limits. By 1973, however, the model shows that those gains were largely realized: indeed, both positive and negative shadow prices averaged closer to zero, which is also reflected in the average potential gain in IVA of less than 1 percent.

Comparing the results for the four developed European countries with the results from the project countries is of interest. The Common Market was still in formation in 1965, and trade was expanding rapidly among the member countries. This is reflected in the European estimates, where the average shadow prices attaching to positive capacity constraints were fairly sizable, although still below those for Chile, the Ivory Coast, and Tunisia. What is striking, however, is that the absolute order of magnitude of potential further gains from contracting industries at their lower bound constraints was much less. Indeed, only for Italy did the estimate exceed 10 percent. This suggests that the efficiency of overall resource allocation in the developed countries and, at least by 1973, in South Korea, substantially exceeded that in the import substitution sectors of the countries covered by the project.

These findings are reinforced by the data in the sixth and seventh columns of table 8.12. There the estimated percentage increase in attainable IVA, given domestic factor availability, is given in column 6, while column 7 indicates what would have happened to DVA in tradable production at the model's solution. For all the project countries except Indonesia and South Korea, the model estimated that maximizing IVA would entail a decrease in DVA. This suggests that the observed allocation of resources in the project countries was in response to the incentives prevailing. For Chile, for example, the implied 3.6 percent increase in IVA in the model's solution would be accompanied by a 4.9 percent *decrease* in DVA, a clear indication that the resource shifts implied by the model were not profit-maximizing for producers under Chile's incentive structure.

By contrast, the positive shifts in DVA for South Korea and the four Western European countries suggest that inefficiencies implied by the model's solution were also reflected in domestic prices, and that those prices provided incentives for resource movements. This is especially pronounced in Germany, where much of the large estimated increase in attainable IVA originated in the inefficiency of the agricultural sector; at domestic prices, too, Germany's comparative advantage in industry was reflected.

For the countries covered by both the Henderson model and individual studies, the two sets of results reinforce each other. Regardless of procedures used, all the import substitution countries show large potential gains through increasing the efficiency of the import substitution strategy and resource allocation.[24] Some of them also indicate large potential gains through expanding some activities, primarily for export. There seems to be little doubt that the existing pattern of production, including inefficiencies, has been the result of the trade regime and of incentives confronting domestic producers.

By contrast, the degree of inefficiency in South Korea appears to have been smaller and to have diminished over the period covered by Hong and by Henderson. By 1973 it appears that the efficiency of South Korean resource allocation resembled that of the developed countries more than it did that of the import substitution developing countries.

9   Conclusions

At the outset of the project the intent was to ascertain the extent to which domestic factor market conditions impinged on the realization of labor-abundant developing countries' comparative advantage in international trade. It was assumed that the appropriate trade data could be assembled and that existing analyses of developing countries' factor markets could be relied upon as an input in analyzing the links between trade strategies and employment.

Perhaps the most striking findings emerging from the trade strategies and employment project were that, on one hand, despite factor market conditions, developing countries' manufactured exports tend to exhibit the factor intensity consistent with their endowment, and that, on the other hand, the scope for further increasing their demand for labor through both trade policies and realignment of domestic factor market incentives is sizable.

Thus, in answer to the questions initially raised, there does not appear to be any conflict between objectives associated with more rational resource allocation and increasing the demand for labor, especially unskilled labor. Indeed, the degree to which the project countries' exportables were intensive in the use of unskilled labor was one of the important findings to emerge from the country studies.

An equally striking finding was the extent to which our knowledge and understanding of factor markets in developing countries is imperfect. Analysis of the interaction between trade strategies and domestic factor markets was generally more constrained by a lack of data and analyses on domestic factor market conditions than by lack of data and analyses on trade strategies.

The project has raised as many questions as it has answered, but answering most of them will require intensive examination and understanding of the functioning of domestic factor markets. The evidence is striking on the size of the divergence in capital/labor costs between sectors of the economy in which labor legislation is enforced and access to credit and import licenses is fairly free and those sectors hiring without constraints and unable to secure favored treatment in obtaining loans or capital goods. Although the estimates in chapter 8 provide some basis for assessing the effects of such differences, a great deal of work remains to be done in understanding factor market interventions and their effects. The orders of magnitude are surely large enough that it is at least plausible that low observed elasticities of employment with respect to output may be explicable in terms of factor market interventions. Regardless of whether those distortions are partly or almost entirely to blame for the failure of employment opportunities to grow, finding ways to remove incentives for using capital-intensive techniques is one component of any effort to increase real incomes and employment opportunities.

Despite data limitations and imperfect understanding of factor markets, the evidence from the country studies and from the project as a whole strongly suggests that there are gains to be had in resource allocation and employment from shifting to an outer-oriented trade strategy. Moreover, the extent of the potential gain very much depends on the degree to which factor markets function appropriately. While alteration of the trade strategy itself may remove one source of distortion in costs of using capital-intensive techniques, it is clear that credit rationing, tax structures, and labor legislation also play important roles.

In many of the project countries, appropriate factor market incentives to producers could have significantly increased the demand for unskilled labor under the existing trade strategy. Likewise, an altered trade strategy could have brought sizable increases in the demand for unskilled labor even in the presence of inappropriate relative prices for factors of production. Obviously, however, the greatest potential for employment gain is in those situations where the shift in policy realigns incentives in both the domestic factor market and the trade regime. The extent to which there may have been interaction between inner-oriented trade strategies and factor market distortions, both leading to high capital/output ratios and low rates of increase in the demand for labor, is striking.

Moreover, the income-distribution implications of the findings seem to accord fairly well with the proposition that inner-oriented trade strategies and measures that increased incentives for using capital-intensive techniques probably contributed to a less equal income distribution than might otherwise have been observed. The very fact that HOS exportable industries tend to be relatively intensive in the use of unskilled industrial labor suggests that additional employment in those industries would increase the rate at which the urban sector could absorb new entrants to the labor force. To be sure, insofar as removal of labor market legislation might reduce the real incomes of industrial workers, there would tend to be a partial offset; however, in most of the countries covered in the project, employed industrial workers were a small elite receiving relatively high earnings at the expense of fewer employment opportunities in the industrial sector and lower earnings for those unable to find employment within it. Paul Schultz's finding, that effective protection tended to increase employers' earnings proportionately three times as much as employees' earnings, even within industries and after adjustment for age and other variables, is also significant in suggesting the compatibility of real income, employment, and income-distribution goals.[1]

Among the many findings of the project, another deserves special note by way of conclusion. That is the degree to which manufactured exports supplied in response to regional arrangements turned out to be relatively high-cost and apparently uneconomic. On one hand the evidence certainly suggests that the potential gains from regional trade in manufactures, if undertaken behind a common wall of protection, are probably relatively small, if not negative. On the other hand it suggests that the large potential gains in real income, growth rates, employment, and income distribution are attainable largely through an outer-oriented trade strategy that would result in increased exports of manufactures to developed countries under fairly uniform incentives.

The first point once again underscores the important conclusion that exports emanating from the ad hoc, specific, and widely varying incentives created under an import substitution regime do not usually provide the resource allocation gains that can result from uniform, across-the-board incentives. While there is undoubtedly scope for gainful intra-LDC trade,[2] it seems clear that the type of trade in manufactures that has been encouraged under regional trading arrangements has generally been more the outcome of the import substitution type of incentives than of the incentives that accompany a genuine outer-oriented trade strategy.

The second consideration, that the major gains from an outer-oriented trade strategy are likely to arise in trade with developed countries because of their very different factor endowments, points to the crucial importance of access to developed country markets in permitting developing countries to achieve maximum gains from appropriate trade policies and well-functioning domestic factor markets. While the inefficiencies of some import substitution regimes are so pronounced that there would in any event be gains by alteration of trade strategies, the magnitude of those potential gains is greater when access to markets is unrestricted and those markets are growing rapidly. This is not the place to assess the prospects for protectionist pressures in the developed countries, except to note that exporting LDCs have been able to increase their shares of world markets despite protectionist pressures and that, in the past, those who have cautioned against an outer-oriented trade strategy because of some form of export pessimism have been proved wrong.

What is clear is that maintaining access to markets of the developed countries is one of the major contributions developed countries can make to the growth prospects of developing countries, especially middle-income developing countries. While appropriate policies in LDCs, with respect to domestic markets, the trade regime, education, and much more, are a necessary condition for increasing prospective rates of growth of real income and living standards, those same policies clearly have a larger potential payoff in a liberal international economy.

Notes

Chapter 1

1. This collection of papers was the outcome of a major study of the issue sponsored by the Ford Foundation. See especially Edwards's summary (1974, p. 29). Logically, the analysis should center on the labor intensity of exportables relative to import-competing goods unless the fraction of income spent on home goods changes with the type of trade regime.

2. These two companion volumes provide a synthesis of the results of that project. See also Little, Scitovsky, and Scott (1970).

3. See also the series of studies done by the OECD. The synthesis volume, which contains references to the individual studies, is Little, Scitovsky, and Scott (1970).

4. That there has been implicit subsidization of capital goods imports has long been recognized. However, there have been very few attempts to qualify or estimate the importance of these subsidies and their effects on choice of techniques in developing countries. Two interesting exceptions are: McCabe and Michalopoulos (1971) and Öngut (1970). See chapters 7 and 8 of this volume for further discussion.

5. These conclusions emerge from the NBER project. An initial version is presented in Bhagwati and Krueger (1973). A more complete statement is contained in Krueger (1978).

Chapter 2

1. See also T. Paul Schultz's pathbreaking paper in the second volume of this series (Schultz 1982). Schultz's work is the first systematic analysis of the link between rates of effective protection and earnings structure in a developing country.

2. There are two sets of models that posit an upper bound on the number of "productive" jobs that can be created. The first is the "technological" explanation, first set forth by Eckaus (1955). According to that view, the labor/capital endowment in the industrial sector of developing countries exceeds the maximum technologically feasible ratio. The alternative is the "two-gap" model, in which a foreign exchange or savings limit prevents further expansion in real output. The model is associated with Hollis B. Chenery and Michael Bruno. See section 2.2.1 for further discussion.

3. See section 2.2 for a definition of the "formal" and "informal" markets.

4. As will be seen in chapter 5, authors who were able to obtain data on labor coefficients for agricultural activities generally found that export-oriented activities in that sector were

consistent with greater labor utilization. However, labor coefficients for agriculture are averages, and there is reason to believe that there may be significant divergences between marginal and average coefficients in the agricultural sectors of many of the project countries. Since the question underlying the project is the implications of a switch in trade strategies that would imply resource reallocation (with marginal, not average, coefficients predominating), the agricultural coefficients were viewed with suspicion. There is less basis for believing that marginal and average differ in the industrial sector than in the rural sector.

5. For an analysis of the role of skills and determinants of the wage structure, see section 2.3.3.

6. Although it is not empirically important for purposes of analyzing the relationship between trade strategies and employment, it is even possible that in a neoclassical labor market an upward shift in the demand for labor could result in decreased employment (if the labor supply curve were backward bending).

7. See Sen (1975) for a fuller discussion of ways the labor supply to the urban sector might be perfectly elastic.

8. For a model of growth and employment in a dual economy, see Jorgenson (1961) and Ranis and Fei (1961).

9. A market is said to be more fragmented the less changes in one part of the market affect other parts. If labor is perfectly immobile between two areas, those markets are entirely fragmented.

10. For a recent treatment of short-term macroeconomic policy in developing countries, see Behrman and Hanson (1979).

11. See especially Behrman (1982).

12. For a recent treatment of macroeconomic aspects of development, see the collection in Blitzer, Clark, and Taylor (1975), which focuses upon input-output models and supply constraints. Nowhere is attention given to aggregate demand.

13. Not all developing countries' labor markets are so regarded among the countries covered here. Hong Kong, Pakistan, and South Korea were generally thought to have well-functioning labor markets in the neoclassical sense.

14. Some believe that the differential may reflect only skill differentials, differences in living costs, and a premium to induce additional migrants as needed. If that were the case it would not constitute a distortion, and the labor market could be regarded as neoclassical.

15. In particular, migrants might be risk averse, in which case expected urban income could be above rural income at equilibrium.

16. Several extensions of the model have been made that endogenize the urban wage. Calvo (1978) developed a model of maximizing trade union behavior that endogenized the urban/rural wage differential. See also Stiglitz (1974).

17. For an exposition of the model in an open-economy setting see Bhagwati and Srinivasan (1974).

18. For a fuller discussion of the question whether there is "disguised unemployment" in rural areas, see Sen (1975, chap. 3). There is also a problem of "balancing" growth to maintain approximately constant terms of trade between agriculture and industry. But opportunities to trade on the international market can obviate the need for balance in that sense.

19. We saw in connection with table 2.1 that in some Latin American countries the agricultural labor force is already fairly small, but that the problem of finding productive urban employment opportunities is a key issue.

20. In contrast to rural labor markets, for which an important question is whether unemployment or underemployment exists other than in the sense of low productivity, there is little dispute that urban unemployment à la Harris-Todaro is a significant phenomenon in a number of countries. Although there are important questions about the reliability of unemployment measures, who the unemployed are, and the causes of unemployment, these questions did not arise in a central way for purposes of analyzing the trade strategies–employment relationship. They are therefore not covered here.

21. For a careful analysis for one country, see Nelson, Schultz, and Slighton (1971) on Colombia.

22. Argentine data are often presented below. There is also evidence of an informal sector in Argentina.

23. See table 6.6 for illustrative data on Pakistan.

24. See chapter 4 for a definition.

25. If exports or import-competing goods originated in firms with above-average productivity within each industry within the modern sector, the bias might be upward.

26. Inducements to use capital-intensive techniques can also lead to a nonoptimal choice of techniques or mix of industries. That topic is covered in chapter 7.

27. Nabli estimates an elasticity of .09 for the period 1961–71 for manufacturing establishments excluding food processing and handicrafts.

28. The situation in Pakistan changed in the early 1970s.

29. See Calvo (1978).

30. Many believe that urban living costs exceed rural living costs by a margin sufficient to explain much of the observed wage differential between unskilled urban and rural earners. There is also a school of thought that alleges that better-paid workers are more productive. On this see Mirrlees (1975).

31. The term "human capital" was developed to indicate that investments in man are as important as investments in machines and other physical capital goods in the development process. See Becker (1975).

32. See Schultz (1982) for the estimation of an earnings function based on Colombian data. For analyses of the links between ability and human capital variables in earnings functions see Griliches (1972) and Behrman et al. (1979).

33. For a review of estimates of rates of return to human capital in developing countries, see Psacharopoulos (1973).

Chapter 3

1. There is a range of commodities whose allocation to export or import categories is ambiguous, and the precept that is simple in theory is not so readily implemented in practice. See chapter 5 below for a discussion of the allocation of commodities and industries to trade categories on the basis of the conceptual framework of chapter 4.

2. In the presence of such distortions, shadow prices can be used to estimate DMRTs. Estimation itself is difficult empirically, though it is conceptually straightforward. See Srinivasan and Bhagwati (1978) for a discussion.

3. There are of course a number of problems in estimating B empirically. With many commodities, weights must be used to form aggregate p's and q's. Sometimes the same commodity is sold at different prices in the domestic market and abroad. Also, price comparisons, not tariff rates, are the appropriate bases for estimating B.

4. To be sure, governments can and do provide rebates to compensate for the cost differential between domestic and imported goods. In some instances these are automatic and may offset the export disincentives. More often, however, the incentives to overstate actual usage in order to get bigger rebates lead the authorities to institute fairly careful checks that are time-consuming and constitute a disincentive to exports.

5. See Díaz-Alejandro (1965) for an analysis of this phenomenon.

6. A number of countries have taxed a major raw material export while encouraging import substitution, but that further increases the bias toward import-competing industries.

7. All countries have policies they term "export promotion." In many instances, however, examination of incentives reveals that the promotion measures are really nothing more than partial offsets to the discrimination exports would otherwise face in light of exchange rate overvaluation and the high domestic prices confronting exporters. What is meant by genuine export promotion in this context is a trade strategy in which, on balance, incentives are not tipped toward import substitution. This might be because a country's

policies were very close to free trade or because incentives for exporting equaled or exceeded those for selling in the domestic market.

8. The effective rate of protection for a given activity is the rate of protection to domestic value added in that activity. If t_j is the nominal tariff (or tariff equivalent) on the jth input to industry i, then E_i, the ERP for industry i, is

$$E_i = \frac{t_i - \Sigma_j \, a_{ji} t_j}{1 - \Sigma_j \, a_{ji}},$$

where a_{ji} is the input of j at international prices per dollar (at international prices) of output of i.

9. ERP estimates are difficult to make, and data are not available for the countries covered in the project other than for the years indicated (except in cases where alternative sources provide noncomparable estimates). See table 3.2, where an indication is given of how trade strategies altered within individual countries over time.

10. See the description of Chile's protective structure in Behrman (1976, p. 144).

11. This discussion draws heavily on the findings of the NBER project on foreign trade regimes and economic development. See Bhagwati (1978) for a full analysis of these issues.

12. In some cases, such as Argentina and Indonesia, "official prices" or "check prices" are established for some commodities, and tariffs are payable on the official price rather than the actual price of the import. This can make straightforward reliance upon the tariff schedule highly misleading if the former is higher.

13. To be sure, a sufficiently high rate of protection through tariffs can achieve the same result. This has been the case in Argentina and Uruguay, where tariff levels have been set so high that the domestic price exceeded the international price by less than the tariff rate ("water" in the tariff).

14. Capital goods imports are generally permitted at low rates of duty. When the exchange rate is overvalued, this can result in a substantial incentive for favored industries to use relatively capital-intensive techniques. See chapter 7 for an analysis of this phenomenon in the project countries.

15. Qualifications to this statement are necessary because the presence of a uniform export subsidy rate does not imply equal incentives to exports when the ratio of value added to output varies across sectors: sectors with high ratios of imported inputs are implicitly subject to a higher rate of incentive than are those with a low ratio of imported inputs if the subsidy per dollar of exports is the same and imported inputs are permitted at a lower price of foreign exchange.

16. Variance can arise chiefly if different activities have very different value added/output ratios, with export incentives based on value of output.

17. Credit availability at low or negative real rate of interest can provide incentives for exporters to use overly capital-intensive techniques. See chapters 7 and 8.

18. Export-oriented regimes often establish export promotion agencies to facilitate marketing and give favored treatment to successful exporters in all government dealings. There is also the intangible—but sometimes very important—value of the government commitment that exporting will continue to be profitable.

19. See the large literature on growth-rate determinants among developed countries, in particular Denison (1967) and Christensen, Cummings, and Jorgenson (1980). Robinson (1971) surveyed the available evidence for developing countries.

20. Heller and Porter (1978) later contended that Michaely should have computed the growth rate of GNP net of exports for his test. They reestimated his relations on that basis and found that they still held. They also reinforced Michaely's earlier finding that the relationship between changing export share and growth is much stronger among higher-income developing countries than it is among low-income developing countries.

21. Data from Hong Kong are used where pertinent in later chapters. Hong Kong appears to conform very closely to free trade, with virtually no tariffs and a bias of unity. See Sung (1979) and Lin, Mok, and Ho (1980) for details.

22. In part this may have been because the growth in export earnings reflects almost entirely the fact that the price of copper was in a slump in 1960 and rose throughout the decade.

23. Among import substitution countries covered in the project, Brazil before 1968, Chile, Colombia before 1967, Tunisia, and Uruguay have all had such episodes (as did Argentina).

24. See Krueger (1978) for a fuller discussion.

25. Balassa (1978a, p. 45) makes much of this point. He cites incremental capital/output ratios for the period 1960–73 of 1.76 for Singapore, 2.10 for South Korea, and 2.44 for Taiwan and contrasts them with corresponding ratios of 5.49 for Chile and 5.72 for India.

26. See chapter 4 for reasons why that might be expected.

Chapter 4

1. Note that, even with factor intensity reversals, *all* industries would employ more labor-intensive techniques at a lower wage/rental ratio under any efficient allocation. This implication would be useful empirically were it not for the impossibility of identifying homogeneous factors across countries.

2. For a given price set, it can never be more profitable to produce three commodities than two. This is what makes the composition of output indeterminate.

3. In the context of a multicommodity model, specialization takes on a different meaning from the one it has in two-commodity models. In the latter, specialization implies a positive production level for only one commodity. With many commodities, specialization means the failure to produce at least as many commodities in common as there are factors of production.

4. If commodity prices were truly imposed at random, it would be highly improbable that either country would have positive production levels for more than a few goods (and there is no assurance whatever that the commodities at either factor intensity extreme would be produced at all). In reality, prices are determined in the market and are related to production costs via supply and demand: at the wage/rental ratio associated with a particular commodity's production, there *are* prices at which other commodities can also be produced at competitive equilibrium; if the factor demands derived from the output mix demanded at those prices are not equal to factor supplies, the wage/rental ratio can adjust as commodity prices alter.

5. The empirical likelihood of such an outcome is open to question, especially if one takes into account transport costs. A simple proof that it could happen in the model set forth above is as follows. If the wage/rental ratio were lower in country 8 than in country 9, then commodity 6 would be cheaper to produce in country 8 than in country 9 at prevailing factor prices and the competitive profit conditions would not be met. Therefore the wage/rental ratios in countries 8 and 9 must be the same. The reverse reasoning can then be used between countries 7 and 8, as a higher wage/rental ratio in 8 than in 7 would imply that commodity 5 could not be competitively produced (see Bhagwati 1972 for a fuller discussion).

6. Whether an industry is an import substitute or an export is simply a matter of the precise nature of the factor endowment relative to other countries and, of course, demand conditions. Consider, for example, country 1 in figure 4.1. It must export commodity 1 and may export commodity 2, depending on whether production is greater or less than domestic demand. It could, however, be using virtually all its resources in the production of commodity 1, so that demand for commodity 2 exceeded domestic production. In that case commodity 1 would be exported and commodities 2 through n imported.

7. In effect, this is the "small country" assumption, and it could not be valid indefinitely, since continued growth, with the rest of the world of constant size, would eventually make the country in question very large. Many of the statements in this section can, however, be interpreted to apply to a situation in which all countries but one are accumulating capital

relative to labor at a common rate and the country in question is growing more rapidly. Formal extension of the model to that case is difficult and is not attempted here. The problem lies in the fact that, as shown by the Rybczynski theorem (Rybczynski 1955), if a country is producing two commodities and its capital/labor endowment increases, output of the capital-intensive commodity must increase more rapidly than the proportional change in the capital stock, while output of the labor-intensive commodity must change less than the percentage change in the quantity of labor (so that, if there was no change in the quantity of labor, output of the labor-intensive commodity would have to decrease). An attempt to describe growth of the world economy would therefore require consideration of demand conditions, since price changes would surely have to be explicitly incorporated into the model.

8. It could happen that production of one commodity ceased simultaneously with the start of the other. In that event there would be no period with a constant wage/rental ratio.

9. It is shown below that introducing transport costs probably smooths the stepwise progression described here.

10. Strictly speaking, the assumptions made are insufficient, if the labor force is growing, to ensure such an outcome: output of the more labor-intensive commodity could be growing, but at a slower rate than the growth of the labor force. This is where the "small country" assumption becomes inadequate.

11. A necessary condition for the validity of the assertion is that food is a normal good.

12. Strictly speaking, this statement is valid only if it is assumed that there is no upper limit to the marginal product of labor in agriculture.

13. If there is "disguised unemployment" in the rural sector, so that workers leave at some fixed wage as urban jobs become available, the real wage would remain constant for a greater interval of capital accumulation and output would increase more rapidly in the urban sector. The composition of output would not start changing until the urban real wage began rising. See chapter 2 for a discussion of the issues involved in identifying the nature of the urban labor supply, and see also Sen (1975).

14. Once import-competing production is adequate to satisfy the domestic market, the domestic price of the good is free to vary within the range determined by transport costs. It could even be less than the international price, but by an amount insufficient to enable exports with competitive profit levels. Thus the domestic price of exportables must be exactly equal to their international price less transport costs; the domestic price of importables can be anywhere from the international price less transport costs to the international price plus transport costs. It must exactly equal the latter only when imports and domestic production are both sold in the domestic market.

15. For a summary of the basic theorems of the HOS model when home goods are present, see Batra (1973, chap. 12).

16. Likewise, if it were assumed that production of home goods required only labor as an input, the analysis would not be affected. Note that intermediate goods also do not affect the analysis insofar as they are all tradable; when they are home goods, the complications discussed above arise.

17. This follows because labor-abundant manufacturing sectors will need less of a transport-cost barrier to enable their firms to compete with the labor-intensive commodities.

18. But see the interesting paper by Hufbauer and Chilas (1975), who attempted to estimate the effect of protection on the extent of specialization among the Western European countries compared with regions of the United States: the authors found that American regions were more specialized than comparable European countries, thus providing another piece of indirect evidence in support of the view that specialization patterns and not comparison of import-competing and export coefficients are the appropriate forms for empirical work.

19. To attempt to formalize an n-country model in which there are distortions in more than one country is an incredibly complex task that will not be attempted here.

20. Travis (1964) has expounded the position that it is trade impediments that prevent the realization of the HOS predictions.

21. See chapter 5 for a discussion of these measures in the project countries.

22. As is evidenced in chapter 8, this probably occurred in some of the project countries.

23. Intermediate goods have not been explicitly dealt with here. If they were, then it would be effective rates of protection that should be correlated with capital intensity.

24. For the most capital-abundant country, protection rates should be positively correlated with the labor intensity of the industry. For countries in the middle, one would have to partition commodities into those more capital intensive and those less capital intensive than the manufacturing sector's factor endowment. The hypothesis is that the height of protection needed to induce domestic production is positively correlated with labor intensity for the commodities on that side of the sector's endowment, and positively correlated with capital intensity for commodities on the other side.

25. The presence of protection, which would induce production in more capital-intensive industries than would occur under an efficient protection pattern, increases the likelihood that there would be greater capital intensity in the import-competing commodities than in export industries. This result holds only for the countries with extreme manufacturing endowments, however.

26. Of course one would have to use the appropriate protection measure, including the tariff equivalents of quotas and the subsidy equivalents of credits and the like and omitting all tariff redundancy. In addition, appropriate measures of capital and labor would, as always, be necessary.

27. Strictly speaking, if factor markets are distorted, the price of home goods will in general diverge from that which would prevail under competition in all markets. It must therefore be assumed in this section that there are no home goods. Since transport costs do not affect the results, because international prices are assumed given, they too will be assumed absent. The world under discussion is therefore one in which there are n manufactured goods and food, with all prices given to the country under consideration by the international market. There are, as before, three domestic factors: land, which is always fully employed in agriculture; capital, which is always fully employed in manufacturing; and labor, which is used in both sectors. It will be seen that there are a number of possible distortions, each of which can be characterized by a set of conditions on the wage and employment of labor. Full employment may or may not be assumed, and the wage may or may not be common between agriculture and manufacturing or within manufacturing.

28. Of course, if one knew the subsidy and tax equivalents of these measures, they could then be treated as protective rates, and empirical work could proceed in the same manner as described for the commodity market distortions.

29. If one regards the "real wage floor" as applying only to the manufacturing sector, the case merges with the full employment, constant differential case discussed next.

30. A difficulty with this interpretation is that there are generally some commodities, such as textiles, produced in both sectors.

31. Recall that it is assumed initially that domestic prices equal international prices. The effects of introducing tariffs in the context of the factor market distortion are examined below.

32. If a labor-abundant country did specialize in producing the capital-intensive good and was on its transformation curve (at D in figure 4.2a), it would be using more labor-intensive techniques of production than other countries whose "true" comparative advantage lay in producing that commodity. It should be stressed again that this could happen only if the distortion-ridden country somehow managed to increase the relative price of the capital-intensive commodity enough to make production profitable at a high real wage with labor-intensive techniques of production. One can doubt whether there are many instances of wrong specialization and full employment.

33. That employment (and output) in agriculture will fall follows immediately from the fact that the real wage increases from its distortion-free level.

34. This can be seen most easily by thinking of the "dual" of the undistorted case. Consider the wage rate that would prevail with complete specialization in commodity 1. Let the wage rise to the point where it pays to produce commodities 1 and 2, that is, to the wage/rental ratio implied by the prices of the first two commodities. Then production of both commodities will be profitable, and, with total capital stock the same, employment must be smaller. Let the wage increase a little more. Now production only of commodity 2 will be profitable; as the real wage rises (for a given price of output and capital stock), employment in the second industry will be smaller. At some point the wage will be that implied by the prices of goods 2 and 3, and production of both will be profitable, and so on. It should also be noted that the value of production of manufactured goods, evaluated at international prices, will decrease with increase in the real wage.

35. The straightforward definition of "labor intensive" in this context is clearly that more hours of labor are employed per unit of international value added in one sector than in the other.

36. If agriculture is labor intensive relative to industry, and the real wage is higher in industry, the reversal could never happen in physical terms, although it might be that labor's share became higher in industry than in agriculture.

37. If the wage differential were between all manufacturing, on the one hand, and agriculture, on the other, the analysis would be the same as for the Harris-Todaro case.

38. For a survey of the literature, see Magee (1973). Corden (1974. chap. 5) has a good exposition of the basic model and its implications.

39. I am indebted to Stephen Magee, who called this representation to my attention.

40. Note that the relative price of the labor-intensive commodity must increase or production would simply become completely specialized.

41. It should be stressed that this result could not be observed unless the relative price of the commodity was above the level that would prevail at free trade. If, for example, textiles are the "efficient" export for a particular country and are observed to be capital intensive relative to other produced commodities, one could rule out the proposition that they were naturally labor intensive unless their relative price was higher domestically than in international markets. This could happen, of course, but it would require subsidization of exports *and* factor market distortion so that the wage/rental ratio facing the export industry was higher than that facing the other industry.

42. One could presumably test whether there had been a reversal of the factor intensities in response to the differential by contrasting the factor-intensity ordering of the country with that of other countries thought to be unaffected by the distortion.

43. See note 42, which also applies here.

Chapter 5

1. Some of the Latin American country authors believed that the T_i statistic did not adequately discriminate between competing and noncompeting imports, because prohibitions against imports of anything produced domestically implied that all goods actually imported were noncompeting.

2. Yun Wing Sung (1979) found that for Hong Kong the T_is had a highly skewed distribution. He therefore transformed the statistic into a related one of $(P_i - C_i)/P_i$. With the benefit of hindsight, it might have been preferable to use the latter statistic throughout, though it is not evident that it affected the results of the individual country studies.

3. See below for a discussion of the shift in Brazil's trade composition.

4. Look at table 3.3 to see the prevalence of this phenomenon.

5. In principle, a country could have a sufficiently distorted incentive system for exports so that some commodities were exported that would not be economic at free trade, and one could have a category of "protected" exportables. This did not arise in practice in any of the country studies, although some country authors did break down exports into "more protected" and "less protected."

6. There are also problems associated with estimating the factor proportions that would probably be used in the development of new import substitution industries. See chapter 1 of Krueger et al. (1981) for a discussion of that issue.

7. See Leamer (1980) for a discussion of the appropriate test of a country's relative factor abundance in this case.

8. This is because, under balanced trade "gross exports," that is, the value added domestically plus the value of imported inputs used in production of exports (not export-ables), equal "gross imports," that is, imports used in domestic consumption plus imports used in production of goods for export. Likewise, "net" exports (gross exports less the value of imports reexported) equal "net" imports (gross imports less the value of imports reexported). With imbalanced trade, the difficulty lies in the fact that gross, not net, exports are observed.

9. For a full exposition of this procedure and its rationale see chapter 1 of the first volume in this series (Krueger et al. 1981).

10. This discussion assumes that a single factor price prevails throughout the country's economy. The existence of factor market distortions in the sense of different factor prices confronting producers in different sectors is taken up in chapters 7 and 8.

11. Recall that in some instances the availability of a domestically produced raw material was judged to be a significant determinant of comparative advantage for a particular manufacturing sector. See section 5.1.2.

12. The absolute numbers are telling in this regard. Monson's (1981) estimates of total labor coefficients indicate that 2,488 man-hours of labor are used for modern-sector HOS exportable production per million FCFA of domestic value added. This compares with 19,933 man-hours for NRB exports. That NRB exports predominate is reflected by the fact that the average over NRB and HOS exports is 18,993 man-hours per million FCFA of DVA.

13. Pulp and paper exports are destined primarily for Chile's LAFTA trading partners; see section 6.2 below.

14. If the Tunisian figure is recomputed to include oil among NRB exports, the Tunisian NRB exports become an exception to the statement above.

15. Westphal and Kim (1977) also based their estimates on output, not on value added. Labor/capital ratios derived that way are not biased, and it is therefore those ratios that are reported in table 5.2.

16. For 1968 Westphal and Kim estimate that the labor/capital ratio in primary exports was 5.69, compared with 15.48 for primary imports. That contrasts with labor/capital ratios of 3.55 for manufactured exports and 2.33 for manufactured import-competing goods. See Westphal and Kim (1977, table VII-10).

17. In correspondence, Hong offered an index of labor intensity of South Korean domestic output and exportables with 1960 = 100. According to these data, labor intensity behaved as follows:

	1963	1966	1968	1970	1973	1975
Domestic output	1.000	.553	.610	.500	.382	.333
Exportables	1.026	.884	.873	.670	.460	.263

This pattern is generally consistent with the Westphal-Kim findings. By 1975, subsidies to using capital were an important component of the export incentive system. See Hong's discussion in Krueger et al. (1981).

18. Thoumi was unable to obtain data to provide estimates comparable to those in table 5.1 for direct-plus-home-goods-indirect labor coefficients. He did, however, calculate the increase in output, value added, and wages and salaries that would result from one peso of direct value added. Import-competing industries had the biggest effect on all three. He indicated the reasons for this result: "The import-competing branches of Colombian manufacturing include the heaviest (most capital-intensive) industries in the country. These industries are also the most energy-and-water-intensive, and the ones in which transporta-

tion costs for their inputs are the highest. The high capital intensity also results in higher banking and insurance inputs" (Thoumi 1981, p. 158).

19. Sung (1979, table 5.9*a*). As a check on his results, Sung made a comparable calculation for the apparel sector. He estimated a depreciation/labor ratio for the United States of 11.1, compared with 0.9 for Hong Kong.

20. The corresponding figures for 1962, in 1973 prices, are: 684 for noncompeting imports, 346 for import-competing production, and 296 for exportable production. See Sung (1979, table 5.11).

21. Recall that Hong did not correct for differences in value added/output ratios, so capital/labor ratios must be used to generate meaningful results.

22. Thoumi's work contains an estimate of the factor content of "noncompeting imports," but that estimate is derived from domestic coefficients. Those coefficients are derived from the subsectors represented domestically, which presumably are different from the noncompeting import subsectors for which an estimate of factor inputs is desired.

Chapter 6

1. See the Corbo and Meller (1982) results on this point, and also Branson and Monoyios (1977).

2. See chapter 7 for a discussion of optimal factor proportions and skill/capital/labor substitutability.

3. See Paul Schultz's study in *Trade and Employment in Developing Countries*, vol. 2, *Factor Supply and Substitution* (Krueger 1982), discussed in chapters 7 and 8 below. Schultz's finding, that part of effective protection shows up in higher earnings to persons in the protected industry, strongly suggests that the Carvalho-Haddad procedure is preferable to using mean earnings when the necessary data are available.

4. Nogues reported that 72 percent of all Argentine exports to LAFTA were import-competing. Further, these exports were the least labor intensive of all Argentina's exports.

5. However, the ordering of capital/labor ratios remains unchanged.

6. For incomplete specialization, there must be at least one set of factor prices at which both commodities could be profitably produced for a given set of world prices. Since figure 6.2 is drawn with the factor prices and world prices indicated, it would not be possible for every country to face common production functions in each industry and simultaneously produce both commodities.

7. Although figures 6.1 and 6.2 both represent "reversals" from L/DVA to L/IVA, they differ fundamentally in that in figure 6.1 there is a set of factor prices (and therefore endowments) at which it would pay both industries to produce, whereas in figure 6.2 it would never pay to operate industry B at any positive level as long as international prices remained as depicted. In the latter case, if some other country were producing both commodities without protection, it would be presumptive evidence of differences in production functions between countries.

8. Not all country authors computed the IVA statistics. Countries covered in the project and not listed in the table are countries for which the data were not available. For Hong Kong, of course, DVA and IVA coefficients are identical and are not reproduced here.

9. It should be noted that L/IVA is undefined when international value added is negative.

Chapter 7

1. In principle, one should also consider the ways the choice of trade regimes affects labor costs. However, it is difficult to pinpoint mechanisms through which such an effect

might arise; some have suggested that multinational corporations may pay different wages than do domestic firms, but, quite aside from the fact that this could happen under any type of labor regime, it is not evident how the practice would affect relative costs of labor between industries. It is also possible that imported capital equipment might generate demand for a different type of labor than does domestically produced capital equipment, but that would affect the domestic labor market through distortions under the trade regime induced by its treatment of imports of capital goods. There is no evidence on these points available from the country studies and little basis for believing that these or other mechanisms are quantitatively significant.

2. Some export promotion strategies, including notably that of South Korea, have been implemented in part by providing exporters with preferential access to credit. Generally such access is valuable precisely because there is credit rationing. The effects of preferential access are therefore discussed below in connection with domestic capital market imperfections.

3. If domestic consumption was smaller, it would be either because imports of consumer goods were less than they would be at equilibrium (because of their higher price) or because exports of consumer goods were greater than they would otherwise be. This latter possibility could occur only if the effective exchange rate for exportables lay above that for import of capital equipment (and above its equilibrium rate in a unified exchange rate system).

4. The transfer would be from exporters receiving fewer units of domestic currency per unit of foreign exchange that they would at equilibrium to import-license recipients.

5. If all applicants know that licenses will be granted in proportion π to the amount applied for, all applicants will apply for $1/\pi$ times their desired quantity of imports, and the rationing mechanisms will be ineffective. To be sure, if there is excess demand for foreign exchange, the actual proportion will be less than π.

6. Ghana, India, the Philippines, and Turkey also had this set of incentives surrounding the industrial sector, as was documented in the NBER project on foreign trade regimes and economic development.

7. South Korea has in recent years begun contracting to erect large projects in foreign countries, notably in the Middle East, so that construction need not be a home good. In the import substitution countries, however, it seems sensible to so regard it.

8. See, for example, McCabe and Michalopoulos (1971). Nogues (1980) also deals with this question for Argentina. See section 7.2.1.

9. For an interesting case study, see Rhee and Westphal (1977).

10. Whether domestic construction represents a viable substitute for imported machinery and equipment is more problematic. There is some evidence that the fraction of construction in total investment rises during periods of extreme restrictiveness of import substitution regimes. However, that phenomenon appears to reflect a diversion of investment away from the industrial and commercial sectors and toward residential construction. See Krueger (1978, pp. 252–57) for a discussion.

11. For an exposition of the view that capital market imperfections are a crucial distortion in LCDs, see McKinnon (1973).

12. Because of "moral hazard" and other uncertainties, it may be rational behavior for banks to determine interest rates and give borrowers less credit than they would wish at those rates. The "moral hazard" and uncertainty argument for credit rationing has been spelled out by Jaffee and Russell (1976). The credit rationing and negative real interest rates discussed here refer to far more extreme circumstances, in which financial institutions would charge higher rates for loans if permitted to do so (and would sometimes do so by under-the-table payments, requiring large minimum balances during the period when loans are outstanding or when other conditions effectively increase the cost of borrowing).

13. For a survey of the rationales for these practices, see Katkhate and Villaneuva (1978).

14. This assumes that the tax does not simply finance fringe benefits desired by workers

in a context in which cash wages might be higher in the nontaxed sector (to compensate for the absence of those benefits).

15. Indeed, it is an interesting question, but one on which the country studies did not shed any light, whether multinational corporations may not use more capital-intensive techniques than their local counterparts precisely because they are induced to locate in the country by tax holidays and exemptions not granted to their local counterparts. Although Lipsey, Kravis, and Roldan (1982) show that use of more capital-intensive techniques is far less widespread than often stated, they could not obtain data on differentials in incentives for domestically owned and foreign capital.

16. It should not be forgotten that the structure of protection constitutes a distortion in the product market. The effect of differentiated tariffs on factor use is considered in chapter 8, along with the effect of the factor market distortions discussed here.

17. The conclusions stated above are those of Carvalho and Haddad, and also of most knowledgeable analysts of the Brazilian economy. It is an unexplained puzzle, therefore, that the index of the price of capital equipment in Brazil rose less rapidly than either the nominal wage or the wholesale price index. Carvalho and Haddad indicate that, from 1955 to 1974, real wages rose 80 percent, while the nominal price of capital goods rose by less than half the increase in the wholesale price index. See Carvalho and Haddad (1981, pp. 59 ff.).

18. There is, however, evidence that investment decisions by individual firms were heavily influenced by foreign exchange availability. See the interesting results reported by Bilsborrow (1977).

19. But see Schultz's analysis of the effect of the trade regime on earnings in Krueger (1982).

20. Data are from Monson (1981), table 6.14.

21. Data are from Monson (1981), table 6.15.

22. This assumption vastly simplifies analysis, since otherwise the value of a credit subsidy hinges upon the tax rate and the value of a tax break hinges upon the fraction interest payments constitute of sales revenue less other costs. When interest payments are subject to tax, the incremental value of either a lower tax rate or an interest subsidy is reduced.

23. However, the average rate of duty collection in Korea has not been very high—duty collections were only 9 percent of imports in 1970. The duty-free provisions were changed to a delayed-payment arrangement after 1974.

24. Among the measures taken during the period of transition from import substitution to export promotion in Korea was a fairly thoroughgoing financial reform that raised nominal interest rates and also lowered the rate of inflation. By the 1970s, however, real interest rates fell sharply.

25. This assumes that the won was not devalued during the period of the loan. For an analysis of the effects of this distortion, see Frank, Kim, and Westphal (1975, chap. 9).

26. A possible exception is Uruguay, but there are not enough data available to judge.

27. Of course, to the extent that different firms or industries had differential access to credit or other privileges, that access affected their demand for capital goods. Since domestic credit market imperfections seem to have been of considerable importance in Tunisia, the statement that all comers had access to imports at the same price is somewhat misleading. See the discussion in Nabli (1981, sec. 10.1.4).

28. Hong Kong is an exception. It is arguable whether Brazil's BNDE loans constitute credit rationing. And the evidence is simply not available for Chile or Colombia.

29. See, for example, Magee (1976, p. 45).

30. If the minimum wage is set at above equilibrium level and employers are induced to hire more skilled, and fewer unskilled, workers than they otherwise would, the resulting "shortage" of skilled workers will be greater than would have resulted had the wage rate for unskilled workers not been constrained. In those circumstances the actual wage paid to

skilled workers would generally be expected to be higher than it would be in the absence of the minimum wage constraint.

Chapter 8

1. Focus throughout the project has been on the link between trade strategies and employment under efficient allocation of resources. Thus, attention is on ways existing trade strategies might have been implemented consistent with greater labor utilization at a positive marginal product and no less international value added.

2. See section 3.1.2 for a definition of the effective rates of protection (ERPs).

3. Note that these data are based on a different set of estimates than those reported in table 8.1. See Nabli (1981) for a discussion of the difference between the two sets.

4. See section 5.1.2 for a discussion of the relation between T_is and ERPs.

5. In the Brazilian case the implications are even stronger. Based on 1970 employment coefficients, the data indicate that employment per million cruzeiros of exports and import-competing products was 11.2 and 16.3 in 1959, contrasted with 16.1 and 15.9 in 1968 and 20.5 and 14.4 in 1974. Thus, observed factor intensities in fact reversed.

6. For purposes of evaluating potential in table 8.10, Monson's estimated labor coefficient for DC importables with below-average protection was contrasted with the average for all DC importables.

7. On an earlier draft of this chapter, one reader raised the question whether the output of the large- and small-scale firms is the same. There is no ready answer to the question, but it is difficult to believe that the systematic pattern seen across all industries reflects only differences in output composition within each industry.

8. There may also be factors associated with the choice of trade regime that influence size of firm regardless of trade category. Carlos Díaz-Alejandro found, for example, that in Colombia import licenses tended to be granted more readily to larger firms (see Díaz-Alejandro 1976, pp. 139ff.). Insofar as licensing procedures, access to foreign exchange, and fixed costs of paperwork bias the allocation of licenses to larger firms, an import substitution regime may affect the overall size distribution of firms.

9. See section 8.3.2 for a comparison across countries. Comparison of mean g_is is somewhat hazardous when the degree of disaggregation differs significantly. But when, as in Korea, the sectoral breakdown remains constant over the set of observations, the reliability of mean g_i as a measure of efficiency of resource allocation is considerably greater.

10. It is also of interest to examine the g_is associated with different sectors and the changes in them over time. The g for cotton yarn, for example, was .37 in both 1966 and 1970. Exports of that commodity were growing rapidly during the period 1966–70. By 1973, g fell to .03, suggesting that the profitability of further expansion of that activity had diminished sharply. A similar pattern prevailed for most other textile activities. By contrast, items such as electrical products and motor vehicles, both of which had sizable negative g's in the 1960s, showed much higher g's in 1973, thus reflecting the shift that was taking place in South Korean comparative advantage.

11. Data are from Bension and Caumont (1981, tables 11.10 and 11.11).

12. Recall from chapter 7 that Carvalho and Haddad believe minimum wage legislation was binding only for a very small fraction of workers by the late 1960s.

13. The proportionate increase in each sector differs both because the estimated elasticities of substitution are sector-specific and because the percentage of social insurance taxes levied on workers in different sectors varied somewhat. See Carvalho and Haddad (1981) for details.

14. It may also be noteworthy that the average proportionate change in labor coefficient of the capital-intensive goods seems to be somewhat greater than that of the labor-intensive

goods. This suggests that the distortions may have worked to increase the observed capital intensity of import-competing industries relative to that of exportables.

15. See Corbo and Meller (1981, Appendix A), for details.

16. Skill coefficients appear unaffected relative to unskilled labor. The reason for this is that Corbo and Meller held the relative price of skilled and unskilled labor constant in their simulation. Since most industries were estimated to have Cobb-Douglas production functions, no change in the ratio of skilled to unskilled labor could have been expected.

17. Note that the q's are defined as output per worker. The estimates in table 8.7 refer to possible increases in labor units per unit of value added. They thus refer to the inverse of the q's.

18. This assumes, of course, that the existing strategy is somehow amended to remove the bias toward choice of capital-intensive techniques for eligible firms.

19. Thailand and Uruguay are omitted from the table for lack of quantitative estimates.

20. He also implemented the model for Kenya, Taiwan, and Turkey. Those results are not reviewed here, since interpretation would require considerable background on those countries. The results are presented in Henderson (1982).

21. Constrained optimization means that limits are placed on the change from base period output values that can occur. These limits are in addition to the usual resource availability and balance constraints.

22. Strictly speaking, the shadow prices attaching to the output limits reflect the gain in international value added that would result from relaxing the capacity constraint (either upward or downward) by a unit. Although both upper- and lower-bound output limits are placed on each activity, only one will have a nonzero shadow price in any solution. A large positive shadow price on an upper-bound constraint indicates that additional capacity would permit a corresponding increase in international value added. A smaller shadow price indicates less potential gain. Negative shadow prices on lower-bound constraints reflect the gain to be had by shifting resources to alternative, more efficient, activities.

23. The force of this qualification can be seen by noting that, even for the West European countries included in Henderson's analysis, the capacity constraints were reached in many sectors. Indeed, it is a property of the model that there will be few (usually only one) marginal sectors in which neither the upper- nor the lower-bound constraint is binding.

24. In the Henderson model there is no way of ascertaining the extent to which the estimated increase in IVA orginates in factor reallocation as marginal rates of substitution between factors are equated across activities rather than in output reallocation at existing factor proportions. Inspection of the magnitude of the output shifts, compared with the relatively smaller magnitude of the realignment of factor proportions, suggests that the increased IVA probably originated more from changing outputs than from realigning factor proportions. But without further work it is impossible to verify this conjecture.

Chapter 9

1. To be sure, there are short-run considerations pertaining to the behavior of income and employment during the transition from one factor market and trade regime to another. Questions pertaining to the transition were not addressed in the project. See Krueger (1978), especially chapters 11 and 12, for a discussion of these issues.

2. In particular, there is considerable evidence that many of the middle-income developing countries persist in protecting their highly labor-intensive industries, such as textiles and footwear, in which they may have lost comparative advantage. Monson's findings for the Ivory Coast and Nogues's conclusions for Argentina are particularly compelling in this regard.

References

Akrasanee, Narongchai. 1981. Trade strategy for employment growth in Thailand. In *Trade and employment in developing countries*. Vol. 1. *Individual studies*, ed. Anne O. Krueger, Hal B. Lary, Terry Monson, and Narongchai Akrasanee, pp. 393–433. Chicago: University of Chicago Press for National Bureau of Economic Research.

Balassa, Bela. 1978*a*. Export incentives and export performance in developing countries: A comparative analysis. *Weltwirtschaftliches Archiv* 114, no. 1: 24–61.

———. 1978*b*. Exports and economic growth: Further evidence. *Journal of Development Economics*, June, pp. 181–89.

Baldwin, Robert E. 1979. Determinants of trade and foreign investment: Further evidence. *Review of Economics and Statistics* 61, no. 1 (February): 40–48.

Batra, Raveendra N. 1973. *Studies in the pure theory of international trade*. New York: St. Martin's.

Becker, Gary S. 1975. *Human capital*. New York: Columbia University Press.

Behrman, Jere R. 1976. *Foreign trade regimes and economic development: Chile*. New York: Columbia University Press for National Bureau of Economic Research.

———. 1982. Country and sector variations in manufacturing elasticities of substitution between capital and labor. In *Trade and employment in developing countries*. Vol. 2. *Factor supply and substitution*, ed. Anne O. Krueger, pp. 159–92. Chicago: University of Chicago Press for National Bureau of Economic Research.

Behrman, Jere R., and Hanson, James A., eds. 1979. *Short-term macroeconomic policy in Latin America*. Cambridge: Ballinger.

Behrman, Jere R.; Taubman, Paul; Wales, T. J.; and Hrube, Z. 1979. *Socioeconomic success*: *A study of the effects of genetic endowment, family environment, and schooling*. Amsterdam: North-Holland.

Bension, Alberto, and Caumont, Jorge. 1981. Uruguay: Alternative trade strategies and employment implications. In *Trade and employment in developing countries*. Vol. 1. *Individual studies*, ed. Anne O. Krueger, Hal B. Lary, Terry Monson, and Narongchai Akrasanee, pp. 497–529. Chicago: University of Chicago Press for National Bureau of Economic Research.

Bhagwati, Jagdish N. 1968. *The theory and practice of commercial policy: Departures from unified exchange rates*. International Finance Section: Special Papers in International Economics, no. 8. Princeton: Princeton University Press.

———. 1972. The Heckscher-Ohlin theorem in the multi-commodity case. *Journal of Political Economy* 80 (September/October): 1052–55.

———. 1978. *Foreign trade regimes and economic development*: *Anatomy and consequences of exchange control regimes*. Cambridge: Ballinger for National Bureau of Economic Research.

Bhagwati, Jagdish N., and Krueger, Anne O. 1973. Exchange control, liberalization and economic growth. *American Economic Association Papers and Proceedings* 63, no. 2 (May): 419–27.

Bhagwati, Jagdish N., and Srinivasan, T. N. 1974. On reanalyzing the Harris-Todaro model. *American Economic Review* 64, no. 3 (June): 502–8.

Bilsborrow, Richard. 1977. The determinants of fixed investment by manufacturing firms in a developing country. *International Economic Review* 18, no. 3 (October): 697–718.

Blitzer, Charles R.; Clark, Peter B.; and Taylor, Lance, eds. 1975. *Economy-wide models and development planning*. Fair Lawn, N.J.: Oxford University Press.

Branson, William, and Monoyios, Nikolaos. 1977. Factor inputs in U.S. trade. *Journal of International Economics* 7, no. 2 (May): 111–31.

Brecher, Richard. 1974. Minimum wage rates and the pure theory of international trade. *Quarterly Journal of Economics* 88 (February): 98–116.

Calvo, Guillermo. 1978. Urban unemployment and wage determination in LDCs: Trade unions in the Harris-Todaro model. *International Economic Review* 19, no. 1 (February): 65–81.

Carvalho, José L., and Haddad, Cláudio L. S. 1978. Foreign trade strategies and employment in Brazil. Rio de Janeiro: Fundaçao Getulio Vargas. Mimeographed.

———. 1981. Foreign trade strategies and employment in Brazil. In *Trade and employment in developing countries*. Vol. 1. *Individual studies*, ed. Anne O. Krueger, Hal B. Lary, Terry Monson, and

Narongchai Akransanee, pp. 29–82. Chicago: University of Chicago Press for National Bureau of Economic Research.

Chenery, Hollis B., and Bruno, Michael. 1962. Development alternatives in an open economy: The case of Israel. *Economic Journal* 72 (March): 79–103.

Chenery, Hollis B., and Strout, Alan. 1966. Foreign assistance and economic development. *American Economic Review*, September, pp. 679–733.

Christensen, Laurits R.; Cummings, Dianne; and Jorgenson, Dale W. 1980. Economic growth, 1947–1973: An international comparison. In *New developments in productivity measurement and analysis*, ed. J. W. Kendrick and B. Vaccara, pp. 595–698. Studies in Income and Wealth, no. 41. Chicago: University of Chicago Press for National Bureau of Economic Research.

Corbo, Vittorio, and Meller, Patricio. 1981. Alternative trade strategies and employment implications: Chile. In *Trade and employment in developing countries*. Vol. 1. *Individual studies*, ed. Anne O. Krueger, Hal B. Lary, Terry Monson, and Narongchai Akrasanee, pp. 83–134. Chicago: University of Chicago Press for National Bureau of Economic Research.

———. 1982. Substitution of labor, skill, and capital: Its implications for trade and employment. In *Trade and employment in developing countries*, Vol. 2. *Factor supply and substitution*, ed. Anne O. Krueger, pp. 193–213. Chicago: University of Chicago Press for National Bureau of Economic Research.

Corden, W. M. 1974. *Trade policy and economic welfare*, London: Oxford University Press.

Denison, Edward F. 1967. *Why growth rates differ*. Washington, D.C.: Brookings Institution.

Díaz-Alejandro, Carlos. 1965. On the import intensity of import substitution. *Kyklos*, fasc. 3.

———. 1976. *Foreign trade regimes and economic development: Colombia*. New York: Columbia University Press for National Bureau of Economic Research.

Eckaus, Richard S. 1955. The factor-proportions problem in underdeveloped areas. *American Economic Review* 45 (September): 539–65.

Edwards, Edgar O. 1974. *Employment in developing nations*. New York: Columbia University Press.

Fields, Gary S. 1975. Rural-urban migration, urban unemployment and underemployment, and job-search activity in L.D.C.'s *Journal of Development Economics* 2, no. 2 (June): 165–87.

Fishlow, Albert. 1975. Foreign trade regimes and economic development: Brazil. Paper presented at NBER conference, Bogotá, Colombia.

Frank, Charles R., Jr.; Kim, Kwang Suk; and Westphal, Larry. 1975. *Foreign trade regimes and economic development: South Korea.* New York: Columbia University Press for National Bureau of Economic Research.

Griliches, Zvi, and Mason, William. 1972. Education, income and ability. *Journal of Political Economy* 80, part 2, (May/June): S74–103.

Guisinger, Stephen. 1981. Trade policies and employment: The case of Pakistan. In *Trade and employment in developing countries.* Vol. 1. *Individual studies*, ed. Anne O. Krueger, Hal B. Lary, Terry Monson, and Narongchai Akrasanee, pp. 291–340. Chicago: University of Chicago Press for National Bureau of Economic Research.

Harris, John R., and Todaro, Michael P. 1970. Migration, unemployment and development: A two-sector analysis. *American Economic Review* 60 (March): 126–42.

Heller, Peter S., and Porter, Richard C. 1978. Exports and growth: An empirical re-investigation. *Journal of Development Economics* 5, no. 2 (June): 191–93.

Henderson, James M. 1982. Optimal factor allocations for thirteen countries. In *Trade and employment in developing countries.* Vol. 2. *Factor supply and substitution*, ed. Anne O. Krueger, pp. 1–82. Chicago: University of Chicago Press for National Bureau of Economic Research.

Herberg, Horst, and Kemp, Murray C. 1971. Factor market distortions, the shape of the locus of competitive outputs, and the relation between prices and equilibrium outputs. In *Trade, balance of payments and growth*, ed. Jagdish N. Bhagwati et al. Amsterdam: North-Holland.

Hong, Wontack. 1981. Export promotion and employment growth in South Korea. In *Trade and employment in developing countries.* Vol. 1. *Individual studies*, ed. Anne O. Krueger, Hal B. Lary, Terry Monson, and Narongchai Akrasanee, pp. 341–91. Chicago: University of Chicago Press for National Bureau of Economic Research.

Hufbauer, Gary C., and John G. Chilas. 1974. Specialization by industrial countries: Extent and consequences. In *The international division of labour: problems and perspectives*, ed. Herbert Giersch. Tübingen: Mohr.

Jaffee, Dwight M., and Russell, Thomas. 1976. Imperfect information, uncertainty, and credit rationing. *Quarterly Journal of Economics* 90, no. 4 (November): 651–66.

Johnson, Harry G. 1965. Optimal trade interventions in the presence of domestic distortions. In *Trade, growth and the balance of payments*, ed. Robert E. Baldwin et al. Amsterdam: North-Holland.

Johnson, Omotunde E. G. 1975. Direct credit controls in a development context: The case of African countries. In *Government credit alloca-*

tion: *Where do we go from here?* ed. Karl Brunner. San Francisco: Institute for Contemporary Studies.

Jones, Ronald W. 1971a. Distortions in factor markets and the general equilibrium model of production. *Journal of Political Economy* 79 (May/June): 437–59.

———. 1971b. A three-factor model in theory, trade, and history. In *Trade, balance of payments and growth*, ed. Jagdish N. Bhagwati et al. Amsterdam: North-Holland.

Jorgenson, Dale W. 1961. The development of a dual economy. *Economic Journal* 71 (June): 309–34.

Katkhate, Deena, and Villanueva, Delano P. 1978. Operation of selective credit policies in less developed countries: Certain critical issues. *World Development* 6, nos. 7/8 (July/August): 979–90.

Krueger, Anne O. 1974. The political economy of the rent-seeking society. *American Economic Review* 64, no. 3 (June): 291–303.

———. 1977. *Growth, distortions, and patterns of trade among many countries*. Princeton Studies in International Finance, no. 40. Princeton: Princeton University Press.

———. 1978. *Foreign trade regimes and economic development: Liberalization attempts and consequences*. Cambridge: Ballinger Press for National Bureau of Economic Research.

———. 1979. *The developmental role of the foreign sector and aid*. Cambridge: Harvard University Press.

———, ed. 1982. *Trade and employment in developing countries*. Vol. 2. *Factor supply and substitution*. Chicago: University of Chicago Press for National Bureau of Economic Research.

Krueger, Anne O.; Lary, Hal B.; Monson, Terry; and Akrasanee, Narongchai, eds. 1981. *Trade and employment in developing countries*. Vol. 1. *Individual studies*. Chicago: University of Chicago Press for National Bureau of Economic Research.

Leamer, Edward. 1980. The Leontief paradox, reconsidered. *Journal of Political Economy* 88, no. 3 (June): 495–503.

Leontief, Wassily. 1953. *Domestic production and foreign trade: The American capital position re-examined*. Lancaster, Pa.: Lancaster Press. Reprinted in Richard E. Caves and Harry G. Johnson, eds., *A.E.A. Readings in International Economics* (Homewood, Ill.: Irwin, 1968), pp. 503–27.

Lewis, W. Arthur. 1954. Economic development with unlimited supplies of labour. *Manchester School* 22 (May): 139–91.

Lin, Tzong-biau; Mok, Victor; and Ho, Yin-ping. 1980. *Manufactured exports and employment in Hong Kong*. Hong Kong: Chinese University Press.

Lipsey, Robert E.; Kravis, Irving B.; and Roldan, Romualdo A. 1982.

Do multinational firms adapt factor proportions to relative factor prices? In *Trade and employment in developing countries*. Vol. 2. *Factor supply and substitution*, ed. Anne O. Krueger, pp. 215–55. Chicago: University of Chicago Press for National Bureau of Economic Research.

Little, Ian; Scitovsky, Tibor; and Scott, Maurice. 1970. *Industry and trade in some developing countries*. London: Oxford University Press.

McCabe, James, and Michalopoulos, Constantine. 1971. *Investment composition and employment in Turkey*. AID discussion paper no. 22. Washington, D.C.: U.S. Agency for International Development.

Macedo, Roberto B. M. 1974. Models of the demand for labor and the problem of labor absorption in the Brazilian manufacturing sector. Ph.D. diss., Harvard University.

McKinnon, Ronald. 1973. *Money and capital in economic development*. Washington, D.C.: Brookings Institution.

Magee, Stephen P. 1973. Factor market distortions, production and trade: A survey. *Oxford Economic Papers* 25 (March): 1–43.

———. 1976. *International trade and distortions in factor markets*. New York: Marcel Dekker.

Michaely, Michael. 1977. Exports and growth: An empirical investigation. *Journal of Development Economics* 4, no. 2 (March): 49–53.

Michalopoulos, Constantine, and Jay, Keith. 1973. *Growth of exports and income in the developing world: A neoclassical view*. AID discussion paper no. 28. Washington, D.C.: Agency for International Development.

Mirrlees, James. 1975. A pure theory of underdeveloped economies. In *Agriculture in development theory*, ed. Lloyd Reynolds, pp. 84–106. New Haven: Yale University Press.

Monson, Terry. 1978. Ivory Coast—data appendix. New York: National Bureau of Economic Research. Mimeographed; available on request from NBER.

———. 1981. Trade strategies and employment in the Ivory Coast. In *Trade and employment in developing countries*. Vol. 1. *Individual Studies*, ed. Anne O. Krueger, Hal B. Lary, Terry Monson, and Narongchai Akrasanee, pp. 239–90. Chicago: University of Chicago Press for National Bureau of Economic Research.

Nabli, Mustapha K. 1981. Alternative trade policies and employment in Tunisia. In *Trade and employment in developing countries*. Vol. 1. *Individual studies*, ed. Anne O. Krueger, Hal B. Lary, Terry Monson, and Narongchai Akrasanee, pp. 435–97. Chicago: University of Chicago Press for National Bureau of Economic Research.

Nam, Chong, 1975. Economies to scale and production functions in South Korea's manufacturing sector. Ph.D. diss., University of Minnesota.

Nelson, Richard R.; Schultz, T. Paul; and Slighton, Robert. 1971. *Structural change in a developing economy: Colombia's problems and prospects*. Princeton: Princeton University Press.

Nogues, Julio, 1980. Trade, distortions, and employment in the Argentine manufacturing sector. Ph.D. diss., University of Minnesota.

Ongut, Ibrahim. 1970. Economic policies, investment decisions, and employment in Turkish industry. In *Labor force and employment in Turkey*, ed. Duncan Miller. Ankara: U.S. Agency for International Development.

Pitt, Mark M. 1981. Alternative trade strategies and employment in Indonesia. In *Trade and employment in developing countries*. Vol. 1. *Individual studies*, ed. Anne O. Krueger, Hal B. Lary, Terry Monson, and Narongchai Akrasanee, pp. 181–237. Chicago: University of Chicago Press for National Bureau of Economic Research.

Prebisch, Raúl. 1959. Commercial policy in the underdeveloped countries. *American Economic Review, Papers and Proceedings* 49 (May): 251–73.

Psacharopoulos, George. 1973. *Returns to education*. Amsterdam: Jossey-Bass/Elsevier.

Ranis, Gustav, and Fei, John C. 1961. A theory of economic development. *American Economic Review* 51 (September): 533–65.

Rhee, Yung W., and Westphal, Larry E. 1977. A micro, econometric investigation of choice of technology. *Journal of Development Economics* 4, no. 3 (September): 205–37.

Robinson, Sherman. 1971. Sources of growth in less developed countries: A cross section study. *Quarterly Journal of Economics* 85 (August): 391–408.

Rybczynski, T. M. 1955. Factor endowment and relative commodity prices. *Economica* 35 (November): 336–41. Reprinted in Richard E. Caves and Harry G. Johnson, eds., *A.E.A. readings in international economics* (Homewood, Ill.: Irwin, 1968), pp. 72–77.

Schultz, T. Paul. 1982. Effective protection and the distribution of personal income by sector in Colombia. In *Trade and employment in developing countries*. Vol. 2. *Factor supply and substitution*, ed. Anne O. Krueger, pp. 83–148. Chicago: University of Chicago Press for National Bureau of Economic Research.

Sen, Amartya. 1975. *Employment, technology and development*. Oxford: Clarendon Press.

Senna, José Julio. 1975. Schooling, job experiences and earnings in Brazil. Ph.D. diss., Johns Hopkins University.

Srinivasan, T. N., and Bhagwati, Jagdish N. 1978. Shadow prices for project selection in the presence of distortions: Effective rates of protection and domestic resource costs. *Journal of Political Economy* 86, no. 1 (February): 97–116.

Stiglitz, Joseph. 1974. Wage determination and unemployment in LDCs. *Quarterly Journal of Economics* 87 (May): 194–227.

Suh, Sang Chul. 1975. Development of a new industry through exports: The electronics industry in Korea. In *Trade and development in Korea*, ed. Wontack Hong and Anne Krueger. Seoul: KDI Press.

Sung, Yun Wing. 1979. Factor proportions and comparative advantage in a trade-dependent economy: The case of Hong Kong. Ph.D. diss., University of Minnesota.

Taylor, Lance, and Bacha, Edmar. 1973. Growth and trade distortions in Chile and their implications for calculating the shadow price of foreign exchange. In *Analysis of development problems*: *Studies of the Chilean economy*, ed. R. S. Eckaus and P. M. Rosensteen-Rodan. Amsterdam: North-Holland.

Thoumi, Francisco E. 1981. International trade strategies, employment, and income distribution in Colombia. In *Trade and employment in developing countries*. Vol. 1. *Individual studies*, ed. Anne O. Krueger, Hal B. Lary, Terry Monson, and Narongchai Akrasanee, pp. 135–79. Chicago: University of Chicago Press for National Bureau of Economic Research.

Todaro, Michael P. 1969. A model of labor migration and urban unemployment in less developed countries. *American Economic Review* 59 (March): 138–48.

Travis, W. P. 1964. *The theory of trade and protection*. Cambridge: Harvard University Press.

Westphal, Larry E., and Kim, Kwang Suk. 1977. *Industrial policy and development in Korea*. World Bank Staff Working Paper no. 263. Washington, D.C.: World Bank.

Author Index

Subject Index

Agriculture, 56, 57, 64–69, 80, 82, 85, 139; capital/labor ratio in, 66; credit in, 124; employment in, 11, 12, 14, 15, 81; labor in, 11, 12, 18, 19, 21–23, 65–66, 67, 68, 81; labor/output ratio in, 98

Argentina, 3, 4, 29, 144, 169; capital costs in, 130–31, 147–48; credit in, 130; government policies in, 130–31, 147–48; import substitution in, 130, 145, 149, 158; labor costs in, 130, 131, 147; labor intensity in, 115, 169–70; and LAFTA, 158; market distortions in, 130–31, 169–70; noncompeting imports in, 103; protection in, 35, 130; taxes in, 130, 131; trade strategy of, 35, 124, 145; unemployment in, 15; wages in, 131

Balance of payments, 44, 48

Banco Nacional de Desenvolvimento Econômico (BNDE), 131–32, 146, 170

Brazil, 3, 5, 7, 14, 23, 28, 29, 39, 48, 169, 181; BNDE in, 131–32, 146, 170; capital costs in, 131, 148; capital intensity in, 162; capital/labor substitution in, 170–73; credit in, 129, 131–32, 146; employment in, 159, 171–73; export promotion in, 131, 132, 146, 159, 160; government policies in, 131–33; import substitution in, 131, 145, 155, 160, 171; labor in, 96, 97, 159–60, 171–73; labor costs in, 27, 132–33, 147; labor skills in, 105, 107; market distortions in, 131–33, 149, 170–73; protection in, 35, 36, 131, 155; taxes in, 129, 133; trade strategy of, 33, 35, 36, 40–41, 45, 46, 87, 89, 145, 159, 177; wages in, 132

Capital, 3; accumulation, 63, 64, 65, 66, 67–68, 69, 70, 139; costs, 120, 121–29, 130–34, 136–41, 142–43, 144, 145–46, 147–48, 149, 162, 186; and credit market, 125–29, 146; deepening, 5, 26, 27; human, 27–28, 105, 107, 143, 191 n.31; as production factor, 59–60, 62, 63–64, 65–66, 67, 68, 70, 71, 72, 74, 75, 77, 79, 80, 81, 92–93, 117; rental on (*see* Wage/rental ratio); skills as component of, 104, 105; subsidies, 5, 125, 171. *See also* Credit; Distortions, market, capital; Goods, capital, imported

Capital intensity, 5, 7, 23, 52, 57–58, 59–60, 62, 63, 64, 68–85 passim, 103, 110, 111, 112–16, 118, 121, 122, 129, 131, 134–42 passim, 144, 149, 163, 167, 168, 170, 171, 175, 176, 177, 186

Capital/labor ratio, 5, 6, 57, 58, 59–60, 112, 116, 117, 155, 163, 164, 168, 169; agricultural, 66; in Hong Kong, 101–2, 103; in import substitution, 50; in manufacturing, 66–67, 68, 69–70, 71, 72, 74, 98–99, 100, 102; in South Korea, 102, 103; urban, 66, 67

Capital/labor substitution, 17, 25–26, 76, 81, 82, 122, 124, 169–75, 177, 181; in Brazil, 170–73